C000202915

FIFTY YEARS OF Ferrari

Others books by the same author:

FORMULA 1 RACING TEAM SERIES
Williams Benetton and McLaren

MCLAREN
The Epic Year

FERRARI
The Battle for Revival

DAMON HILL
On Top of the World

WILLIAMS
Triumph out of Tragedy

DAMON HILL
From Zero to Hero

THE QUEST FOR SPEED
Modern Racing Car Design and
 Technology

DRIVING FORCES
Fifty Men Who Have Shaped Motor
 Racing

WILLIAMS
The Business of Grand Prix Racing

FIFTY FAMOUS MOTOR RACES

DEREK BELL
My Racing Life

FERRARI
The Grand Prix Cars

BRABHAM
The Grand Prix Cars

MARCH
The Grand Prix and Indy Cars

JACKIE STEWART'S PRINCIPLES OF
 PERFORMANCE DRIVING

FIFTY YEARS OF
Ferrari

A Grand Prix and sports car racing history

ALAN HENRY

Foreword by Jody Scheckter

© Alan Henry 1997

Alan Henry has asserted his right to be identified as the author of this work

All rights reserved. No part of this book may be reproduced or transmitted in
any form or by any means, electronic or mechanical, including photocopying,
recording or by any information storage or retrieval system, without written
permission from the publisher.

First published 1997
Reprinted in 2000
British Library cataloguing-in-publication data:
A catalogue record for this book is
available from the British Library.

ISBN: 1 85960 008 5

Library of Congress catalog card no. 97-72304

Haynes North America Inc.,
861 Lawrence Drive, Newbury Park,
California 91320, USA.

Published by Haynes Publishing, Sparkford,
Nr Yeovil, Somerset BA22 7JJ, UK.

Tel: 01963 442030 Fax: 01963 440001
Int. tel: +44 1963 442030 Fax: +44 1963 440001

E-mail: sales@haynes-manuals.co.uk
Web site: www.haynes.co.uk

Designed and typeset by
G&M, Raunds, Northamptonshire.
Printed and bound in France by
Imprimerie Pollina s.a., Luçon, France n° 81404

Contents

Acknowledgements

IN GATHERING INFORMATION for this book, I have effectively drawn on 25 years' experience accumulated as a Formula 1 journalist and author. That means I am indebted to the many people I have spoken to on the subject of Ferrari. Thus, in no particular order, I must thank: Phil Hill, Cliff Allison, Tony Brooks, Niki Lauda, Jody Scheckter, Michael Schumacher, Carlos Reutemann, Alain Prost, Nigel Mansell, John Barnard, Harvey Postlethwaite, Brenda Vernor, Luca di Montezemolo, Mauro Forghieri, Doug Nye, the late Denis Jenkinson, the late Peter Coltrin, Nigel Roebuck, Maurice Hamilton, Eddie Irvine, Paul Frère, Victor Pigott, Jean Alesi, Ivan Capelli, Gerhard Berger, Giorgio Ascanelli, Steve Nichols, David Piper, Jo Ramirez, Rob Walker and Stirling Moss.

Apologies to those I have left out. It would be nice to think they will be included in the first reprint.

Alan Henry
Tillingham
Essex
March 1997

Jody Scheckter: Just driving for Ferrari is nearly as good as winning the Championship. (LAT)

Foreword

by Jody Scheckter,
1979 World Champion in a Ferrari 312T4

B Y THE TIME I joined Ferrari for the 1979 season, I had accumulated five and a half seasons of Formula 1 experience with McLaren, Tyrrell and Wolf. The first time Maranello approached me was just after I had competed in my second Formula 1 race for McLaren, when they offered me a drive alongside Niki Lauda; and I was secretly summoned to Maranello by the Commendatore several times during the following years, but things never worked out until mid-1978 when I signed for Ferrari to start the 1979 season.

A lot of people in motor racing thought I had taken leave of my senses. I had something of a reputa-tion for being rather moody, I suppose, and the critics were out in force predicting that a combination of Scheckter and the Italian tempera-ment would end in disaster.

One of the first thoughts you got on going to the Ferrari factory was 'why don't they win more races?' because their facilities in those days were so superior to anything else in Formula 1 in terms of manpower, machinery and backing.

Winning the World Championship was so very special for me. It was all I had wanted to do from my very first race in Formula 1, but I must say that just driving for Ferrari is nearly as good as winning the Championship.

In a way, when you are driving for Ferrari you are really driving for Italy, and I think that is what makes it such a special experience being a Ferrari driver and being treated as such a special guest of that country.

I was also very privileged to have been able to clinch the Championship in a Ferrari at Monza. I wish every person could at least experience that for one day of their life! After that, there was nothing else for me to achieve, so I announced my retire-ment six months later.

I hope Alan Henry's latest book gives you, the reader, a taste of what made my two years at Ferrari so very special.

June 1997

Prologue

On 11 May 1947, two Ferrari 1.5-litre Tipo 125s were fielded in a sports car race at Piacenza, driven by Giuseppe 'Nino' Farina and Franco Cortese. For motor sport historians and race fans alike the world over, that date has come to be regarded as one of the most significant lines ever drawn in the shifting sands of motor racing folklore. It was the moment when a proper Ferrari car raced for the first time.

Fifty years later to the very day – on 11 May 1997 – the Monaco Grand Prix took place through the tortuous streets of that fairytale Mediterranean principality. Although Ferrari has no great claim to success in this, the most romantic, ostensibly, of all Grand Prix races – five wins since its first in 1955 can hardly be described as a record of Olympian proportions – it was perhaps appropriate that Michael Schumacher should have added a sixth such victory in this most recent edition of the historic event.

Enzo Ferrari would have approved of such a neat and tidy pigeon-holing of his company's racing achievements, although the truth of the matter is that imposing such a convenient chronology on the Ferrari story is no more than a comfortable coincidence. Sceptics – and there are many – would also doubtlessly point out with some glee that bracketing Ferrari with the Monaco Grand Prix has an element of unconscious irony in the sense that both man and event have not always been as they have seemed.

Just as Enzo Ferrari was sly, Machiavellian, conspiratorial and melodramatic when it came to cultivating an image, which did not always stand the test of detailed scrutiny, so Monaco beneath the glitz is not always the superb motor race its organisers would like us to believe. In many ways, man and event spent most of their time acting out a charade. Yet they have both made their undeniable contribution to the complex and intricate tapestry which is the history of motor racing.

Celebrating the 50th anniversary of Ferrari's racing cars within the confines of a single volume is, on the face of it, a challenge calculated to overwhelm even before the first word is written. To examine every car, let alone every race, in even cursory detail would require a tome alongside which the *Encyclopaedia Britannica* might be classed as a pamphlet. Besides, the number of volumes already focusing on the achievements of the Prancing Horse are enough to fill a tidy library of their own.

The route I have chosen is therefore more of a tour d'horizon than blow-by-blow. By reference to various significant events, and by drawing on interview material with key players, I have sought to construct a framework around which to record, not so much what happened, but what it was all like; and where Ferrari's individual and specific efforts fell within the racing world, what merit attached to them in terms of opposition beaten, and what impact those achievements had on associated events within the wider motor sporting spectrum.

I have also found myself spending what might be considered a disproportionate emphasis on particular events, or personalities, which have tickled my personal fancy. The reader may find, for example, that the Rodriguez brothers, the Marquis de Portago, relationships between the Ferrari Dino 246 drivers, David Piper's recollections of racing as a Ferrari sports car privateer and Niki Lauda's time at Maranello represent stories within the story, so to speak. Nevertheless, I hope they will be enjoyed and taken to add some insight and further depth to the overall picture.

Throughout the exercise I have found, time and again, that Enzo

Ferrari himself was the ultimate motor racing self-publicist. His racing heyday was certainly not played out against the public relations hype which, of commercial necessity, came to surround motor racing in the 1980s and 1990s. Yet there are many within the sport today who regard themselves as 'PR professionals' who seem to be merely scrambling around on the nursery slopes when compared with this automotive Greta Garbo who spent a great deal of his life saying one thing whilst implying another.

It is also worth keeping in mind that Ferrari, as much as any other single personality, was responsible for shaping the way in which Formula 1 motor racing has developed over the past two decades. Bernie Ecclestone may be rightly identified as the commercial powerhouse of the sport's fortunes, yet the shrewd British entrepreneur was one of the very first to realise that the teams had to carry Ferrari with them unless they were to be disruptively divided.

When Enzo Ferrari died in August 1988, at the age of 90 years, the last link to the pioneering days of motor sport was effectively severed. He was the man who had fielded the works Alfa Romeo competition programme in the 1930s, then fallen out with the famous Turin company and set out to carve his own furrow in what proved to be a uniquely individualistic style.

On a personal level, Enzo Ferrari's life was a bundle of contradictions and complexities. His firm was nigh bankrupt when, in 1969, he was rescued from almost certain extinction by the sympathetic intervention of Fiat supremo Gianni Agnelli.

Even so, squaring up to this potential disaster was as nothing compared with the death in the summer of 1956 of Ferrari's eldest son Dino from nephritis, a kidney complaint, four years after contracting muscular dystrophy. The last paragraph of the *The Enzo Ferrari Memoirs* sums up his inner feelings:

'I feel alone after a life crowded by so many events, and almost guilty of having survived. And I feel, too, a certain detachment, for in this arid earth that is myself, the plant of hope can thrive only if watered by a son's love.'

These words were written in 1963 long before Ferrari formally acknowledged the existence of his illegitimate second son, Piero Lardi. In fact, Enzo Ferrari gained something of a reputation as a libertine during his lifetime, embracing Piero as a member of his family only after the death of Dino's mother Laura in January 1978. A girlfriend of Chris Amon recalls the Old Man moving his hand above her knee during a lunch at the factory. Enzo Ferrari had married young and had something of a sparky relationship with his wife for much of their life together, which lasted for more than 50 years.

After Dino's death, his father withdrew increasingly to his Maranello fortress, the racing progress of his cars in the field monitored by a succession of acolytes, many of whom were more interested in protecting their own backs in the highly politicised Maranello environment rather than objectively reporting the facts of what was happening. This, of course, was quite understandable, particularly when Ferrari's cars were not performing competitively – which was often – for the Old Man did not receive bad news lightly.

With Dino taken from him, Ferrari also increasingly seemed to gain a degree of perverse pleasure from fostering a destructive sense of internal rivalry amongst the drivers he employed. A firmly nominated team leader was seldom appointed, Ferrari preferring that they raced each other's wheels off in order to establish a pecking order.

Naturally, this often conspired to blunt the team's overall competitive edge, making it easier for the opposition to press home its attack. Perhaps Ferrari resented the fact that these drivers were alive and his beloved Dino was not. Yet, paradoxically, he could be remarkably warm and sympathetic to some of the men he employed behind the wheel, whilst at the same time virtually ignoring the very existence of some others.

He was notably approving towards Peter Collins, Gilles Villeneuve and Chris Amon, yet brutally unsympathetic to the likes of Phil Hill and Eugenio Castellotti.

When Jean Behra was killed at Avus, only a week after throwing a punch at Ferrari team manager Romolo Tavoni in the pits at Reims, there was not so much as a wreath from Maranello at his funeral. Yet when Chris Amon reached his 40th birthday, over a decade after last driving one of the Italian cars, he received a congratulatory message, penned, as always, in Ferrari's distinctive purple ink.

Ferrari recalled writing that particular missive: 'When he turned 40, I sent him a photograph and signed it "To the best and most lucky racer." Who knows if his children – he had twins in 1980 – will believe how close he came to being one of the greatest aces of racing?'

Whatever the results they achieved from year to year, Ferrari's racing cars always carried with them an aura of what might be termed classical romanticism based almost entirely on a sense of tradition and historical continuity – but they were seldom pacemakers in the most absolute sense of the word. A close examination of their Formula 1 history, for example, reveals that only from 1975 to 1977 could they seriously and consistently be regarded as representing the best engine/chassis combination of the era.

In that respect, one might reasonably argue that, taken as a whole, Maranello has done a pretty poor job over the period of five decades. I appreciate that this might be regarded as unfashionably heretical talk in a year when the rest of the motor racing community prepares to offer ritual obeisance to the marque's achievements, but it is an undeniable truth that Ferrari frequently squandered its resources just as it seemed poised on the verge of consistently great things.

Reviewing Ferrari's first 50 years of motor racing at a time when Maranello could be poised to scale remarkable heights – thanks, in part at least, to the presence of Michael Schumacher on the team's driving strength, could also represent something of a double-edged sword. Possibly only Alberto Ascari, Niki Lauda and Alain Prost matched the German driver's perceived status during their respective Ferrari eras. Yet even they found themselves unseated when the Prancing Horse stumbled and sought solace in the employment of others.

Schumacher could be the man who makes the crucial difference. Eighteen years have passed since Jody Scheckter won the last World Championship for Ferrari, and the German superstar could conceivably end the drought for the Nearly Team of the Formula 1 firmament. Those who steer the fortunes of the most famous motor racing team in the world, almost 10 years after the death of its founder, must certainly be hoping so.

Yet, for all that, Ferrari continues to exert that almost narcotic sense of mystical fascination on its many disciples. This book probes that magical aura and discovers what made the man, and his racing team, tick.

Chapter 1

Starting out

Enzo Ferrari was born in 1898. Queen Victoria was on the British throne and most of the globe carried the red tint of her empire beyond the seas. Motor cars were in their infancy and modern Italy had not long since been created from an uneasy bunch of loosely associated nation states.

Only 38 years had passed since the states of Modena, Romagna, Tuscany, Parma, Umbria, Marches, Naples and Sicily had come together as the makings of a single country; much less since Lombardy and Venetia joined this federation. To put things in even clearer perspective, Piedmont, which included such cities as Turin and Genoa, would not become part of Italy until after the First World War, in which Enzo Ferrari served.

So what sort of a man was Enzo Ferrari? Sure enough, there are sufficient credible resources remaining to testify to his nature as the owner of the company which carried his name. Yet what of those days before the Second World War when he carried Alfa Romeo's racing fortunes on the back of his Modena-based Scuderia? What was he really like?

One must remember that Ferrari was 49 by the time Cortese and Farina took to the tracks with the first Tipo 125s; he was 53 by the time Froilan Gonzalez scored the marque's maiden Grand Prix victory at Silverstone in 1951; he was 57 when his son Dino died in 1955, and he had just turned 60 when Mike Hawthorn became Britain's first World Champion driver at the wheel of one of his cars three years later.

Thus Ferrari was a comparatively old man, you might contend, at the time of his most celebrated exploits. At best, he was certainly no spring chicken. So how did he make the leap, bridging the chasm which separated the distinctly underprivileged son of a rural metal worker, a youngster called up to serve in the Italian army in 1917 who was allotted the mundane task of shoeing mules? How did he make the jump from the gutter to the exalted position as de facto chief of Alfa Romeo's racing department – in barely a decade?

The nearest thing to an autobiography we can refer to is the *The Enzo Ferrari Memoirs*, published in the UK as long ago as 1963 when its subject was 65. By then he was already referring to 'treading the sunset road', although, as it happened, he still had another 25 years ahead and would continue to exert a powerful influence over his own company's destiny right through to the final months of his life.

Ferrari's personal memoirs tell his story with remarkably little in the way of convincing or detailed explanation. The volume lacks a degree of personal underpinning, if you like. Yet the image of a man who lived on his wits comes across strongly.

At the end of the First World War he took his letter of discharge from the army along to a job interview at Fiat, only to find there was no opportunity available. The Italian labour market was flooded with ex-servicemen and Enzo Ferrari was not to be numbered amongst the lucky ones.

Aged barely 20, Ferrari spent much of his time frequenting the Bar de Nord on Turin's Porta Nuova, getting to know people and making connections. He got a job with CMN, a fledgeling car maker which concentrated on converting commercial vehicles left over from the war. Through this association he got the chance to start racing himself at a time when drivers were far from the celebrity figures they would subsequently become (ironically) under the patronage of team owners like Enzo Ferrari. In 1920 he finished second at the wheel of an Alfa Romeo in the Targa Florio.

Clearly, as a driver, he was not bad, yet precise details of his racing exploits have proved extremely difficult to pin down. Historian Griffith Borgeson has investigated this area more deeply than most and, in response to his probing, the Italian Automobile Club produced a list of only 21 events in which Ferrari could be said definitely to have competed between 1919 and 1931.

Throughout the 1920s Ferrari spent a lot of time judiciously massaging his commercial and engineering connections. He also began surrounding himself with a loyal cabal of close collaborators, including Gioacchino Colombo – the man who would eventually design the first Ferrari car after masterminding the Alfa 158s under Ferrari's patronage – and former Fiat technician Luigi Bazzi, a man who would survive into the 1960s as possibly Enzo's longest-standing lieutenant, having originally joined him in 1923.

Bazzi had joined Alfa Romeo as long ago as 1922 after a spell in Fiat's experimental department, and would later become tagged as the man who conceived the fearsome twin-engined Alfa Romeo 'Bimotore' in the 1930s. Not only was he a valued technical guiding hand, but his long association with Enzo Ferrari enabled him to help smooth over the differences of opinion and temperamental problems which made working with his boss an increasingly unpredictable, sometimes tempestuous, challenge in later years.

During his time with Alfa Romeo, Bazzi was also responsible for tempting the highly respected engineer Vittorio Jano to leave Fiat to join the rival firm. Bazzi, who had also worked with Fiat, was at least partly responsible for persuading Ferrari that Jano was the right man for the job. Within months of joining Alfa, the ex-Fiat man was putting the finishing touches to the historic supercharged 2-litre P2 which made its competition debut in 1924.

There were many important dates in Enzo Ferrari's personal life, one of which was surely 17 June 1923, when a sequence of events gave rise to what

The man himself – Enzo Ferrari, photographed in 1962 when he was 64 years of age. (Phipps Photographic)

is unquestionably regarded as one of the most widely identified logos used by any car maker in history. On that day he was entered by Alfa Romeo in the Circuit of Savio at Ravenna, winning the race commandingly with his 3-litre machine against significantly more powerful opposition.

After the event, a man elbowed his way through to the front of the excited crush immediately surrounding Ferrari and shook the winner warmly by the hand. It turned out that this was the father of Francesco Baracca, the legendary First World War Italian fighter ace who shot down no fewer than 35 enemy planes during the conflict.

Baracca's squadron had sported a yellow shield in the centre of which was a prancing horse, and now his family presented Ferrari with their son's squadron badge as an acknowledgement of his courage and audacity behind the wheel of a racing car. Thus was born the famous 'Prancing Horse' symbol which is carried by every road and racing Ferrari to this day.

In 1929, two years before the birth of his son Dino, when Ferrari actually retired from driving, he severed his formal links with Alfa Romeo to establish the Modena-based Scuderia Ferrari which, effectively, would continue as the competition arm of the famous Turin car maker throughout much of the following decade.

The concept of the Scuderia Ferrari was originally mooted during a dinner in Bologna during 1929. Co-founders of the team with Enzo Ferrari were the Ferrara-based Caniato brothers, Augusto and Alfredo, heirs to a textile fortune, and keen amateur racer Mario Tadini who later earned himself a considerable reputation in hill-climb events. Tadini and the Caniato brothers were well-heeled amateur racers whose financial support was crucial to

Ferrari fielded what amounted to the works Alfa Romeos during the 1930s, and the team chief struck up a close personal relationship with Tazio Nuvolari. Here, Nuvolari urges Ferrari's pit crew to hurry up during a refuelling stop at the 1935 German GP at Nürburgring. (C. Posthumus)

Ferrari in those early days, but the team soon expanded to become what amounted to a small, autonomous division of the Alfa company.

As a natural result of this expansion, the Scuderia Ferrari soon outstripped its initial concept of an association of like-minded amateur racers, to become a fully established team, highly professional by the standards of the day, which fielded cars for such established stars as Tazio Nuvolari, Giuseppe Campari, Achille Varzi and Louis Chiron. Yet Ferrari was also proud that his team also produced plenty of its own fledgeling talent, most notably Antonio Brivio, Guy Moll, Tadini and Carlo Pintacuda.

One particularly shrewd observer from this period was René Dreyfus who had switched from Bugatti to drive for the Scuderia Ferrari at the start of the 1935 season. Having gone from being part of the family at Bugatti, Dreyfus was now aware of a profound change in his environment. With Ferrari he was very much aware of being no more than a hired hand.

'The difference between being a member of the Bugatti team and Scuderia Ferrari was virtual night and day,' recalled Dreyfus almost 50 years later. 'I lived with [Meo] Constantini [the Bugatti team manager], I visited with Ferrari. That was the literal fact, but there were subtle contrasts which made it even more true.

'With Ferrari, I learned the business of racing, for there was no doubt he was a businessman. Enzo Ferrari was a pleasant person and friendly, but not openly affectionate. There was, for example, none of the sense of belonging to the family that I had with the Maserati brothers, nor the sense of

Tazio Nuvolari's Scuderia Ferrari Alfa Romeo P3 heads for victory in the 1935 German GP at Nurburgring, one of the greatest victories of his career. (Eoin Young Collection)

spirited fun and intimacy that I had with Meo Constantini.

'Enzo Ferrari loved racing, of that there was no question. Still, it was more than an enthusiast's love, but one tempered by the practical realisation that this was a good way to build a nice, profitable empire. I knew he was going to be a big man one day, even then when the cars he raced carried somebody else's name. I felt sure that eventually they would carry his.

'Ettore Bugatti was Le Patron; Enzo Ferrari was The Boss. Bugatti was imperious; Ferrari was impenetrable.'

Dreyfus unquestionably had a keen eye for detail, not to mention a clever turn of phrase.

The 1935 season would also be distinguished by one of Scuderia Ferrari's most remarkable successes, the victory by 43-year-old Nuvolari in the German GP at the wheel of the team's three-year-old Alfa Romeo P3.

The Mercedes-Benz and Auto Union opposition were clear favourites to win, but a combination of mechanical misfortune and driver error left Nuvolari running second in the closing stages of the race, but carving into the lead held by Manfred

von Brauchitsch's Mercedes W25.

Anxious to fend off the Italian challenge, the German driver over-taxed his tyres, with the result that the Merc's left-rear tyre flew apart midway round the final lap, and Nuvolari ducked through to win. It was just the sort of giant-slaying act of which Enzo Ferrari approved and it cemented his personal affection for the little driver from Mantua to whom he seemingly remained devoted right up to Nuvolari's death in 1953.

'There are few men who understood the public and what it wants as well as he did, or who knew how to feed their myths,' he wrote.

'Nuvolari, unlike almost all the other racers of yesterday and today, never began a race beaten, never fell behind in the middle [of the contest] and always battled ferociously regardless of the car. The crowds understood his passion and tenacity, and this was the stuff from which the myth was born.' In truth, one must suspect that Enzo Ferrari really meant 'legend' rather than 'myth'.

Ferrari's personal motor racing successes in the 1920s also gained him a certain national distinction. After winning the Acerbo Cup race at Pescara he was awarded the title 'Cavaliere', then later 'Cavaliere Ufficiale' and finally, in 1928, 'Commendatore'.

However, after the Second World War all such titles awarded by the Fascist regime were investigated in detail. No impropriety was found to attach to Ferrari in this connection and it was made clear that he could apply for reconfirmation of the honour, but the title lapsed. Even so, he would continue to be referred to as 'Commendatore' by some people right through to the end of his life, although he would, more often than not, respond by saying: 'Just call me Ferrari.'

So we can see that Enzo Ferrari was clearly an independent-minded operator. He frequently crossed swords with Ugo Gobatto, one of Alfa Romeo's directors who was entrusted with administering the link between the parent company and Scuderia Ferrari. The breach with Alfa finally came in 1939 after Ferrari conceived a very violent and specific dislike of Gobatto's latest nominee, the Spanish engineer Wilfredo Ricart.

A quarter of a century later, Ferrari still could not contain his dislike of Ricart and delivered a crushing, if measured, condemnation of the man he blamed for the final rift with Alfa Romeo.

'The crisis of conscience which led me to abandon Alfa Romeo was brought about especially by the arrival of a Spanish engineer called Ricard [sic],' recalled Ferrari with what must surely have been a deliberate decision to misspell the surname of the incomer he clearly categorised as something of a demon.

'He appeared almost surreptitiously, having been engaged for reasons that I never properly found out – perhaps political or commercial opportunism was behind his engagement.'

'This Spaniard, who spoke four or five languages, captured – this is the only word for it – the trust of Gobatto.'

'With sleek, oiled hair and smart clothes that he wore with a somewhat Levantine elegance, Ricard affected jackets with sleeves that came down far below his wrists and shoes with enormously thick rubber soles. When he shook hands, it was like grasping the cold, lifeless hand of a corpse.'

Ferrari admitted that, one day, he asked Ricart the reason for his extraordinary shoes with their huge soles. The engineer replied quite seriously that this was an obvious precaution because 'a great engineer's brain should not be jolted by the inequalities of the ground and consequently needed to be carefully sprung.'

'Nonplussed and worried by curious statements of this kind, I broached the matter with Gobatto,' recalled Ferrari with distinctly mischievous undertones, 'admitting that the Spaniard was undoubtedly a most interesting person, but insisting that his superior brain should fit him for much more elevated spheres of activity than the mere designing of racing cars. Gobatto rounded on me, perhaps because he thought I was jealous.'

Clearly, you crossed Enzo Ferrari very much at your own peril.

In fact, at the heart of Ferrari's disagreement with Alfa Romeo was the Milanese company's intention to re-enter motor racing under its own name in 1938, the Alfa Corse organisation absorbing the Scuderia Ferrari operation and transferring the Tipo 158 development – which was essentially a Ferrari design and concept – back to Milan.

Enzo Ferrari clearly felt affronted by this challenge to his own personal domain. Reading between the lines, it was now only a matter of time before he picked a fight with the Alfa management and went his own way. In that respect, Ricart's arrival represented something of a convenient peg from which to launch on to a path of confrontation with Alfa Romeo. The moment had arrived to plough his own individualistic furrow.

One can only assume that Ferrari worked out a financially beneficial severance package with Alfa Romeo, since he confides that he was bound by a clause preventing him from any motor racing activities, save with an Alfa Romeo machine, for the next four years. Yet, by the same token, one does not have to read far between the lines to see that Ferrari regarded such a restriction as offering the maximum leeway for his plans.

By 1940 he had manufactured a couple of eight-cylinder, 1.5-litre sports cars, designed by former Fiat engineer Alberto Massimino, which were supplied to local Modenese drivers Alberto Ascari and the Marchese Lotario Rangoni Machiavelli di Modena, a wealthy local aristocrat who would later be killed in a wartime bomber crash. These cars were used to compete in the 1940 Mille Miglia and, although they carried no formal designation apart from '815' – standing for eight cylinders, 1.5 litres – they were widely and correctly regarded thereafter as the first Ferrari cars.

Alberto Ascari

THERE ARE THOSE who firmly believe that Alberto Ascari was the best driver of the post-war era, whose true ability was never displayed in its proper perspective due to his early death in 1955 after dominating the 1952 and 1953 World Championships at the wheel of Ferrari's Formula 2 Tipo 500s.

The son of the legendary Antonio Ascari, who was killed at the wheel of an Alfa Romeo during the 1925 French Grand Prix at Montlhéry when Alberto was barely seven, Ascari junior's own racing career began on two wheels as a member of the Bianchi team before the Second World War. As previously mentioned, he had the distinction of driving the first Ferrari-built racing car – the enigmatically titled '815' – in the 1940 Mille Miglia, and he also finished ninth in that year's Tripoli Grand Prix at the wheel of a Maserati.

During the war, Ascari and his close friend Luigi Villoresi built up a thriving business hauling fuel to Mussolini's armies in North Africa, an activity which also had the secondary benefit of exempting him from national service. After hostilities came to an end, he returned to racing at the wheel of a Cisitalia and scored his first four-wheeled victory on 28 September 1947 driving a Maserati sports car at Modena.

By now married with a young son, Ascari had already toyed with the idea of turning his back on motor sport, but Villoresi persuaded him otherwise. Consequently, through 1948 they raced under the Scuderia Ambrosiana banner in a pair of Maserati 4CLT Grand Prix cars – Alberto winning the San Remo Grand Prix and finishing runner-up in the British race at Silverstone.

Ascari and Villoresi's switch to Ferrari's factory team in 1949 signalled the start of Alberto's most successful period, the 32-year old fully capitalising on the absence of Alfa Romeo to win the Swiss Grand Prix at Berne ahead of Villoresi, then leading the Italian GP from start to finish in the latest two-stage supercharged Tipo 125.

With Alfa Romeo returning to the scene in 1950, when the first official World Championship contest was inaugurated, Ferrari had a patchy time in terms of hard success as the team struggled to develop the Lampredi-designed 4.5-litre non-super-charged V12. Yet Ascari accurately signalled what was to come by scoring a decisive victory in the non-title Gran Premio de Penya Rhin at Barcelona, the last major event on the European calendar.

The following season saw Froilan Gonzalez, not Ascari, score Ferrari's maiden Championship Grand Prix success with victory at Silverstone, but Alberto's great

opportunity came in 1952. Concerned about the shortage of current Formula 1 cars, the FIA decreed that the World Championship would be staged for Formula 2 cars for the following two seasons. He won nine races with the 2-litre Ferrari Formula 2 Tipo 500

across two seasons to win the title crown on both occasions.

In 1954 Formula 1 was restored for the World Championship under the new 2.5-litre non-supercharged regulations, but Ascari decided to turn his back on Ferrari, instead

signing to drive Gianni Lancia's technologically advanced Tipo D50. Unfortunately the new car was not ready to race before the end of the season, for much of which Ascari was left twiddling his thumbs on the sidelines.

Lancia generously released Ascari to drive a Ferrari 625 in the Italian GP at Monza, where he gave arch-rival Juan Manuel Fangio's Mercedes W196 a great run for its money before the Maranello machine suffered engine failure. Finally, the Lancia D50 was readied in time for the Barcelona race where Ascari demonstrated its awesome potential by qualifying on pole position and shooting into a commanding lead, only to be thwarted by clutch trouble.

Yet it seemed as though Ascari had set the tone for a successful 1955, underlining the D50's potential with victories in the non-championship Naples and Turin Grands Prix at the start of that season. He then crashed spectacularly into the harbour at Monaco when poised to take the lead of that particular Grand Prix.

Ascari survived this unexpected ducking with nothing more than a shaking and a broken nose. The following Thursday he turned up unexpectedly at Monza where Lancia had again given him permission to drive a Ferrari, this time a sports car shared with Eugenio Castellotti, in the next Sunday's Supercortemaggiore 1000km race.

Although not originally having intended to drive in this mid-week test, he borrowed Castellotti's helmet and went out for what he planned would be just a few exploratory laps. On his third lap Ascari crashed at the fast Vialone left-hander and was fatally injured.

His death was a shattering body blow for Gianni Lancia after all that expense and endeavour involved in developing the Tipo D50. Within a few months of Ascari's passing, Lancia had withdrawn from Formula 1 and – irony of ironies – the entire D50 project was passed across into the custody of Enzo Ferrari.

Alberto Ascari scored a dominant victory in the non-title 1950 Penya Rhin GP at Barcelona's Pedralbes circuit with the 4.5-litre non-supercharged Ferrari 375.

Throughout the Second World War Ferrari kept his company in business by carrying out specialist machine tool work, moving out from his original premises in Modena during 1943 to establish a new plant on land he already owned in the village of Maranello. In due course this would come to be regarded as the capital of the world for successive generations addicted to high performance automobiles.

The aftermath of the Second World War saw Europe pretty much in ruins, and motor racing apparently low on the list of most people's personal priorities. Yet the first flickers of enthusiasm for the sport's possible revival were literally coaxed out of the dying embers of the conflict. Before the war, a new set of regulations for Grand Prix racing had been envisaged for 1941, the sport's governing body having settled on engine capacities of 4.5 litres unsupercharged or 1.5 litres supercharged, and these rules were eventually formally instigated for the start of the 1947 season.

Ferrari's 1.5-litre Tipo 125, powered by its Gioacchino Colombo-designed V12 engine, duly made its race debut at Piacenza on 11 May 1947, and Ferrari's first outing in a Grand Prix was officially registered on 16 May 1948, when Prince Igor Troubetzkoy – who gained more celebrity status by being one of Woolworth heiress Barbara Hutton's six husbands – drove a 2-litre Tipo 166 at Monaco. The official World Championship was as yet two years away from its instigation, but a little slice of history had already been written by the man who so boldly turned his back on Alfa Romeo almost a decade earlier.

Later that same year, after Raymond Sommer emerged victorious in a sports car race at Turin's Valentino Park circuit, Ferrari admitted to casting his mind back to the moment in 1918 when he was turned down for that job with Fiat. 'It was a very cold one [winter],' he wrote. 'I found myself out in the street again, my clothes feeling as though they were freezing to me.

'Crossing Valentino Park, I brushed the snow off a bench and sat down. I was alone, my father and brother were no more. Overcome by loneliness and despair, I wept. Many years later, in 1947, after Sommer had won the first post-war Turin Grand Prix with the 12-cylinder Ferrari, I went and sat on that same bench. The tears I shed that day, though, were of a very different kind!'

Ferrari's first proper Formula 1 car was the Colombo-designed supercharged Ferrari 125 which made its debut in the Italian Grand Prix staged in Turin's Valentino Park on 5 September 1948. A great deal of technical consideration had gone into the V12 engine configuration, for although Ferrari admitted that his enthusiasm for this layout had originally been fired by the American Packard V12 engines, there were firm practical justifications for not following the Alfa Romeo eight-cylinder route.

A word on Ferrari's type numbering now seems timely. Generally the cars were identified by their individual cylinder capacity. Therefore, the 12-cylinder 125 had a 1500cc engine (12 x 125 = 1500), the 12-cylinder 375 a 4.5-litre, the four-cylinder 500 Mondial a 2-litre, the 12-cylinder 250TR a 3-litre unit, and so-on.

However, this was later varied in the late 1950s when the Ferrari Dino 246 represented a 2.4-litre six-cylinder, the 156 a 1.5-litre six cylinder, the 158 a 1.5-litre eight cylinder and the 1512 a 1.5-litre 12-cylinder. The advent of the 3-litre Formula 1 produced the 312 – a 3-litre 12-cylinder – which was supplanted by the 312B range – the 3-litre, 12-cylinder boxer – and then the 312T range, 3-litre 12-cylinder (boxer) with the 'T' identifying it as the transverse gearbox version.

By the mid-1980s, Ferrari type numbering came off the rails in a big way. The 126C now represented a 120-degree six-cylinder (turbo), then the 156/85 was the 1.5-litre six-cylinder turbo for 1985 and the F186, 187 and 88 just identified the year of the Formula 1 machine concerned. Then we had the 640 V12 in 1989 which introduced a new series, and this was changed again in the early 1990s to the point that the 1997 car was the F310B – a second generation Formula 1 car with a V10-cylinder engine.

Returning to the first Formula 1 type 125, the short-stroke configuration chosen by Colombo offered potential for higher revs and the additional advantage of a stiffer crankcase, reduced bearing loads and a lighter, lower cylinder block. Alfa Romeo's 158s were clearly the main opposition at this time, although Maserati's supercharged 4CL was regarded as the next best challenger giving away around 50bhp to the 'Alfettas' which developed a claimed 275bhp at 7500rpm from their two-stage supercharged engines.

Talbot continued to campaign a 4.5-litre unsupercharged machine which was definitely inferior to the Italian opposition, but fields were unpredictable in size and there was no obligation on the part of any individual team or manufacturer to contest any particular race.

In that respect the development of Grand Prix racing was a distinctly piecemeal affair in those immediate post-war years, with race organisers

Luigi Villoresi

BORN ON 16 May 1909, Luigi Villoresi began racing at the wheel of a Lancia Lambda in 1931, but his first really important competition outing came in the Mille Miglia two years later when he shared a Fiat Ballila with his younger brother Emilio.

By 1936 Luigi had gained a measure of success, finishing sixth at Monaco at the wheel of a Maserati 4CM, and he remained loyal to the marque for much of the immediate pre- and post-war period. In 1938 he was recruited to the Maserati factory team in an effort to counter the speed of the newly arrived (and Ferrari-designed) Alfa Romeo 158s, one of which, ironically, was now being driven by brother Emilio, who was emerging as one of Villoresi senior's most formidable rivals.

Luigi remained with the Maserati works team into the 1939 season and carried on racing after Emilio was killed on 20 June whilst testing an Alfa 158 at Monza. After the war, Villoresi resumed racing and won the Italian championship in both 1946 and 1947, simultaneously encouraging the career of his close friend Alberto Ascari. He joined Ascari in the Ferrari team for the start of the 1949 season and won the Dutch Grand Prix at Zandvoort, eventually accompanying Ascari when he switched to the Lancia team at the start of 1954.

Ascari's death during an impromptu test at Monza in May 1955 deeply affected Villoresi. He did not race Formula 1 again until the following year when, after a bad accident in the Rome Grand Prix, he retired for good at the age of 46.

Luigi Villoresi heading for third place in the 1949 Silverstone International Trophy race with one of the single-stage supercharged 1.5-litre Ferrari 125s. (LAT)

getting by as best they could whilst being perpetually subject to the technical readiness of the competing teams. Bernie Ecclestone and his well-drilled squad of Formula One Constructors' Association members, guaranteeing race organisers a firm package in exchange for a fixed fee, was still more than a generation away in the future.

There were other aspirants on the Formula 1 stage at the time, yet most appeared only fleetingly. The futuristic Cisitalia-Porsche flickered briefly on the racing stage, the French CTA Arsenal appeared in 1947 and 1948 before disappearing for good and, as far as Britain was concerned, efforts to build a national racing car, seemingly designed and operated by committee, resulted in the BRM project getting off the ground, albeit shakily.

Meanwhile, Ferrari's new bespoke Grand Prix cars certainly did not disgrace themselves at Turin. The race was held in pouring rain and resulted in a commanding victory for Jean-Pierre Wimille's Alfa 158, while Sommer took the survivor of three Ferrari 125s to a close third place behind Luigi Villoresi's Maserati.

Farina and Prince Bira had driven the other two Ferrari 125 Formula 1 cars at Turin in 1948 and the former made up for the disappointment of retiring after making contact with a straw bale by winning the Circuit of Garda, based on the lakeside village of Salo, after both Ferrari entries had retired from the Grand Prix Autodromo at Monza.

The final outing for the 125s in 1948 came at the Grand Premio de Penya Rhin on Barcelona's now long-defunct Pedralbes circuit where Bira and Farina both retired with transmission failure. Yet again demonstrating his keen commercial edge, Ferrari hired out the third 125 to local

Spanish driver Jose Pola, who presumably paid handsomely for the privilege of breaking its V12 engine.

In 1949, Ferrari decided to sell two 125s to privateers, one being to the British driver Peter Whitehead and the other to Vandervell bearing magnate Tony Vandervell. This latter machine would become the first 'Thinwall Special', a competition test bed for Vandervell's Thinwall bearings. It would also lay the preliminary groundwork for Vandervell's own Vanwall Grand Prix machines which would drive Ferrari's Dino 246 cars into the ground less than 10 years later.

By the mid-1950s, of course, Formula 1 would be well supported by many teams and manufacturers, but this was far from the case in 1949 when Alfa Romeo temporarily withdrew from the Grand Prix arena. The Milanese firm was worried about Ferrari's burgeoning opposition and equally nervous about the potential threat from the British BRM, although it would be many years before Britain's so-called national racing car would pose any sort of realistic competitive challenge.

In addition, Alfa's efforts had been undermined by the loss of three of its top drivers. Achille Varzi had been killed the previous year when he flipped his 158 while practising in the rain for the Swiss Grand Prix at Berne's Bremgarten circuit, and Jean-Pierre Wimille was killed at the wheel of a little Simca-Gordini in Buenos Aires in January 1949. In addition, Count Carlo-Felice Trossi had been laid low by cancer and would eventually die on 9 May 1949 following a long illness.

Alfa Romeo's decision to stand aside, albeit fleetingly, meant that Ferrari pretty well had the scene to himself. Not that things went

smoothly by any means, for Tony Vandervell soon returned his Ferrari 125 to Maranello with a stiff note from the British industrialist to the effect that he was certainly not satisfied with the new car's performance.

If Ferrari was becoming accustomed to fobbing-off customers who complained, he certainly met his match in Tony Vandervell who sent a long technical explanation to the Italian car maker detailing precisely what his technicians thought was wrong with the Tipo 125. This delightful correspondence was analysed in some detail by the late Denis Jenkinson and Cyril Posthumus in their superb volume *Vanwall: The story of Tony Vandervell and his racing cars* (Patrick Stephens Limited, 1975).

What was clear from this exchange of letters was that Ferrari was very aware of the benefits of technical collaboration with Vandervell, for his Ferrari engines were experimenting extensively with the use of Vandervell's new Thinwall bearings. By mid-1950 it was agreed that Vandervell should take delivery of the latest two-stage supercharged Ferrari 125 to replace the original car. It certainly hadn't been a pleasant experience for Tony Vandervell, whose exchanges with Enzo Ferrari more than ever convinced him that his own engineers should be capable of building a better Formula 1 car. So, in the long term, it would prove.

Meanwhile, Ferrari's factory team was enjoying an increasing level of success. In particular, Maranello's morale was boosted with Ascari and Villoresi's 1–2 success in the Swiss GP at Bremgarten, and Villoresi winning at Zandvoort. But it was becoming clear that Ferrari needed more power to defeat the Maserati 4CLT/48s, and a two-stage supercharged version of the Tipo 125 was produced by the team's

Froilan Gonzalez

ENZO FERRARI ONCE observed that Froilan Gonzalez, the rotund Argentinian, often got himself into such a lather at the wheel of a racing car that he found himself wondering why he chose to compete at all.

Yet Gonzalez, the son of a Chevrolet dealer from the provincial town of Arrecifes – about three hours' drive from Buenos Aires – was a keen athlete from a young age. In addition to being successful in road races like Fangio, Gonzalez was a first-rate swimmer, a crack shot and a competitive cyclist.

He first made his name in a Ferrari 166 by trouncing the old pre-war supercharged Mercedes-Benz W163s in two non-championship Argentine races in the opening weeks of 1951. Later that same season he would storm to Ferrari's first World Championship victory in the British GP at Silverstone at the wheel of one of the factory 375s.

In 1952 Gonzalez switched to Maserati and stayed there until the end of the Formula 2 World Championship period the following year, rejoining Ferrari in 1954 when he repeated his British GP victory with the Tipo 625, vanquishing the entire Mercedes-Benz works team in the process.

Sadly, his career petered out after he crashed a sports Ferrari in practice for the Tourist Trophy at Dundrod in 1955. He was almost 38 years old when he had his final Formula 1 outing, at the wheel of a Ferrari Dino 246 in the 1960 Argentine GP at Buenos Aires.

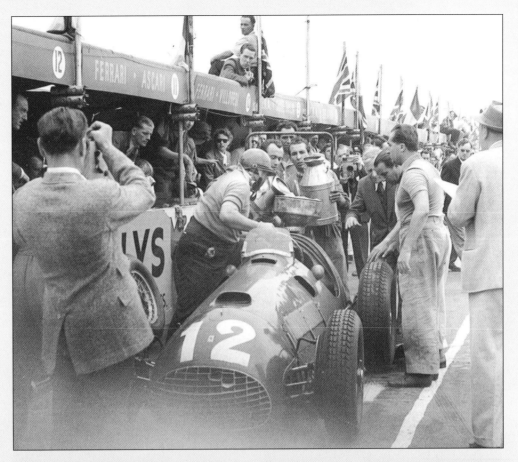

A historic moment – Froilan Gonzalez (left) watches anxiously as the Ferrari crew refuels his 1951 British GP-winning Ferrari 375 at Silverstone. Alberto Ascari, who had retired earlier, is standing by the car's left rear wheel. (LAT)

Gonzalez on his way to his historic 1951 Silverstone victory, hunched up over the steering wheel, urging the Ferrari ever onward. (LAT)

new designer Aurelio Lampredi in time for Ascari to score a flag-to-flag victory at Monza.

Despite this, behind the scenes there was tension building up in the Ferrari design department. Aurelio Lampredi had originally joined the company in 1946 at the age of 29, but found he could not get on working under Colombo's direction and left for a brief stint with the Isotta Fraschini organisation. But Ferrari wooed Lampredi back to Maranello later that year, after which he became increasingly responsible for Formula 1 engine development.

Colombo's position was usurped when Ferrari gave Lampredi total responsibility for the technical operation of the Grand Prix team as from the start of the 1950 season. The older

engineer's reaction was uncertain; initially he found himself unable to argue against Ferrari's logic, but he soon began to wonder whether there was any serious point in staying on developing sports cars including the 212s and 166MMs.

At the end of 1950 Colombo received an invitation to return to Alfa Romeo. Ferrari was displeased. He threatened not to allow him to go unless he first agreed to allow a company representative to check his lodgings and make certain he was not taking any Ferrari technical drawings with him.

It was said that Ferrari even tried intimidating Colombo by making a telephone call to the Modena Chief of Police and asking for such a search to go ahead right away – unless Enzo

phoned back within minutes countermanding the instructions. It was an extraordinary example of the paranoia and tunnel vision so often displayed by self-made businessmen, particularly feudal patriarchs like Ferrari. It would not be the last time that Ferrari would resort to emotional theatrical blackmail in an attempt to get his own way.

By the end of the 1949 season the Tipo 125 two-stage supercharged V12 was nudging the 300bhp barrier, and there was the promise of some even closer racing to follow in 1950 with the news that Alfa Romeo would be returning to the Formula 1 scene. However, both Ferrari and Lampredi had by now concluded that a 4.5-litre non-supercharged V12 would be a far better route to pursue – Lampredi reckoning that it would be much easier to develop around 80bhp per litre from such an engine than the 225bhp per litre required from

Reg Parnell takes a look over his shoulder as he hustles Tony Vandervell's 4.5-litre Ferrari – dubbed 'Thin Wall Special' – to victory in the 1951 Festival of Britain Trophy race at Goodwood.

Colombo's supercharged 1.5-litre unit.

Development pressures meant that Ferrari's new V12 was not ready until the Belgian GP at Spa on 18 June 1950, prior to which event the team soldiered on with its two-stage supercharged 1.5-litre cars. The new car started as a 3.3-litre engine, then evolved to a 4.1 in time for the GP des Nations at Geneva on 30 July, then the full 4.5-litre unit arrived for the Italian GP at Monza.

There, Ascari gave Fangio's Alfa 159 a real fright, leading for two glorious laps before the new Ferrari suffered an engine failure. Undaunted, he took over test driver Dorino Serafini's sister car and, despite gearchange problems, hauled it back from sixth place to second at the chequered flag, just over a minute behind Fangio's winning Alfa.

Throughout the first part of the 1951 season it was clear that Ferrari was now hovering on the verge of his first World Championship Grand Prix victory. The performance of the Tipo 375s was enhanced by the fact that they did not need to make as many pit stops as the fuel-hungry Alfa 159s, and it would eventually be Froilan Gonzalez who finished the job in the 1951 British Grand Prix at Silverstone.

Ferrari could now see a chance of actually winning that year's World Championship and this prospect was enhanced by Ascari's dominant victory in the first post-war Championship German GP to be held at the Nürburgring. Having been defeated by Ferrari twice now, Alfa Romeo was very definitely on the run. Ascari and Gonzalez scored another 1–2 at Monza where five Tipo 375s were ranged against the supercharged challengers from Milan.

There was now a single round of the World Championship remaining – the race scheduled for 28 October at

Juan Manuel Fangio had a somewhat strained relationship with Enzo Ferrari during his racing career, even though he used this 2-litre supercharged Formula 2 Ferrari to great effect in Brazil, Argentina and Uruguay early in 1952 – before signing for the Maserati works team.

Barcelona. Rather foolishly, under the circumstances, Ferrari decided to experiment with Pirelli tyre sizes for this crucial event, and the decision to use smaller 16-in diameter tyres, rather than the 17-in covers used throughout the year up to that point, caused the 375s to start throwing treads from early in the race. Fangio therefore won for Alfa Romeo, with the gallant Gonzalez second, and Ferrari missed out on his first title crown.

Pensioned off. In 1952 the old 4.5-litre Ferrari 375s were largely redundant through the advent of the Formula 2 World Championship regulations. Here, Luigi Villoresi has a rare 1952 outing in one of the works cars, contesting a formule libre event at Silverstone.

At the end of the season Alfa Romeo withdrew from racing after failing to secure any financial support from the Italian government. This left race organisers across Europe in an acutely nervous frame of mind, wondering how many fully-fledged Formula 1 cars would actually be ready for the start of the 1952 season.

The acid test would come at the Turin Grand Prix on 6 April where it was optimistically hoped that the BRM team, which had spent much time over the winter testing at Monza, would attend to offer Ferrari some worthwhile opposition. Yet BRM withdrew at the last moment.

It was the last straw for motor racing's then governing body, the CSI. The decision was taken to rubber-stamp the official 1952 and 1953 World Championships under the 2-litre Formula 2 regulations, leaving Ferrari's Tipo 375s along with the supercharged BRMs to justify their existence with outings in a handful of Formula 1 non-championship events over the next couple of seasons.

Ferrari, meanwhile, was not only well equipped for the Formula 2 challenge, but was also taking the long view and preparing a new 2.5-litre engine for the new technical regulations which were due to come on stream at the start of the 1954 season. Not for the last time would he be running ahead of the prevailing game.

Chapter 2

Getting to grips
with the sports car epics

FERRARI'S EARLY FORAYS into sports car races were conducted with the cycle-winged 125s which Farina and Cortese had used on that historic day at Piacenza in May 1947. Two weeks afterwards, Cortese scored the marque's first victory in a race at Rome's Caracalla circuit, and he was soon joined by Tazio Nuvolari – 12 years and a world war after his Nürburgring success in the Scuderia Ferrari Alfa P3 – which saw the veteran from Mantua winning a minor-league event at Forlì.

These successes would provide the bedrock on which Ferrari built the commercial success of his company. The policy was to build winning cars and then sell them to private owners. With no substantial financial infrastructure to support his organisation, his cars were, in effect, as good as their last race. Happily, just as with the Scuderia Ferrari during the 1930s, there seemed to be plenty of financially well-placed competitors prepared to join his party.

In that crucial respect he was assisted by the likes of Raymond Sommer and the two Counts Besana, Gabriele and Soave, who purchased two of the cycle-winged 166SCs, as well as the well-heeled White Russian Prince Igor Troubetzkoy who was a welcome early Ferrari customer.

At the start of the 1948 season, Gioacchino Colombo joined the company and one of his first tasks was to develop the original V12 engine into the 2-litre 166, which was to firmly establish the marque as a decisive force in the many Italian domestic sports car events.

Clemente Biondetti, already twice a winner of the Mille Miglia, drove one of the first distinctive new 166 berlinettas, with bodywork by the Turin-based Carrozzeria Allemano, to victory on the Tour of Sicily. He would repeat that success to score the third of his four career victories in the Mille Miglia, but it was the performance of Tazio Nuvolari in an open 166SC – loaned by Troubetzkoy – which really

Tazio Nuvolari ready to start the 1948 Mille Miglia in Count Igor Troubetzkoy's Ferrari 166 which had been borrowed back by the factory for the occasion. (Colombo collection)

By the closing stages of the 1948 Mille Miglia, Nuvolari's Ferrari had lost its bonnet and right front cycle wing, yet was leading the event by a huge margin. He was only forced to retire with a broken spring almost within striking distance of the finish. (Colombo collection)

Clemente Biondetti's Allemano-bodied 166 berlinetta – effectively the very first GT Ferrari ever built – about to leave the Florence control on the 1948 Mille Miglia. Biondetti inherited a comfortable victory after Nuvolari's retirement. (Colombo collection)

went down into the history books.

By this stage Nuvolari was unwell and ageing prematurely, dogged by the first signs of the TB-related illness which would take him to his grave five years later. He had spent much of the previous winter taking things easy, on the advice of his doctors, but had decided to drive in the 1948 Mille Miglia at the wheel of one of Piero Dusio's Cisitalias. Yet problems in testing resulted in Dusio sending his driver a telegram informing him that the car would not be ready. This was on 27 April, barely five days before the Mille Miglia was due to start.

Ferrari stepped in and Troubetzkoy willingly relinquished his own 166SC for the veteran Nuvolari. What followed was almost impossible to believe. By the time the field reached Ravenna, Nuvolari's Ferrari was already in the lead. At Rome he was even further ahead, although his car had lost a cycle wing and the bonnet.

Nevertheless, by the time he reached Florence, Nuvolari was almost half an hour ahead of Biondetti, snug in the big closed berlinetta. Then at Reggio Emilia, a broken spring forced him out of the battle. Biondetti went through to win as Nuvolari, drained and exhausted, was taken away to rest in a nearby hospital.

Ferrari visited him in an effort to boost his spirits, telling him to buck up, there was always next year's race to look forward to. 'Ferrari,' he replied, 'at our age there aren't many days like this left. Remember that, and try to enjoy them as much as you can.'

In fact, the following year Nuvolari would be back again in the Mille Miglia. Again he was leading Biondetti's Ferrari by nine minutes when his tiny Cisitalia roadster ran through a large puddle and swamped its engine. Biondetti went by to score a record fourth victory in this remarkable road race; but for Nuvolari the game was up and his career effectively ended on this cruelly disappointing note.

Biondetti's winning Allemano-bodied 166 was the first Ferrari competition coupé and, from the start of the 1950 season, Gioaccino Colombo spent most of his time developing this range of customer competition car, now that Aurelio Lampredi had taken sole responsibility for the Formula 1 end of the operation.

The 1949 season had seen three versions of the 166 produced with bodywork by Touring of Milan. One was the 166 Inter, described by Colombo as 'a transitional model intended primarily to use up remaining stock', a 166 Sport designed for road use and the 166MM which was a 140bhp racer with stylish open two-seater 'barchetta' bodywork.

The 166MM was a hit from the moment of its unveiling at the Turin Motor Show on 15 September 1948. Its racing debut took place in the 1949 Mille Miglia where Biondetti drove one such machine to score his fourth successive victory.

The 1949 season also saw the 166MM's prestige enhanced by its victory in the Le Mans 24-hour race where Chinetti shared the driving with Britain's Lord Selsdon. In what was effectively a reversal of his 1932 Le Mans win sharing an Alfa Romeo with Raymond Sommer, Chinetti drove virtually the entire 1949 race single-handed with barely an hour's intervention at the wheel by the inexperienced English blue-blood.

For the 1950 season, the 2-litre 166 engine was further expanded to 2.3-litres and was christened the 195S, being available in either barchetta or 'Le Mans' coupé trim. The new car's debut took place in the 1950 Targa Florio in the hands of Alberto Ascari, but was forced to retire from this event, but then continued to score its first major success in the Mille Miglia.

This event would later come to be described as 'the double-breasted Mille Miglia' as it was won by industrialist Gianino Marzotto, one of the four racing sons of a great Valdagno-based industrial dynasty. Marzotto's success attracted enormous media

Historic turning point. The Ferrari 166MM shared by Luigi Chinetti and Lord Selsdon passes the pits at the 1949 Le Mans en route to the Italian marque's maiden victory in the French endurance event. (LAT)

Luigi Chinetti

IRONICALLY, IT COULD be argued that Luigi Chinetti started out as an even more famous personality than Enzo Ferrari. Born in Milan in 1905, he was seven years younger than the man whose interests he would eventually represent in the USA, having qualified as an engineer and worked briefly for his father before joining the Alfa Romeo competitions department.

Resourceful and ambitious, Chinetti eventually cajoled and persuaded his way behind the wheel of a 2.3-litre Alfa which he shared with Raymond Sommer to win at Le Mans in 1932. It was often subsequently recalled that

Luigi Chinetti, photographed late in his life. (Michitake Isobe)

Chinetti was unwell for most of the race, and that Sommer consequently had to do the lion's share of the driving, but this contention was vigorously rebutted by the Italian through to the end of his life. Two years later he would repeat that success with Philippe Etancelin under the Scuderia Ferrari banner, but his links with Alfa Romeo were severed at the end of 1935 when Italy invaded Ethiopia.

Like René Dreyfus, Chinetti decided that he would not return to Italy after Mussolini's latest colonial adventure, for he was a devout anti-Fascist and had already been living in Paris for several years. Even a strongly worded request from Alfa director Ugo Gobatto could not shake Chinetti's resolve over this particular issue.

Just after the outbreak of the Second World War, Chinetti was hired by the charismatic Lucy O'Reilly Schell – mother of future Formula 1 driver Harry Schell – to prepare the two Maserati specials she was entering in the 1940 Indianapolis 500 to be driven by Dreyfus and René Le Begue. He accepted the invitation with alacrity, even though the party sailed for New York on an Italian liner and he spent much of the voyage deeply concerned that he might be interned.

As with Dreyfus, who was Jewish, this proved pretty well a one-way trip for Chinetti who stayed on in the USA and was eventually granted citizenship in 1946. After the war he briefly returned to Paris to tie up the loose ends of his garage business, met up with Enzo Ferrari again and, after briefly importing his new sports cars to France, returned to the USA and established a completely new operation in rented premises on New York's West 49th Street during 1948. His first sale was a 166 Spider delivered to millionaire and future Le Mans team-owner Briggs Cunningham.

Chinetti scored Ferrari's maiden Le Mans victory in 1949, sharing with the British Lord Selsdon, and that success helped boost not only Ferrari's image in the USA, but also

Chinetti's as an entrepreneur. From then on the American distributorship made steady progress and, by the mid-1960s, was reputedly responsible for the sale of around 35 per cent of the entire Maranello road car output.

Chinetti could certainly match Enzo Ferrari for individualistic behaviour. Just as Ferrari could keep international celebrities waiting at his pleasure for hours at a time at Maranello, for no better reason than the inner knowledge that they would not bridle at such treatment, so Chinetti could prove equally temperamental in dealing with his US customers. Many people felt that, once a car had been purchased from Chinetti, the normal dealer/customer relationship had somehow succumbed to a bizarre role reversal.

Rather than Chinetti catering for every whim of the well-heeled clients who patronised his business, he often gave them the impression that he was really doing them something of a favour dealing with their expensive cars. On the face of it, this might have been frustrating in the extreme for those who signed the cheques, but in terms of sustaining the Ferrari mystique, Chinetti was adopting precisely the correct strategy.

On the international racing scene, Chinetti's North American Racing Team (NART) campaigned with consistent zeal and enthusiasm with plenty of tacit factory support. Despite this, Luigi was delighted when his cars upstaged the works Ferrari entries, something they did quite often.

In 1961 he brought the dazzling Mexican duo of Pedro and Ricardo Rodriguez to Le Mans in NART's 250 Testa Rossa. Smashing lap record after lap record, at one point the teenage twosome looked as though they might humble the factory cars in a straight fight.

Ferrari's team manager politely sent an 'invitation' to Chinetti to the effect that he might rein in his two tempestuous talents. Chinetti declined and, as it turned out, the

NART Testa Rossa wilted under the mechanical strain. Nevertheless, Pedro would go on to win twice at Daytona for NART, and it was Chinetti who was responsible for arranging Ricardo's works Ferrari Formula 1 drive at the end of the 1961 season at the beginning of what would be a tragically brief Formula 1 career.

In 1964, when Enzo Ferrari flew into a fury over the CSI's refusal to accept the central-engined 250LM as a properly homologated GT racer, NART would enter the works Formula 1 Ferraris in distinctive blue and white livery for the last two Grands Prix of the season, after Ferrari surrendered his entrant's licence to express his annoyance at the action of the sport's governing body.

Chinetti also had the satisfaction of scoring Ferrari's last victory at Le Mans in 1965 when Masten Gregory and Jochen Rindt barnstormed the NART 275LM to victory after the faster works 330Ps and the rival Ford 7-litre Mk2s failed to last the distance. Thereafter, Chinetti would continue to support Le Mans with a variety of Ferraris long after the works team withdrew to concentrate exclusively on Formula 1.

Throughout his time as an entrant at Le Mans and many other classic endurance races, Chinetti would shamelessly charge wealthy privateers for the privilege of driving his cars. It didn't matter, he insisted, whether or not they were the most highly talented drivers of all time.

If they were promising, and had no money, then there was always the chance of Chinetti giving them a drive anyway. But if they were rich, they paid, no matter what. Even more so than Enzo Ferrari, Luigi Chinetti made it his business to ensure that nobody took a ride on the Maranello dream boat with a cut-price ticket.

attention, not only because of the ease with which he won the race, but the fact that he stepped out of his car at the Brescia finishing line wearing a double-breasted grey suit, white shirt and tie. For weeks afterwards, apparently, the Italian newspapers and magazines could talk of little else.

Gianino Marzotto, and his brothers Vittorio, Paolo and Umberto – all racing Ferraris to a greater or lesser extent in the early 1950s – were sons of the powerful Count Gaetano Marzotto, a man with wealth, influence and trenchant views such as to make an impact on even Enzo Ferrari's independent mentality. They were good customers, of course, but it was Ferrari's estimation that Gianino Marzotto ranked with the Marquis de Portago as one of the few amateur racers who could genuinely stand comparison with the professionals.

In addition to Colombo's 2.3-litre V12, Aurelio Lampredi began the evolution of a second family of sports car engines enjoying the same cylinder configuration. The first such unit was the 275S 3.3-litre which would eventually lead to the unveiling of the new Ferrari 340 America at the end of the year. This engine represented the first stage in the process which would lead to the 4.5-litre V12 naturally aspirated Formula 1 engine, but on the sports car stage the 166 variants continued to exert a worthwhile presence for the next couple of years.

The 275s 'barchettas' made their race debut on the 1950 Mille Miglia, handled by Ascari and Villoresi, but neither made the finish. These two machines were also present at Le Mans to supplement a trio of 166MMs. Chinetti, sharing with Pierre-Louis Dreyfus (no relation to René), handled one of the 195S models, but the early pace was set by the French blue Touring berlinetta

which Sommer was sharing with Dorino Serafini. Alas, none of the Ferraris made it to the chequered flag.

However, the 2.3-litre 195S helped Giovanni Bracco to win the 1950 Italian Hill-climb Championship and Chinetti kept the 166MM in the limelight with a fine victory in the Paris 1000km at Montlhéry, again sharing with Jean Lucas.

In 1951, Luigi Villoresi would win the Mille Miglia at the wheel of one of the 4.1-litre Ferrari 340 Americas which sported purposeful Vignale bodywork designed for the most part by Giovanni Michelotti. No fewer than three such cars were entered, the other two being handled by Vittorio Marzotto and Ascari, but of the trio only Villoresi survived to win.

Ferrari followed this up with a dismal time at Le Mans with only Chinetti/Lucas finishing in eighth place. But the Prancing Horse redeemed its reputation after what had developed into a somewhat dreary 1951 sports car racing season, when Piero Taruffi and Luigi Chinetti won the second Carrera Panamericana road race, their 212 Inter Vignale coupés finishing ahead of team-mates Ascari and Villoresi at the end of this 1936-mile epic which ran from Tuxtla Gutierrez to Ciudad Juarez on the US/Mexican border.

For the 1952 season Ferrari, three types of sports car engines were used. There were two new versions of the Colombo V12 – the 2.7-litre 225S and the 2.9-litre 250S – and a developed 4.1-litre Lampredi V12 dubbed the 340 Mexico. A promising newcomer by the name of Eugenio Castellotti demonstrated the potential of the 225S when his 'barchetta' won an event at Syracuse in convincing style, but the Mille Miglia would again prove the most formidable challenge, as amongst the Ferrari opposition

Chinetti at work. The Italian drove most of the 24-hours at the 1949 Le Mans in the Ferrari 166MM to score his third victory in the event. The previous two occasions had been in 1932 and 1934, both at the wheel of Alfa Romeos. (LAT)

were a trio of factory Mercedes-Benz 300SLs driven by Rudi Caracciola, Karl Kling and Hermann Lang.

Ferrari's works armoury was slightly blunted for this classic race. Ascari was off competing in an abortive Indianapolis foray and Villoresi was recovering from injuries sustained in the Swiss Grand Prix. Maranello thus put its shoulders behind Piero Taruffi's efforts, providing him with what looked like a 225 Vignale spider, but powered by a 4.1-litre V12 developing around 260bhp. In addition, there was an experimental 230bhp 250S-engined berlinetta coupé for hill-climb ace Giovanni Bracco.

Even by the standards of the Mille Miglia, this promised to be an epic. Bracco led at Ravenna on the southbound leg with an advantage of around five minutes over Kling's Mercedes, but by the time the field reached Rome the German driver had

gone ahead. On the northward sprint home, Taruffi nosed ahead of Kling by the time they reached Siena, only to fall victim to transmission seizure as he began tackling the Futa and Raticosa passes.

What followed from Bracco was, in Enzo Ferrari's words, probably 'the most spectacular success of all my racers.' Bracco was a man who liked his drink and would eventually die prematurely, partly it was said due to this inclination. He was two minutes down on Kling when his Ferrari arrived at Florence, but he looked at his co-driver and promised they would be leading by the time they reached Bologna.

Fortified by a bottle of Chianti – and reputedly an endless supply of brandy fed to him by his co-driver – the chain-smoking Bracco simply hurled the 250S berlinetta across the Futa and Raticosa passes to arrive in Bologna over a minute ahead of

Kling. On the final sprint back to Brescia, Bracco added another three minutes to that advantage. Many years later, a German journalist would write that Kling never quite recovered from his Mille Miglia defeat at the hands of Bracco and his Ferrari.

The 1952 Monaco Grand Prix was run for sports cars, with the first five places falling to Ferrari, with Vittorio Marzotto's Vignale spider leading home the parade. However, come Le Mans it was a very different story, with Mercedes posting a convincing 1–2 finish after a blistering early pace set by Ascari and Villoresi in the Mille Miglia-winning 250S ended with the car succumbing to transmission failure after barely an hour of frantic competition. One by one the other Ferraris hit trouble until only the 340 America of André Simon and Louis Vincent was around to survive in fifth place at the finish.

The simultaneous evolution of the Lampredi and Colombo V12s continued through the 1953 season. For those Ferrari customers who wanted to compete in the popular 2-litre sports car category, there was a new 166MM, while the Lampredi development line continued to be represented by the 4.2-litre Type 340. Of more significance altogether was the instigation of an official World Sports Car Championship based on seven races, with individual marques scoring on the basis of 8–6–4–3–2–1 for the first six places.

In the face of opposition from Aston Martin, Jaguar and Cunningham, no works Ferraris contested the opening race at Sebring, and the private US entries failed to get the job done. The second round of the championship was the Mille Miglia where Lancia and the 3.5-litre Alfa Romeos represented a formidable level of opposition for Maranello to tackle. To fend them off, Ferrari pinned its hopes on the powerful 4.1-litre V12 installed in two Touring-bodied roadsters and two Vignale-dressed coupés. In addition there were three 250MMs in the field, two Pininfarina berlinettas and a Vignale roadster.

Initially the Alfa Romeos of Consalvo Sanesi, Karl Kling and Juan Manuel Fangio seemed to have the race in the palm of their hands. But in a repeat of Bracco's great sprint over the Futa Pass the previous year, Gianino Marzotto got ahead of Fangio on that demanding section of the race, his 250MM berlinetta thereafter pulling away to consolidate the Italian industrialist's second win in the great race, by over 11 minutes from the Argentine driver.

By this stage in the company's history, Ferrari had established a firm commercial base from which to take advantage of lucrative sales to private entrants. The rich and famous flocked to Maranello, including diletante racers such as film director Roberto Rosselini and playboy Porfirio Rubirosa (who would die many years later at the wheel of his road-going Ferrari GT in an early morning accident in the Bois de Boulogne). Ferrari was only too delighted to take their lire, realising that such associations simply added to the Maranello image and mystique.

The 1953 Le Mans 24-hour race followed next on the Championship schedule, but the Jaguar C-types emerged as the dominant forces on the smooth Sarthe circuit. In a race marred by the death of American Ferrari privateer Tom Cole, who crashed his 344MM at White House, Paolo and Gianino Marzotto salvaged some dignity for Maranello with fifth place, but the Championship lead was now in Jaguar's hands.

Paolo Marzotto at speed at Le Mans, 1953, in the 4.1-litre 340MM coupé in which he and brother Gianino finished fifth, the best placed surviving Ferrari in the race. (LAT)

Alberto Ascari and Luigi Villoresi gave the Jaguar C-types a brisk run for their money at Le Mans in 1953, but eventually retired with clutch problems on Sunday morning. (LAT)

Beating Jaguar at Le Mans

SINCE CHINETTI'S NEAR-SOLO effort yielded Ferrari's first Le Mans victory in 1949, Maranello had to wait for another five years before duplicating this achievement. In 1950 all five Ferrari entries retired, and in 1951 – when playboy Porfirio Rubirosa was amongst those representing the marque – the race produced a similarly dismal outcome, with Chinetti and Jean Lucas the best placed Ferrari in eighth place.

The 1951 race was won by Jaguar, the British manufacturer coming back to duplicate that feat in 1953, after the 1952 race fell to Mercedes-Benz. Ferrari still hadn't quite got a handle on Le Mans, but it would not be long before the Italian marque became synonymous with this most technically challenging of all international motor races.

In 1954, Jaguar unveiled its aerodynamic D-type and brought it to Le Mans for the first time as a successor to the valiant C-types which had scored the company's previous two victories. Ranged against them was a trio of 4.9-litre Ferrari 375s driven by Froilan Gonzalez/Maurice Trintignant, Robert Manzon/Louis Rosier and Umberto Maglioli/Paolo Marzotto.

The Maranello trio stormed away at the head of the field in the opening stages with Stirling Moss, in the D-type he was sharing with Peter Walker, keeping in touch for the time being. The new Jaguars were delayed on Saturday evening with blocked fuel lines and, as dusk turned to darkness, so Gonzalez and Trintignant pounded away into the distance.

By the end of the night the leading Ferrari was the only survivor of the original Maranello threesome. Maglioli and Marzotto

The 4.9-litre Ferrari 375, shared by Maurice Trintignant and Froilan Gonzalez, to score Maranello's second win at Le Mans in 1954. (LAT)

had retired even before nightfall with rear axle failure, while Rosier and Manzon ground to a halt in the small hours of Sunday morning with a broken gearbox.

By breakfast time on Sunday the rain was lashing down and the stage set for a truly epic chase. Although Gonzalez and Trintignant could afford to take things steadily, any unnecessary delay would bring the sole surviving D-type, driven by Duncan Hamilton and Tony Rolt, within striking distance.

The Englishmen having nothing to lose and everything to gain, threw caution to the wind and ran the D-type as hard as they dared for the remainder of the race. The rain eased mid-morning on Sunday, then intensified again as lunchtime approached. With

two hours left, the Ferrari was still almost two laps ahead of the Jaguar. Time was running out.

Yet there was very nearly a cruel sting lurking in the tail of this Le Mans as far as Ferrari was concerned. With only 90 minutes left, Trintignant brought the Ferrari 375 in for a routine stop. Gonzalez jumped aboard, but the V12 refused to fire. After a few seconds he jumped out again and sat on the pit counter as the mechanics fumbled with the sparking plugs. Rolt was in sight, the Englishman intent on stopping for new goggles, but he was waved on by his excited pit crew. Now the Jaguar was back on the

same lap as the leading Ferrari.

Still the Ferrari mechanics fiddled beneath the bonnet. Suddenly, the engine burst back into life. Gonzalez leaped in and accelerated back into the fray, now barely a minute and a half ahead with the V12 engine sounding less than totally healthy.

Thunder and lightning now lashed the circuit as Hamilton took over the D-type for the final hour, sprinting to within a minute and a half of Gonzalez in the closing minutes. Then the rain eased, the track started to dry slightly and the Argentine driver eased away to score Ferrari's second ever Le Mans win by just under three minutes.

Gonzalez takes the chequered flag to beat the Jaguar D-type at Le Mans in 1954.

Despite having to nurse a fragile rear axle, Mike Hawthorn won the next round at Spa-Francorchamps, posting another Ferrari victory in the absence of the key rival works teams. Then Ascari and Villoresi blitzed the opposition to win the first ADAC Nürburgring 1000km race in a new 4.5-litre Vignale-bodied roadster.

Ferrari failed to contest the Tourist Trophy at Dundrod and declined any works participation on the final round of the championship, the Carrera Panamericana. Private team owner Franco Cornaccia did, however, have four 4.5-litre berlinettas at his disposal. It was a tragic race, however, for one of these cars driven by wealthy amateur Antonio Stagnoli was involved in a fatal accident, and Lancia emerged with a dominant 1–2–3 finish, although Guido Mancini's fourth place in one of the Ferrari 4.5s at least secured a Maranello victory in the first official World Sports Car Championship.

The 1953 season was also distinguished by the introduction of another engine configuration from the Lampredi line, the former being a development of the 500 Formula 2 engine which was enjoying such front-line World Championship success at the time. Lampredi had originally been attracted to the four-cylinder configuration because of its weight advantages, enhanced low-speed torque and reduction in the number of moving parts.

However, from the start of 1954 the front-line Ferrari sports car effort revolved round the mighty 4.9-litre Lampredi V12s developed from the 1951 Formula 1 engine. These 375-Plus models were fearsome beasts but bombed spectacularly in the Mille Miglia where Ascari's 3.3-litre Lancia D40 saw them off, and Maranello had to be content with second place thanks to Vittorio Marzotto in the 2-litre type 500 'Mondial'.

Froilan Gonzalez put the 4.9 V12's prowess on show at Silverstone where he won the sports car supporting race to the International Trophy event, having just won the main event of the day in the team's Formula 1 machine. The burly Argentine driver was on hand, together with Maurice Trintignant, when they finally broke Maranello's disappointing run at Le Mans to score that memorable victory over the Tony Rolt/Duncan Hamilton Jaguar D-type (see sidebar).

Jaguar then avenged its defeat at the Sarthe by taking the first three

The Ferrari 750 Monzas of Eugenio Castellotti/Piero Taruffi and Umberto Magliolli/Maurice Trintignant in nose-to-tail formation during the 1955 Tourist Trophy race at Dundrod. (LAT)

places in the Reims 12-hour race, after which Ferrari increasingly relied on the new generation of four-cylinder engines. Despite this, to round off the year US private owner Erwin Goldschmidt made available his own 375-Plus for Umberto Maglioli to use in the Carrera Panamericana, and the Italian driver won convincingly. For the moment this effectively marked the end of the works Ferrari V12 sports cars, for the company decided to concentrate on the Lampredi four and six cylinder engines for the 1955 season.

The 2-litre 500 Mondial had proved extremely promising in 1954, but the engine was progressively enlarged, first to 2.9 and then to 3-litres. For 1955 these were supplemented by a bewildering array of Lampredi-designed six-cylinder engines; a 3.7-litre unit derived from adding two cylinders to the Formula 1 type 625 engine and the 4.4-litre unit developed from the 735S.

The opening round of the Championship in Buenos Aires fell to the local ex-works 375 driven by Enrique Diaz Saenz-Valiente and Jose-Maria Ibanez after the works 3.7-litre car of Gonzalez and Trintignant was disqualified for entering the pits incorrectly, and the 750 Monza of Maglioli and local old hand Clemar Bucci was excluded for an unauthorised push-start. It was not a promising note on which to begin the new season.

Into the works Ferrari team for 1955 came Eugenio Castellotti, a dynamic young blood on whose talent Ferrari was relying for another Mille Miglia victory. No luck. The 1955 race produced the classic and crushing Mercedes victory for Stirling Moss and Denis Jenkinson, although Castellotti used the brute power of the 4.4-litre Ferrari to catch and pass the German car in the opening stages of the race.

According to Jenkinson, from his matchless vantage point at Moss's shoulder, Castellotti drove the opening stages of the race like a lunatic, the big Ferrari yawing through the corners with armfuls of understeer, its inside rear tyre spinning furiously. Sure enough, tyre problems would eventually lead to his retirement and, with Paolo Marzotto's sister car suffering a similar fate, it was left to Piero to finish third for Ferrari behind the victorious Moss/Jenkinson and Fangio in a second Mercedes 300SLR.

Only a matter of weeks after the Mille Miglia came tragedy when one of Ferrari's favourite sons, Alberto Ascari, was killed at Monza whilst taking an impromptu test in a Ferrari 750 Monza, which Castellotti had been down to race in the following weekend's Supercortemaggiore GP at the famous Milanese circuit. Come the race, there was more disappointment in store for the Prancing Horse as Jean Behra's Maserati 300S beat Mike Hawthorn's Ferrari Monza to score a decisive victory.

For Le Mans there were three 121s (or 735LMs) fielded for Maglioli/Phil Hill, Castellotti/Paolo Marzotto and Trintignant/Harry Schell. It was a disaster in more ways than one, for the French event produced one of the sport's most tragic ever accidents when Pierre Levegh's Mercedes 300SLR vaulted into the crowd opposite the pits and killed more than 80 onlookers.

Mercedes later withdrew its entries on the specific instructions of the German company's board of directors,

Privateer Harry Schell at the wheel of his own Ferrari 750 Monza at Goodwood in August 1955. (LAT)

leaving Hawthorn and Ivor Bueb to notch up Jaguar's third Le Mans success. Almost as a footnote, all three of Ferrari's leading works entries failed to make the distance.

By this stage in the season it was becoming clear that Ferrari's big capacity sixes were insufficiently reliable, so the team reverted to four-cylinder cars for the balance of the season, using a 3.4-litre unit in a 750 Monza chassis. Yet this move did little to stem the generally disappointing results, and the Ferrari team was again taken to the cleaners by Mercedes-Benz come the Tourist Trophy at Dundrod.

Despite all this drama, there was still an outside chance of Ferrari hanging on to the World Championship at Targa Florio. These hopes rested on Castellotti's shoulders once again, and he actually overtook Moss's Mercedes in the early stages of the rough and ready Sicilian road race which made Le Mans look like a leisurely jaunt round Silverstone by comparison.

Only this late refuelling stop prevented the Ferrari 860 Monza, shared by Fangio and Castellotti, from winning the 1956 Nürburgring 1000km sports car race. (LAT)

Unfortunately, just when it seemed as though Maranello had saved the day, Castellotti's co-driver Robert Manzon suffered a puncture and had to change a wheel at the roadside, allowing the Mercedes of Peter Collins and Fangio to score a 1–2 finish and clinch the title crown for the German manufacturer.

At the end of the 1955 season, Aurelio Lampredi quit Maranello to take a senior engineering position with Fiat. His place was taken by a new team of engineers including Vittorio Bellantani, returning from Maserati, the veteran Alberto Massimino and the very promising 28-year old Andrea Fraschetti. In addition, Ferrari's inheritance of all the Lancia equipment following the Turin company's withdrawal from racing, brought the veteran and highly respected Vittorio Jano into the fold.

For the 1955 season the 750 Monza was replaced with the new Massimino-developed four-cylinder 2-litre 'Testa Rossa' which would take on Maserati's highly competitive rival machine in the hotly contested and extremely popular 2-litre sports car racing class. This machine had independent front suspension, at last replacing the transverse leaf spring arrangement which had done sterling service for so long.

As far as drivers were concerned, Phil Hill, Eugenio Castellotti and Olivier Gendebien were retained, but supplemented now by the great Fangio, Peter Collins, 'Fon' de Portago (of whom much more later) and Luigi Musso.

With Stirling Moss and Jean Behra in the Maserati factory line-up, it was obvious that Ferrari was going to be up against it in a big way as far as the Sports Car World Championship was concerned, with Maserati opening the score with a win at Buenos Aires, where Moss was partnered by Carlos Menditeguy in the victorious 300S.

Collins would then win the Tour de Sicily on his first outing in a Ferrari sports car, while the Mille Miglia yielded a Ferrari grand slam with Castellotti winning in 290MM from Peter Collins/Louis Klemantaski followed by Luigi Musso second and third in their LM860s, Fangio fourth in a 290MM and Gendebien fifth, winning the GT class in a 250GT berlinetta.

Maserati won at the Nürburgring thanks to Moss and Behra pouncing when the Fangio/Castellotti 860MM had to make an unscheduled late refuelling stop. Following the 1955 catastrophe, Le Mans was run under 2.5-litre regulations in 1956, and Ferrari arrived with the 625 Le Mans, powered by a specially adapted

Mike Hawthorn's 4.1-litre Ferrari 335S, which he shared with Luigi Musso, was an early casualty in the 1957 Le Mans 24-hour race. This was a similar machine to that in which de Portago had been killed during the Mille Miglia. (LAT)

Castellotti at speed with the Ferrari 860 Monza in the 1956 Swedish GP at Kristianstad. He and Fangio led for more than half distance before the car let them down. (Roebuck collection)

version of the four-cylinder Formula 1 engine. Gendebien and Trintignant managed to finish third behind the Ron Flockhart/Ninian Sanderson Jaguar D-type and the Aston Martin DBR1 of Stirling Moss/Peter Collins, the last-named having rejoined the British team.

Finally, despite the retirement of the 860 Monza of Fangio and Castellotti, which led the first half of the Swedish GP at Kristianstad, Ferrari clinched its third World Sports Car Championship with a victory for Phil Hill and Gendebien in a 290MM. Events would now unfold into the 1957 season to change the face of international sports car racing and set Maranello on course for its most consistent spell of success so far in this ever-changing and complex category.

Chapter 3

The Formula 2 championships and beyond

Ferrari began the 1952 'Formula 2 championship' season in an extremely well-ordered situation. Aurelio Lampredi finalised a four-cylinder 2-litre engine, in addition to a 2.5-litre derivative for future Formula 1 use, and this was installed in one of the most elegant of all Ferrari single seaters, the Tipo 500.

The car made its competition debut in the 1951 Modena GP where Ascari and Villoresi completely dominated both practice and the race. From the start of the 1952 season, Ferrari's 500s were racing across Europe every weekend, contesting a full programme of non-title events in addition to the championship races. The works cars were handled by Ascari, Villoresi and Piero Taruffi, occasionally by Nino Farina and French driver André Simon.

Ranged against them were the sleek new Colombo-designed six-cylinder Maseratis for Fangio, Gonzalez and Felice Bonetto, plus the six-cylinder Gordinis of Robert Manzon and Jean Behra. However, Maserati's prospects received a major blow when Fangio suffered injuries in the Autodrome GP at Monza on 8 June 1952 which would keep him out of racing for the rest of the season.

Fangio had originally also signed to

drive the BRM V16 Formula 1 challenger, but with the abandonment of a pukka World Championship for proper Grand Prix machinery, he was committed to only a handful of non-title events for the British team.

He drove the BRM at Dundrod, in Northern Ireland, and was hoping for a lift to Monza in Prince Bira's aeroplane. Unfortunately Bira left without him, leaving Fangio to fly to Paris, then drive through the night to Monza. Exhausted, he started from the back of the grid and crashed out

Alberto Ascari won both the 1952 and 1953 World Championships at the wheel of a 2-litre Ferrari 500 Formula 2 car.

on the second lap, damaging his neck badly enough to preclude him from racing for the rest of the season.

The Formula 2 championship thus became Ascari's playground. With Fangio out of the picture, he was the dominant force on the international racing stage. His smooth, stylish approach paid dividends and his list of successes was awesome, reading like something from the Prost/Senna era of McLaren-Honda domination 36 years later.

In 1952, Ascari won the European (Belgian), French, British, German and Italian GPs. The following year he picked up where he had left off with successes in the Argentine, Dutch and Belgian races before his 13-month record of unbroken championship success was stemmed by team-mate Mike Hawthorn's stupendous victory over Fangio's Maserati in the French GP at Reims.

Ascari then picked up the threads of his achievement to win again in the British and Swiss GPs, guaranteeing himself a second straight World Championship. Away from the major events the Ferrari 500s imposed similar domination on the non-title events, winning battles at such long-abandoned tracks as Comminges, Modena, Posillipo, La Baule-Escoublac and Les Sables d'Olonne.

Yet there were always the occasional problems. At Buenos Aires in the opening race of the 1953 season, Farina crashed into a group of wandering spectators, killing 10 of them. Then Hawthorn was almost deprived of the opportunity to make his name in the French GP at Reims when Ferrari threatened to withdraw his cars after an argument over the outcome of the traditional 12-hour sports car race which immediately preceded the GP on the classic French circuit.

The 4.5-litre Ferrari coupé driven by Umberto Maglioli and Piero Carini was withdrawn from the sports car event after the organisers announced that no more of its lap times would be recorded. It was alleged that its crew had infringed a rule stipulating precisely at what time the competing

The Ferrari 500s of Farina and Ascari lead the Maseratis of Fangio and Onofre Marimon in the 1953 Italian GP at Monza, a race which Fangio won at the final corner after Marimon caused Ascari to spin off the road.

Hawthorn makes his name

MIKE HAWTHORN ENJOYED an enduring relationship with Enzo Ferrari, although he would only win three Grands Prix during his on-off five-year career with the Maranello team. An extrovert, devil-may-care – some would say selfishly uninhibited – personality, he was the son of former motorcycle racer Leslie Hawthorn and was born in the Yorkshire town of Mexborough in 1929.

Mike's father eventually moved south to live close to Brooklands, and established the Tourist Trophy Garage in Farnham, Surrey. Shortly after the war, both father and son began racing Riley sports cars in British club events, and Mike's career was given a major boost in 1952 when Bob Chase, a friend of the family, bought a Formula 2 Cooper-Bristol at the wheel of which Hawthorn junior seriously began to make his name.

By the end of 1952 he had developed a sufficiently prominent reputation to be invited to Modena for a test drive with a view to a full-time Ferrari seat the following year.

By the time the championship contest reached Reims, the Ferrari/Maserati battle was reaching its peak. From the start, Gonzalez raced into the lead for Maserati, running a light fuel load and intending to make a refuelling stop, but planning to draw the Ferrari opposition into a prematurely bruising contest.

In his wake, the remaining red cars from the two famous Italian constructors weaved and jinked around the sun-baked circuit in ever-changing formation, the Ferraris of Ascari, Hawthorn, Villoresi and Farina locked in combat with the Maseratis of Fangio, Felice Bonetto and Onofre Marimon.

After 30 laps Gonzalez came in to refuel and just failed to get back into the fray ahead of Fangio and Hawthorn who raced past the pits locked in wheel-to-wheel combat. For the balance of the race the contest developed into a cut-and-thrust battle between the young Englishman and the former World Champion – Ferrari and Maserati running side-by-side down the long straights through the cornfields and each man crouching as low as possible behind his windscreen in an effort to squeeze every last ounce of speed from his car.

It was clearly only going to be sorted out on the final lap, and with Fangio finding difficulty engaging first gear, the odds were stacked against the Argentine ace on this particular day. Coming into the Thillois right-hander for the last time, Hawthorn judged things perfectly to dive inside the Maserati and he just held off Fangio by a second in the final sprint to the chequered flag.

It was a memorable weekend for Hawthorn in more ways than one. The night before this classic victory, a dalliance with a local young lady resulted in his fathering a son, a fact which remained a secret for over 30 years before it was uncovered by historian Chris Nixon during the preparation of his exhaustive joint biography of Hawthorn and Peter Collins entitled *Mon Ami Mate* (Transport Bookman Publications, 1991).

This remarkable story earned considerable exposure in the national British daily papers more than three decades after Hawthorn's death in a road accident. Unfortunately – although perhaps inevitably – the fruits of Nixon's investigative prowess caused a degree of offence to some older members of the British motor racing community, who believed that it would have been better to let sleeping dogs lie.

Mike Hawthorn (No. 16) made his name with a brilliant victory in the 1953 French GP at Reims. Here, in the early stages of that race he leads team-mate Luigi Villoresi's similar Ferrari 500. (LAT)

cars could turn off their lights during the early dawn. For some hours it seemed as though Ferrari would stand by his threat and withdraw his Formula 2 machines, but at the last moment they were wheeled out on to the Grand Prix grid and Hawthorn was able to drive into the history books with a brilliant win over Fangio.

When it came to preparing for the new 2.5-litre Formula 1 the following year, although the new Tipo 553 'Squalo' had made its debut in 2-litre form at Monza in 1953, it quickly became clear that this Lampredi-designed machine was short on development. As a consequence, the mainstay of Ferrari's 1954 challenge was initially the Tipo 625, a chassis unchanged from the previous year's Formula 2 machine.

The Maranello team thus started the 1954 season in Buenos Aires with a trio of 625s for Mike Hawthorn, Giuseppe Farina and Froilan Gonzalez. Already in the opposition pipeline were the Lancia D50 and Mercedes-Benz W196, not to mention the Maserati 250F, and it was to the rival Italian team that Fangio was loaned by Mercedes for his home Grand Prix as the German machines were not yet ready.

Fangio won the race commandingly with Farina, by now probably past his best as a Formula 1 force, trailing home a distant second. Gonzalez was third, with Maurice Trintignant's private 625 fourth, but it was clear that the 625 was no match for Fangio in a Maserati. The Ferrari team consequently returned to Europe feeling more than a little apprehensive about what might lay in wait for them once the World Championship season got fully into its swing.

Lampredi, meanwhile, had been working hard and had produced a couple of substantially revised 'Squalos' for the non-championship

The Ferrari type 553 'Squalo' was Aurelio Lampredi's four-cylinder offering for the new 2.5-litre Formula 1 which started in 1954. (LAT)

Syracuse Grand Prix on 11 April. The wheelbase had been lengthened, and its distinctive side fuel tanks had been supplemented by another in the tail. Its four-cylinder engine had a claimed modest 5bhp increment over the unit which had powered the 625s.

Yet these modifications were insufficient to overcome the driver resistance to the 'Squalo's' handling characteristics. The car seemed to offer high levels of basic adhesion, but, when pushed to the limit, its loss of grip was sudden and in no way progressive. Farina refused to adapt his driving style to cater for these characteristics and, while Gonzalez proved more flexible, Lampredi waged a lengthy intra-team battle with Hawthorn in a largely unsuccessful quest to coax the English driver into adjusting his approach.

At Syracuse, Ferrari's frustrations

The 'Squalo' made its first appearance in 2-litre form at the 1953 Italian GP at Monza. Although the car was not initially promising, two such examples were raced in this event by Umberto Maglioli and Piero Carini just to earn Maranello a special 7 million lire prize for the constructor who fielded two brand new cars at Monza! (Publifoto)

Aurelio Lampredi (right) was the architect of the non-supercharged early V12 Formula 1 Ferraris. His four-cylinder designs were less successful, as Mike Hawthorn (centre, arms folded) and Harry Schell seem ready to confirm. (LAT)

burnt out. Farina won the race to provide some consolation, but Hawthorn languished in hospital for several weeks before fully recovering from the burns.

Gonzalez went on to win the non-championship Bordeaux Grand Prix in a 625, then won both his heat and the final of the Silverstone International Trophy – using a 'Squalo' in the former sprint and taking over Trintignant's 625 for the main race, after his 553 seized its engine while being warmed up prior to the start.

Fangio won for Maserati again come the Belgian GP at Spa-Francorchamps, but although Farina had successfully squeezed the further revised 'Squalo' briefly into the lead, the entire contemporary Formula 1 equation was rewritten in time for the French GP at Reims where Mercedes unveiled the new W196.

Gonzalez was now emerging as the most consistent of the factory Ferrari drivers, and he drove his 'Squalo's' heart out in the opening stages of the race in a vain effort to keep in touch with Fangio and his Mercedes team-mate Karl Kling who surged to a dominant 1–2 debut victory. Gonzalez's steed eventually suffered an engine failure, as did both the 625s of Hawthorn and Trintignant. That left Robert Manzon's private 625 to finish third, a lap down on the Mercs. The pressure on the Prancing Horse was inexorably increasing.

The need for further development on the Tipo 553 'Squalo' was threatening to overwhelm the Ferrari team, coming as it did in the middle of the season. After Reims it was decided to fit the good-handling 625 chassis with a hybrid engine incorporating the crankcase and bottom end of the original engine, but with a new cylinder head and block from the 553. It

were compounded when Hawthorn, who had opted to drive a 625, clipped a wall, rupturing a fuel tank which caused the car to burst into flames.

Gonzalez stopped his 'Squalo' to go to the help of his team-mate, but the blazing 625 rolled into the Argentine driver's stationary car and both were looked quite a promising step forward after Hawthorn won the non-title GP de Rouen-les-Essarts, six days before the British GP at Silverstone where Gonzalez put on a tremendous demonstration to win at the wheel of a 625/553 on a day when the streamlined Mercedes W196s were simply at sea on the featureless airfield circuit.

Sadly, Gonzalez was unable to repeat this performance in the German GP at Nürburgring where he was overcome with grief at the death of fellow Argentine driver Onofre Marimon who crashed his Maserati 250F during practice. Fangio regained the winning edge for Mercedes with Hawthorn second after retiring his own car early and then taking over the off-form Gonzalez machine.

Ferrari was clearly now floundering around as far as the technical specifications of his Formula 1 cars were concerned and this was never more obvious than at Monza where no fewer than six cars were fielded for the Italian GP. Ascari, on loan from Lancia, drove another variation of the 625 fitted with a 553 engine; Hawthorn and Trintignant had similar chassis fitted with the first version of the hybrid 625/553 engine, Umberto Maglioli had a standard 625 and Gonzalez an original 553 'Squalo'. In addition, Manzon had a 625/553 entered on a semi-works basis.

Ascari's presence in the team perhaps underlined the reality that Ferrari's regular drivers were really only good second-raters in absolute terms, Hawthorn and Gonzalez admittedly being inspired on their day but not really world class on a consistent basis.

By lap 10, Ascari had moved his 625 variant through into a six-second lead over Fangio's Mercedes W196 streamliner. Eventually Ascari's overworked four-cylinder Ferrari wilted after 49 laps and Fangio eventually won, but only after Moss's Maserati subsequently retired with an oil leak. Hawthorn was second with Gonzalez, who took over Maglioli's 625 after his

Farina exiting La Source hairpin during the 1954 Belgian GP at the wheel of the Ferrari 553 'Squalo'. He led briefly, but retired after 15 laps.

Start of the 1954 Belgian GP at Spa-Francorchamps with the Ferrari 'Squalos' of Farina and Gonzalez flanking Fangio's winning Maserati 250F on the front row of the grid.

own 553 broke its gearbox, storming home a determined third.

On paper, this wasn't a bad result, but Hawthorn was clearly dissatisfied, as he later recalled after a bout of testing prior to the final race of the season at Barcelona: 'All this time Ferrari had been working hard to cure the faults of the Squalo, which had proved so disappointing, and we assembled at Monza to try a new version, with coil spring front suspension instead of the transverse leaf spring.

'It was improved out of all recognition and had become a very nice little car. Maglioli and I spent some time driving it round, and then Gonzalez, who was recovering after his Dundrod accident, said he would like a try. He

had done only a few laps when the de Dion tube broke away as he was going round Curva Grande. We heard the engine note die away and rushed round to find the car stopped after a hectic series of swerves with one back wheel at a very peculiar angle . . .'

This revised 'Squalo' was taken to Barcelona for Mike to drive in the Spanish GP. Yet its presence in Spain paled into insignificance, for this was the race at which the long-awaited Lancia D50, with its beautiful four-overhead-camshaft V8 engine, made its race debut with Ascari and Villoresi allocated a car apiece.

The Lancia D50's development period had been so protracted that many observers, incorrectly but with

good reason, began to speculate that it might be fitted with a four-wheel drive system. The first prototype had turned a wheel for the first time in February 1954. It had originally been intended that the D50 should make its race debut at Reims – perhaps with a view to stealing Mercedes-Benz's thunder – then it was to be Monza. Eventually it did not come to a starting grid until eight months after Ascari and Villoresi tried it out on Turin's Caselle airport for the first time.

The workmanship which had gone into the Lancia D50 attracted instant acclamation from the Formula 1 pit lane. Its 90-degree V8 engine was mounted at an angle of 12-degrees within the chassis, in order that the propeller shaft would run to the left of the driver's seat, thereby ensuring

Froilan Gonzalez emerged victorious with the 553 'Squalo' in one of the heats for the 1954 Silverstone International Trophy, but its engine seized just prior to the final and he had to transfer into one of the 625s. (LAT)

that the car was as low as possible. The engine itself was installed as a semi-stressed unit within the chassis, in effect doubling as the upper tube in a complete space-frame.

The D50 was also distinguished by its distinctive pannier tanks mounted between front and rear wheels; the right-hand tank contained fuel, the left-hand tank a smaller fuel tank with an oil cooler mounted ahead of it. The resultant weight distribution made for a high level of adhesion, calling for the sort of sensitive touch on fast corners which Ascari was more than capable of providing. Pre-race testing at Monza had seen Alberto lap three seconds quicker than Fangio's

fastest Mercedes W196 time from the Italian GP.

To judge by contemporary technical information, the Lancia D50 also weighed in as one of the lightest Formula 1 cars of its era. At 1367 lb (620kg), it was significantly lighter than the Mercedes-Benz W196 which tipped the scales at 1587 lb (720kg) fitted with streamlined bodywork and 1521 lbs (690kg) as a conventional open-wheeler. The Ferrari 625 was a claimed 1433 lb (650kg), while the 553 'Squalo' was reckoned to be

lighter at 1300 lb (590kg).

Ascari blitzed the opposition in practice at Barcelona. He qualified the new Lancia on pole position and was pulling away at around 2 sec a lap when the clutch packed up. That allowed Hawthorn's Ferrari to get the upper hand in a battle with Harry Schell's Maserati 250F and run out the winner ahead of Luigi Musso's Maserati and Fangio's slowing Mercedes. It was Hawthorn's second Grand Prix win for Ferrari.

Chapter 4

The Lancia-Ferraris and Dino 246s

IMAGINE IF THE Williams Formula 1 team went bankrupt and the RAC Motor Sports Association financed the transfer of all its cars and other key technical assets to McLaren – and then threw in another half a million pounds for good measure in an effort to buttress Ron Dennis's efforts racing against the might of Ferrari.

Sounds like something from the wildest recesses of a Formula 1 journalist's imagination? Perhaps so. But this is in effect what happened in 1955 as Ferrari inherited the superb Vittorio Jano-designed Lancia D50s when Gianni Lancia's team hit the financial rocks shortly after Alberto Ascari's untimely death in May of that year.

By the time of this disaster, the writing seemed very clearly on the wall for Ferrari as the team squared up for 1955. Moss joined Fangio in the formidable Mercedes-Benz line-up, while Hawthorn opted to switch to the British-based Vanwall team, reasoning that such a move would enable him to spend more time concentrating on his family's garage business in Farnham, Surrey, in the wake of his father Leslie's death in a road accident in 1954.

Ferrari began the 1955 season in a precarious state, using the two-year-old, now coil-sprung Tipo 625s equipped with five-speed gearboxes and driven by the journeyman Trintignant and Farina, the Italian veteran now well past his best.

Fangio and Moss scored a Mercedes 1–2 in the Argentine GP season-opener at Buenos Aires, with Trintignant a solid third sharing his 625 with Maglioli and Farina. For the start of the European season there was another revamped machine available, the Tipo 555 'Super Squalo' which was built up round a completely different chassis frame, the new machine making its debut in the Turin GP at Valentino Park.

Ascari, Villoresi and the newly-signed Eugenio Castellotti delivered a 1–2–3 grand slam for the Lancia D50s, and Ascari rammed home the message by winning at Naples and dominating the Pau GP before he retired, allowing Jean Behra's Maserati through to win.

Amazingly, considering how outclassed the 625 had become, Trintignant bagged a fortuitous win at Monaco, but only after the Mercedes of Fangio and Moss retired and Ascari took his unscheduled ducking in the harbour. Castellotti finished second ahead of the Behra/Cesare Perdisa Maserati and the arthritic Farina.

Further back in the field, Piero Taruffi became so fed-up with the handling of his 'Super Squalo' that he came into the pits and handed it over to Paul Frère, the Belgian semi-professional racer who was the team's reserve driver.

Frère later shed some interesting light on the way in which the Ferrari team operated, having failed to persuade manager Mino Amarotti that changes should be made to improve the 555's handling characteristics.

'That car was a real beast round Monaco,' he remembered, 'as it just wanted to plough straight on at the two tight hairpins. I hinted that it might be a good idea to disconnect the front anti-roll bar, but Amarotti was responsible for technical matters at the races and I am sure he was really upset by my suggestion.

'He did not want to take the responsibility for modifying something which was part of the original design – for which he was not responsible. If he had taken my advice, and then something had gone wrong, then he most certainly would have been held responsible for it back at the factory. He just wasn't prepared to do it.'

Four days after Monaco, Ascari was

killed testing that sports Ferrari at Monza. Lancia's most crucial human asset had been snatched away, and Gianni Lancia, together with the entire Italian motor sporting fraternity, was bereft. Although Castellotti was allowed to take a single D50 to the Belgian GP at Spa-Francorchamps, financial problems were weighing heavily on Gianni Lancia's shoulders and he decided that he would have to retire from Formula 1 racing thereafter.

Thanks to the combined efforts of the Italian Automobile Federation and Fiat, a deal was struck whereby Ferrari took over the entire inventory of Lancia D50s, plus the associated spares, with the promise of the equivalent of £30,000 a year in financial support for as long as the Maranello team continued to race the cars. Enzo Ferrari clearly thought it was Christmas and, bearing in mind the abject failure of his latest Lampredi-engined cars, a lifeline which he could hardly have expected.

On 26 July 1955 the formal hand-over of six D50s and a host of other equipment took place before representatives of the Italian Automobile Federation. Neither Ferrari nor Gianni Lancia were present on this symbolic occasion, Enzo perhaps keenly appreciating his good fortune and not allowing his pride to be publicly dented by what, in truth, amounted to a fairly comprehensive, if oblique, humiliation for his organisation.

Lampredi left Ferrari soon afterwards to join Fiat's road car division, so the Lancia D50 designer Vittorio Jano moved across to Maranello with his V8-engined creations while former Maserati and Alfa engineer Alberto Massimino – who had helped Ferrari with the original '815' development back in 1940 – concentrated on trying to sort out the 555's handling quirks.

Alberto Ascari sits in the superb Lancia-Ferrari D50 prior to the start of the non-title 1955 Pau Grand Prix. (Jesse Alexander)

Massimino had stayed with Ferrari, first time round, until 1943 when he had joined the technical staff of Alfieri Maserati, but renewed his association with the Prancing Horse in the role of technical consultant from 1952 onward.

On the driver front, meanwhile, Hawthorn had fallen out with Tony Vandervell and had actually accepted an offer from Lancia shortly before the team withdrew from Formula 1. Nevertheless, Enzo Ferrari was happy to welcome the Englishman back into the Maranello fold, for by now he could do with all the decent drivers he could get his hands on.

Ferrari stumbled on with the 555s to little effect during the summer of 1955 and it was not until Monza that the Lancia D50s – now dubbed Lancia-Ferraris – made a return to the racing scene. However, the Monza race turned out to be another fiasco for the Prancing Horse.

The D50s were entrusted to Farina, Castellotti and Villoresi while Hawthorn, Trintignant and Maglioli handled a trio of further revised 'Super Squalos'. However, although the Lancia-Ferraris were clearly capable of getting on terms with the Mercedes W196s, they had been designed to run on Pirelli rubber, but Ferrari was contracted to run Belgian Engelbert tyres.

Unfortunately, on Engelberts, the Lancia-Ferraris developed a worrying habit of throwing their tyre treads on the punishing banked section of the Monza Autodrome. Consideration was given to running the cars on

Pirellis, but the Englebert representatives hinted that this would represent a breach of contract by Ferrari, so the end result was – perhaps inevitably – that the D50s were withdrawn from the race, leaving Castellotti to transfer to a 555, the Italian driving his heart out to finish a superb third behind the Mercs of Fangio and Taruffi.

This troubled season ended with Hawthorn and Castellotti driving the Lancia-Ferraris in the non-championship Oulton Park Gold Cup where they finished second and seventh respectively, Mike being roundly beaten to victory by Stirling Moss at the wheel of a borrowed Maserati. For the 1956 season, it was difficult to see how anything could get any worse for the Ferrari team.

Yet in 1956, at least Ferrari had the services of Juan Manuel Fangio. After winning the previous year's World Championship, Mercedes-Benz decided that it had accomplished its mission and withdrew from Formula 1. For his part, Fangio frankly toyed with the idea of retirement. However, the Argentine government had fallen the previous summer and he decided to postpone his retirement for another year – in fact he would eventually race on to the middle of 1958.

With Moss now at Maserati, and both BRM and Vanwall making serious strides, Ferrari knew he had to think things through carefully before deciding on the right technical package for the new season. Eventually – and as expected – he opted for a development of the Lancia D50s, but not before trying such wayward cocktails as a Lancia V8 installed in a Tipo 555 'Super Squalo'. Olivier Gendebien wrestled this particular hybrid to fifth place in the Argentine GP at Buenos Aires, reporting it to be a pretty awful creation.

Fangio was joined in the team by Castellotti, plus newcomers Luigi Musso and Peter Collins. Musso, who was 31 when he joined the Prancing Horse, had made his name at the wheel of a private Maserati 250F over the previous couple of seasons. He was the youngest of three sons of an Italian diplomat who had spent much of his career in China. Luigi grew up to be not only an accomplished racing driver, but also a fine horseman, a talented fencer and a crack shot.

Musso gained a reputation for being rather aloof, but the gregarious Collins had an even, sunny temperament which seemed to strike a favourable chord with Enzo Ferrari. The son of a successful Kidderminster motor trader, Collins had cut his teeth in the rough and tumble of 500cc

Ferrari cocktail. This 555 was fitted with a Lancia V8 engine for the 1956 Argentine GP. Gendebien drove it to fifth place, but it was not judged to be a success.

Formula 3 racing in the immediate post-war years and was a contemporary of Stirling Moss. He partnered Moss in the financially threadbare HWM team during 1951, then dallied briefly with BRM and Vanwall before being signed for Ferrari in 1956.

Yet if Collins was a popular golden boy, Fangio simply didn't hit it off with Ferrari on a personal level. Recollections from the *The Enzo Ferrari Memoirs* reveal a degree of apparent paranoia on Ferrari's part as regards his relationship with Fangio; perhaps they were each a little bit too famous and high profile for each other's taste.

For all that, Fangio's partnership with Ferrari could hardly be described as unsuccessful. He opened the year with a victory in the Argentine GP, following this up with wins in the non-title Mendoza GP before heading back to Europe to post a third victory at Syracuse, in this race using a revised D50 model which featured full-width bodywork to envelop the hitherto separate pannier fuel tanks.

Yet Fangio was clearly not totally

Eugenio Castellotti and Luigi Musso racing for the lead in the 1956 Italian GP with their Lancia-Ferraris, seemingly unconcerned about possible durability problems with their Englebert rubber. Castellotti spun off, Musso had a puncture. (LAT)

Juan Manuel Fangio won the 1956 World Championship at the wheel of a Lancia-Ferrari, here seen at Monaco before he damaged it against the wall at Tabac and took over team-mate Peter Collins's sister car to finish second. Fangio would later describe it as 'my strongest race'. (Jesse Alexander)

Fangio and Ferrari may not have got on when they worked together, but any tensions had clearly evaporated before this meeting in the early 1980s. (IPA)

Collins running in second place and Fangio forcing his way erratically through the field, in the process of which he hit the wall at Tabac with such force that he broke the location of the De Dion tube. He eventually abandoned this car to Castellotti and took over Collins's mount to finish a fighting second, only 6.1 seconds behind the victorious Moss after setting a new lap record on the 100th and final lap.

The Belgian GP yielded the first World Championship Formula 1 victory for Peter Collins after Fangio's Lancia-Ferrari stopped on the circuit with transmission failure, the Argentine ace somehow convincing himself that there had been some more jiggery-pokery on the part of Ferrari to favour his team-mates.

Paul Frère, the Belgian racing journalist, finished second in the Spa event, standing in for Luigi Musso who had been injured in an accident during a sports car race at the Nürburgring. Frère would subsequently voice the candid opinion – just as he had done the previous year on the subject of the 'Squalo' – that Ferrari's meddling with the technical specification of the D50 had effectively undermined their competitive edge. In Frère's judgement, Maranello had pandered to the whims of the drivers by attempting to make the Lancia's handling more progressive, but at the expense of their ultimate road holding capability.

'I rather agree with those who say that Ferrari's revamping of the Lancia D50 was mechanical heresy,' he told the author in the mid-1970s. 'After all, the side tanks of the original D50, which maintained the weight distribution little altered over a race distance, were certainly a better solution than having most of the fuel hanging out of the back.

comfortable with the Lancia-Ferrari, and his performance at Monaco was regarded by many seasoned observers as one of the most erratic of his career, even though the Man Himself later recalled it as 'possibly my greatest drive, perhaps even better than the Nürburgring in 1957.'

As Stirling Moss drove away into the distance to win convincingly at the wheel of his factory Maserati 250F, Fangio spun at Ste Devote going into the second lap and barged back into the fray in a wild manoeuvre which sent Luigi Musso's sister car and Harry Schell's Vanwall careering into the straw bales.

The battle then settled down with

'When all these cars were handed over to Ferrari, the design was very new, and I think if Jano had been allowed to go ahead with his original development, the D50 might have become a better and longer-lasting machine than the Ferrari version.' It was also speculated that some personal friction between Jano and Ferrari engineer Vittorio Bellantani was at least partly responsible for this divergence of technical opinion.

For the French GP at Reims, Musso's substitute was a vivacious Spanish blue blood, the Marquis de Portago, regarded by many as one of the most colourful and engaging personalities ever to appear on the international motor racing scene.

Nicknamed 'Fon', this 27-year-old's full name was in fact Don Alfonso Antonio Vicente Blas Angel Francisco Borjia Cabeza de Vaca y Leighton, 17th Marquis de Portago, the son of a Spanish nobleman by his marriage to Olga Leighton, a one-time Irish nurse who was the widow and heir of Frank J. Mackey, founder of the Household Finance Company.

Raised in Biarritz while his father fought against Franco in the Spanish Civil War, de Portago developed into a fine all-round sportsman, riding twice in the Grand National – on Garde-Troi in 1950, and on Icy Calm in 1952, although failing to finish on both occasions – and actually financing the Spanish Olympic bobsleigh team. In 1952, after poor races by two of his horses at Hurst Park, he complained to Scotland Yard that they had been doped. He was also an outstanding polo player, yachtsman and shot.

'Fon's' father died in 1941 after which he and his mother decamped to the United States where they lived in New York's Plaza Hotel. By the time he was racing seriously in the mid-1950s, 'Fon' and his wife were living

Fangio and Ferrari: the uneasy alliance

IT SEEMS THAT the seeds of the mutual distrust between Juan Manuel Fangio and Enzo Ferrari may have been sown as early as June 1949 when Fangio had been loaned a Formula 2 Ferrari to race at Monza. From the outset, he led the field ahead of Ascari, Villoresi, Bonetto and Cortese, but then slowed gradually, allowing his rivals to catch up.

Ferrari recalls preventing Fangio's mechanic from intervening with a plan to signal his driver to come into the pits to refuel, the team chief feeling that the mechanic would rather see Fangio delayed by force-majeure than being beaten out on the circuit.

Ferrari had correctly concluded that Fangio had slowed in order to allow his engine oil to cool, after which he speeded up and won the race. But there was clearly an exchange of words between driver and entrant which left personal tensions unresolved.

After Fangio's retirement from racing, he published a volume of memoirs which really jangled Enzo Ferrari's sensibilities. 'It is true that he made use of somebody else's pen in order, through this book, to make certain allegations and launch some rash and ingenuous accusations,' responded Ferrari firmly.

'This was quite in keeping with his style, however. I nevertheless did not rise to this provocation; there was someone who was making use of Fangio and, if I were drawn into an argument, this would only boost sales of the book, which was obviously the aim.

'In his memoirs, the story of 1956 is a sort of thriller, a concoction of betrayals, sabotage, deceit and machinations of every kind – all perpetrated to lay him in the dust.'

in Paris in what was regarded as Millionaire's Row – 40 Avenue Foch – where they had become familiar items on the social circuit, in particular as dinner guests of the exiled Duke and Duchess of Windsor.

By 1953 de Portago had become interested in motor racing and rode with Luigi Chinetti – never one to miss what today might be described as a 'financially qualified' potential customer – in that year's Carrera Panamericana.

Immediately after this escapade 'Fon' teamed up with Harry Schell – Chinetti had worked for his mother Lucy and first came to America to mechanic for them at Indianapolis, remember – and they purchased a 250MM Vignale Spider which had

previously been used to win the 1953 Portuguese sports car championship.

Painted in two-tone black over yellow livery, with 'Espana-USA' emblazoned on its flanks, the ambitious duo decided to take it to Buenos Aires for the 1954 1000km race. Rather late in the day it was established that 'Fon' didn't know how to use a manual gearchange, and Schell hadn't the patience to teach him. The result was that de Portago drove only two laps – 10km – of the race, leaving Harry to drive single-handed throughout. The following year he would purchase a Maserati 2-litre sports car – and the company's respected chief mechanic Guerrino Bertocchi spent an afternoon showing 'Fon' how to use a manual shift!

Stirling Moss amuses the Ferrari mechanics by trying the cockpit of the little Formula 2 Dino 156 in the pit lane at Monaco. The car was not raced, although all the team's drivers tried it in practice and were impressed with its potential. (Edward Eves)

'Fon' de Portago relaxing with a cigarette in the cockpit of his Lancia-Ferrari before the 1956 British GP at Silverstone. (LAT)

In 1955 de Portago purchased an ex-works Ferrari 625, but shunted it and broke a leg while practising in the wet for the Silverstone International Trophy. 'That took care of the summer,' he noted wryly. 'I couldn't race again until the end of August.'

However, by 1956 de Portago was maturing into a much more reliable and consistent performer, as evidenced by a superb victory on the Tour de France at the wheel of a Ferrari 250GT. The combination of Chinetti's shrewd patronage and the size of his own wallet was to prove irresistible and eventually earned de Portago a place as reserve driver on the Ferrari Formula 1 team.

Fangio, Collins and Castellotti had their hands full at Reims fighting off a challenge from Harry Schell in the much-improved Vanwall, which was now showing every prospect of developing into a very serious Grand Prix car. The Ferrari threesome had to pull every trick in the book to fend off the ambitious Franco-American and could only breathe again when the Vanwall eventually retired with a broken ball joint on the linkage to its fuel injection pump.

Fangio retired again from this race, this time from a leaking fuel pipe, allowing Collins to win narrowly from Castellotti in a Lancia-Ferrari 1–2. Yet it was a somehow muted triumph with the team's mechanics all wearing black armbands as a gesture of respect to the memory of Dino Ferrari, the owner's son, who had died a few days earlier.

Fangio then won at Silverstone ahead of Collins, who had taken over de Portago's Lancia-Ferrari mid-way through the race, and the Argentine ace continued towards his fourth World Championship title with yet another victory in the German GP at Nürburgring.

Behind Fangio in this particular race, there was a lot of swapping around between the other Lancia-Ferrari drivers during the course of the afternoon, and at one point the Ferrari pit resembled a scene from Barnum and Bailey rather than front-line Formula 1 competition.

Castellotti came in to retire his car with a faulty magneto and was instructed to take over Musso's car, the Italian returnee still having trouble from a recently-healed arm, a legacy from that sports car shunt earlier in the season. However, just as Musso drew in, so Collins arrived, almost unconscious from fumes from a leaking fuel line.

In the ensuing chaos, Castellotti jumped into Collins's car, instantly realised his mistake and hopped out again before finding his correct berth in Musso's machine. Meanwhile, after a short break to recover, Collins took over de Portago's machine which was now running fourth, moving it up to third and then spinning off into a ditch.

'Fon' de Portago's first great success came when he won the 1956 Tour de France in this Ferrari 250GT, seen here during a circuit race on the cobbles at Rouen's Nouveau Monde hairpin. (LAT)

'Fon' de Portago (far right, leaning on Stirling Moss's Mercedes 300SL) at Montlhéry during the 1956 Tour de France. Moss (holding paper) seems to be making a point, while Jean Behra and Olivier Gendebien listen intently. The winning Ferrari is on the left. (LAT)

After the race, de Portago told Collins that he should have pushed the car back on to the road, rather than simply abandoning it out on the circuit. The two men then set off in Peter's Ford Zephyr in an attempt to resolve the theory, only for the Englishman to be vindicated when it turned out that a tow rope and many helping hands were needed to drag the bedraggled Lancia-Ferrari back on to the circuit.

Come the Italian GP at Monza, Ferrari entered no fewer than six cars, the regular five drivers plus the German aristocrat Wolfgang von Trips. In retrospect, this Robert Redford lookalike was perhaps offered his first Formula 1 drive in an over-generous gesture by Enzo Ferrari. Unfortunately he crashed heavily during practice at Curva Grande, returning to the pits to explain, in a rather crestfallen fashion, that the car had suddenly veered out of control.

The team's understandable reaction was to blame von Trips for the shunt, and the wrecked Lancia-Ferrari was left in one of the paddock garages and not seriously examined until the Tuesday after the race. Only then was it discovered that von Trips's car had suffered a pre-impact failure of one of its steering arms. Had that problem been identified before the start of the Italian GP, Ferrari might have spared itself another bruising experience in front of his team's home crowd.

Ironically, Ferrari's home race turned into a repeat of the previous year's debacle as Englebert still appeared unable to produce a sufficiently durable tyre for the bumpy Monza bankings. This situation was aggravated by an absurdly uncompromising nationalistic battle between Musso and Castellotti which saw both men drive their cars into the ground and out of the race.

Fangio, meanwhile, knew that third place would be sufficient to clinch the 1956 World Championship and had no intention of becoming embroiled in such a contest. 'Before the race I took Castellotti and Musso to one side and told them that one of them should win,' he said.

'It was sufficient for me to finish third. I said that if they didn't force the pace too much and sat behind me, I would move over 10 laps from the finish and let them race to the flag. But they said they wanted to run the race their way. From the start they forced the pace like madmen, locking wheels under braking and spinning their tyres everywhere. I could see that neither of them would be there at the finish.'

Both Italian drivers were in early for fresh tyres and then Fangio wobbled into the pit lane with a broken steering arm after only 19 laps. Sixteen laps later, Collins came in for a precautionary tyre check and unhesitatingly handed over his car to Fangio – a suggestion which had earlier been declined by Luigi Musso, who having relinquished his car to Fangio at the start of the year in Buenos Aires, probably thought it was someone else's turn. Meanwhile, Castellotti was also out early, having spun into a barrier.

After Stirling Moss's Maserati had been delayed by a fuel leak, Musso was presented with a commanding lead with only four laps of the race to run. But coming off the banking flat-out, Musso suffered a steering arm breakage, a front tyre burst and he slid across the full width of the start/finish apron, only stopping a matter of feet from the pit wall.

That left Moss a somewhat fortuitous winner for Maserati, but Fangio's second place was good enough for the World Championship

crown. Yet it was worth remembering that Fangio had appropriated cars from his team-mates on no fewer than three occasions during the course of the season – Buenos Aires, Monaco and Monza – and, given the number of cars fielded by the team, its record of five wins out of the seven Championship races was only to be expected given the strength of the mediocre opposition.

Enzo Ferrari put Fangio's 1956 World Championship into brisk perspective when he wrote: 'Musso and Collins stepped down for the sake of Fangio, obviously with my consent. Had Collins not handed his own car over to Fangio twice, he would with mathematical certainty have become World Champion that year, as he well deserved. Instead, Collins and Musso met their deaths without ever being able to win this coveted distinction.

'I had a high opinion of Peter Collins, both as a driver and as a man and Fangio needs a lot of pluck to say that he was an outcast when he was with Ferrari, forgetful even of the sacrifice his own team-mates made for him.'

If Ferrari had seen enough of Fangio, then the feeling was clearly mutual. With Stirling Moss displaying his nagging sense of patriotism with a move to Tony Vandervell's Vanwall team for 1957, the position of team leader at Maserati fell vacant and Fangio opted for another spell with what he clearly regarded as a much more convivial and sympathetic Italian motor racing environment.

That left Collins, Castellotti and Musso remaining in the Ferrari squad, to be joined by Mike Hawthorn, the Englishman returning for a third stint with the Prancing Horse. The team began the season in Buenos Aires where no fewer than six Lancia-Ferraris were fielded, three being heavily revised cars built up on Maranello-based chassis frames. The exorcism of the original Lancia D50 design would be virtually complete before the end of the 1957 season.

The year opened with Fangio cementing his return to Maserati with another victory in the Argentine GP, heading a 1–2–3–4 grand slam for the Trident. A week later, the Lancia-Ferraris performed more competently in the Buenos Aires City GP at the same circuit, Peter Collins winning the second heat in a car shared with Formula 1 new boy Masten Gregory. But that didn't prevent Fangio winning on aggregate yet again.

The run-up to the World Championship season proper was punctuated by two significant developments. First, the non-title Syracuse GP in April saw the debut of a car officially designated the Ferrari 801, which was in fact the final derivation of the D50 with close-fitting bodywork and all the fuel carried in a tail-mounted tank. Moreover, as if to underline the degree of technical uncertainty prevailing at Maranello, the 801 had its V8 mounted as a semi-stressed member in the manner of the original D50 – reverting to the 1956 development which had seen the incorporation of added longitudinal bracing tubes in the previous car's engine bay.

In parallel to this development, Ferrari unveiled a brand new 1.5-litre Formula 2 Ferrari at the Naples GP, a car which was to develop into the Drivers' Championship winning Dino 246 in time for 1958.

Enzo Ferrari would subsequently heap much of the responsibility for the design of this new V6 on to the shoulders of his son Dino, from whose death from muscular dystrophy and nephritis in 1956 he never full recovered. He was only 24, and had earned

Hawthorn and Collins: remembering the fun times

MIKE HAWTHORN AND Peter Collins brought a suitably light-hearted approach to the Ferrari Formula 1 line-up and their time together has subsequently been eulogised by many historians. Yet the fact of the matter is that Hawthorn was simply not sufficiently consistent, and Collins was the better driver. Both men seemed more devoted to living life with gusto, yet could sometimes display an uncharitable streak, jointly freezing out several team-mates – most notably Luigi Musso – and simply did not display the level of single-minded professionalism which so characterised Stirling Moss and Tony Brooks.

In particular, much has been written about Hawthorn's gallant last lap at Nürburgring in 1957 when he fought like a tiger not to lose any more ground to Fangio's winning Maserati 250F. Yet there are those who believe that if Mike and Peter hadn't messed around in the early stages of the race, running side-by-side on the straights and generally having a lark, Fangio might well have been deprived of what is rightly regarded as his best ever victory.

'Even though Peter and I had been beaten, we enjoyed every moment of it,' Hawthorn later reflected. Yet given the fact that at one point they were over half a minute ahead of the Fangio Maserati, even allowing for the fact that it was on fresh tyres following its refuelling stop, the Ferrari drivers really could have been expected to come away from this race with a win.

Hawthorn was unquestionably the less consistent performer behind the wheel. When he was on-form, he could be superb, but there were many other occasions when he seemed to be taking his time, unwilling or unable to over-drive in an effort to compensate for a car's apparent deficiency. Yet the patchy nature of his record may have been directly related to the fact that he suffered from a kidney complaint which would have almost certainly prevented him from surviving beyond middle age.

Collins, on the other hand, was a rich kid who liked the high life. Popular and gregarious, his skill behind the wheel of a Formula 1 car was unquestionable. Yet friends always had the impression that Grand Prix racing was only part of Peter Collins's life, that he could clearly envisage a future beyond retirement from the cockpit. With a lovely young wife, a boat in the harbour at Monaco and considerable expectations, he was genuinely Britain's 'golden boy' of international sport.

an engineering degree in Switzerland before working with Vittorio Jano on the development of the new V6.

In reality, it is hard to see how the technically inexperienced Dino could have made such an authoritative decision as to the configuration of the new engine. Jano, at the very least, must have been the man who guided Dino's hand, yet the sense of tragedy

and melodrama surrounding the premature death of Ferrari's eldest son has made it almost impossible to unravel the truth of the matter from a distance of 40 years.

In his memoirs, Ferrari quotes proudly from a letter Dino wrote him in the summer of 1955, expounding the view that an eight-cylinder engine would be the ideal configuration for the forthcoming Formula 2 rules which were scheduled to start in 1957. Eight years later, with V8 engines by then ruling the roost in the 1.5-litre Grand Prix formula, Enzo Ferrari would look back with pride and refer to the 'prescient intuition' possessed by his son.

In truth, it seems all vaguely embarrassing in retrospect. 'I remember how carefully and with what competence Dino read and discussed all the notes and reports that were brought to him daily from Maranello,' writes Ferrari referring to the bed-ridden state endured by his son towards the end of his life.

'For reasons of mechanical efficiency, he finally came to the conclusion that the engine should be a V6, and we accepted this decision. There

was thus born the famous 156, which was to burst into song for the first time in November 1956, five months after Dino passed away.'

Carlo Chiti, who would take over the leadership of Ferrari's Formula 1 design team in 1957 as replacement for the talented engineer Andrea Fraschetti – killed while testing a Formula 2 Ferrari at Modena – later cast doubt on the veracity of Ferrari's version of events as regards the development of the V6 engine. He believed that Jano had designed the engine at his Turin flat 'on the quiet' when still bound by his Lancia contract not to work for another car maker. Ferrari, says Chiti, was just covering Jano's tracks with this story of the contribution made by his son Dino.

However, while the Dino 246

Formula 1 engine was being developed during 1957, the mainstream Formula 1 Ferrari squad was having a dismal time. Morale was dented considerably when Castellotti was killed in a testing accident at Modena before the start of the European season, while the plain fact of the matter was that the Ferrari 801s did not shape up against the Vanwall and Maserati opposition.

The season ended without a single Grand Epreuve victory recorded by Ferrari – the first occasion since 1950 that this had occurred. Yet things would be reassuringly different when the Dino 246s took to the circuits in 1958. By then the V6 engine had grown from 1.5-litres to 1.8, then 1.9-litres. In October 1957 Collins and Hawthorn had used 2.4 and 2.1-litre versions respectively in what amounted to a final shakedown in the non-championship Moroccan Grand Prix at Casablanca. Collins led until he spun off, and the 2.4-litre engine was duly fixed as the standard unit for the 1958 Championship assault.

By now Vanwall represented the most formidable opposition, but the reality is that both the British cars and the Dino 246s would have only a single season of competitive potential ahead of them before they were overwhelmed by the central-engined Formula 1 revolution.

Stirling Moss put the writing firmly on the wall with his amazing victory at the wheel of Rob Walker's Cooper in the 1958 Argentine GP – a race for which he was released by Tony Vandervell as the Vanwalls were not competing.

The Dino 246 scored its first race victory in the 42-lap Glover Trophy at Goodwood on Easter Monday, 1958, when Hawthorn won easily after Jean Behra's BRM crashed at the chicane. Luigi Musso followed that up with an

No sentiment here. The 1957 Ferrari 801s were pushed out to grass and left to rot in a lean-to behind the main factory. (Graham Gauld)

Mike Hawthorn took the 1958 Drivers' World Championship at the wheel of the distinctive Ferrari Dino 246, although he won only a single round of the title battle. (LAT)

easy win at Syracuse and then Peter Collins took his turn with a third success in the Silverstone International Trophy. Yet the reality of the situation was that the rival Vanwalls were generally superior and, had it not been for their intermittent unreliability, the Ferraris would have been decisively outclassed for much of the season.

The bottom line was that Hawthorn won commandingly at Reims, where Musso, over-driving wildly in the hope that a big pay day might enable him to clear his reputed gambling debts, flew off the road and was killed.

'On the eve of the race, he had, in fact, received a message; a few words typed on a buff telegram that urged him to make an all-out effort,' Ferrari would later reflect mysteriously.

Collins, meanwhile, was experiencing some problems with his employer. The Englishman had been one of Enzo Ferrari's favourites, the team chief admiring his open and sunny disposition. However, the relationship changed subtly after Peter married an American girl, Louise King, and he

began to believe that the romance had taken the edge off his hunger in the cockpit.

Just prior to the Reims race, team manager Romolo Tavoni announced that Collins would only be driving the Dino 156 in the Formula 2 supporting race. This was classic Ferrari driver agitation – most agreed that the Commendatore wrote this particular manual – but Collins, supported by Hawthorn, replied robustly to the effect that if he wasn't going to be allowed a run in the Grand Prix, then he wouldn't be driving in either race. Tavoni relented, so Collins also drove the Formula 2 race and finished second, before finishing fifth in the Grand Prix.

Carlo Chiti later suggested another reason behind Collins's apparent demotion. Mino Amorotti, who had been responsible for managing the works Ferrari Testa Rossa squad at Le Mans in 1958, reported back that Hawthorn and Collins deliberately destroyed their gearbox. Amorotti, who'd been a prisoner of war in East Africa, reportedly hated the guts of the British and somehow got it into his mind that Collins and Hawthorn were trying to help the rival Aston Martin team.

Ferrari accordingly decided to punish Collins by demoting him to the Formula 2 car at Reims. It was a classic example of the problems arising from Enzo Ferrari shutting himself away within his Maranello fortress and no longer attending the races. It meant that he was totally dependent on reports from his own foot soldiers out in the field, many of whom were working to their own personal agenda.

Collins later scored a beautifully executed victory in the British GP at Silverstone, but was killed a fortnight later chasing Brooks's Vanwall round the Nürburgring in the German GP. In many ways Collins's passing has slipped into perspective as a Formula 1 watershed; the day the music died for a generation of devil-may-care sportsmen. From this moment on, Formula 1 would increasingly become the province of the committed professional.

Certainly, Hawthorn continued the season in a subdued and rather depressed frame of mind. To him those two years at Ferrari with Collins had been non-stop fun, an endless series of jolly japes punctuated by some intermittently serious motor racing. Now the fun was over and, although he won the World Championship from Moss by a single point at Casablanca, the celebrations were muted in the aftermath of another serious accident which left Vanwall driver Stuart Lewis-Evans fearfully injured, soon to die.

Hawthorn announced his retirement at the end of the season only to be killed in a road accident on the Guildford by-pass on 22 January 1959 at the wheel of his 3.4-litre Jaguar. It was the end of an era.

Phil Hill finished ninth overall, and fifth in the Formula 2 class, with this Dino 156 in the tragic German Grand Prix which cost the life of his team-mate Peter Collins.

Although Hawthorn and Collins were the Ferrari stars of 1957 and 1958, there were others in their shadows who were just starting out on their professional careers as members of the Maranello line-up. One such was Californian Phil Hill who had initially battled his way on to the international racing ladder at the wheel of a privately-entered Ferrari sports car.

Hill had originally cut his competition teeth at the wheel of an MG TC sports car in West Coast club events back in 1950, after which he decided on a career as a professional mechanic and attended a course at the Jaguar factory in Coventry before returning to California with his own XK120.

That was followed by a brief flirtation with a mechanically fragile ex-Scuderia Ferrari Alfa Romeo before Luigi Chinetti invited him to Le Mans in 1951 to stand in as reserve driver for the 4.1-litre Ferrari V12 which the NART boss was sharing with Jean Lucas. The car finished eighth, and Hill didn't get a drive, although he did manage to take the wheel with Chinetti at Reims where he was standing in for his injured compatriot Bill Spear.

Chinetti quickly concluded that Phil had above-average potential and arranged to make available a Ferrari for him in the USA the following year. This was the 212 export 'barchetta' which had won the 1951 Tour de France in the hands of Pagnibon and Barraquet and served him well on the US domestic scene.

In 1952 Hill's apprenticeship continued when he was invited to drive Texan oil magnate Allen Guiberson's Vignale-bodied 212 coupé in the Carrera Panamericana road race which Ascari and Villoresi had used to finish second in that race the previous year. Phil recalled that he didn't really know what to expect of the event. 'The only thing I remember about the whole affair is that I suffered a terrible attack of the "Aztec quickstep" which I began to think I would never survive.'

Nevertheless, he finished sixth and returned to compete in 1953. On that occasion he was lucky to survive when his Ferrari plunged over a cliff, but he returned again in 1954 to finish a close second in the 4.1-litre Spider which Ascari and Farina had used to win the 1953 Nürburgring 1000km.

'By this time I was convinced that I just had to cross the Atlantic,' he remembers. 'I decided that I'd got to go and barnstorm around Europe, so I loaded up my Ferrari on a boat from Houston in Texas and set off for Catania.

'Believe it or not, it was on that boat that I received a message from Ferrari himself to go to Maranello as soon as I arrived. I was there like a shot to be confronted by the question "do you want to race at Le Mans with Maglioli?" Of course, there was no question; I agreed immediately.'

Thus was Phil launched into his first Ferrari works drive in the fateful 1955 Le Mans race which earned a grim place in the history books for Pierre Levegh's terrible accident when his Mercedes 300SLR vaulted into the crowd opposite the pits, killing more than 80 spectators. By any standards, it was a deeply unsettling experience.

'Here I was, the new-guy American, trying to take in everything that was happening, while at the same time trying to understand the reasoning of the team manager who was for ever urging one to go flat out, while at the same time telling you not to risk bending the car under any circumstances,' he remembers.

Although Hill's status within the team would be steadily enhanced over the following five years, he recalls that he was always aware of Enzo Ferrari's intimidating presence in the background. He didn't like his drivers to rest on their laurels, and that was made very clear by some not-so-discreet pressuring from the touch-lines.

'Ferrari never liked complacency,' said Hill, 'and I found myself always getting pushed around in the Formula 1 team, particularly during my first year in 1958.' He concedes there was a lack of sympathy between his own focused attitude and what he regarded as the devil-may-care attitude displayed by Collins and Hawthorn.

Even so, Phil was successful in his own way gaining access to the Ferrari Formula 1 line-up in the first place, forcing the Old Man's hand by accepting a Maserati drive for the 1958 French GP. Ferrari, particularly aware of Hill's fine reputation as a sports car driver, forbade him to accept the drive. But Phil successfully called his bluff and gained a place in Maranello's Formula 1 squad as a result.

Hill played a crucial role in helping Hawthorn to win the Championship, dutifully obeying team orders and dropping back to third place behind Mike in the closing stages of the Casablanca race. By then he was pretty well secure in the knowledge that he would stay on in the Maranello Formula 1 line-up for 1959, joined by Olivier Gendebien, Jean Behra and former Vanwall star Tony Brooks, while Dan Gurney and Cliff Allison were poised on the touchlines awaiting their chance.

Brooks came to Ferrari with quite a reputation, having been Moss's equal in the Vanwall team over the previous two seasons. Quiet, almost taciturn, this British former public schoolboy who had trained as a dentist was the absolute antithesis of the likes of Musso, Castellotti and Behra. Clearly, at the wheel of the Dino 246, now extensively revamped with de Dion rear end, coil spring suspension and elegant new Fantuzzi bodywork, Brooks was regarded as a very strong title contender from the outset.

Yet beneath that quiet exterior, Brooks had a very firm personal philosophy towards his sport which made quite an unusual motor racing personality. 'Motor racing was always only part of my life,' he explained. 'I think I was blessed with a lot of natural ability; I tried hard, but I never tried to the point that I might risk killing myself.

'In my book, you should never drive to the point where you experi-ence fear. I would drive to the very best of my ability, and persevere with a car if it was mechanically deficient in a non-dangerous way. I was fortu-nate enough that I could win races without going into that fear zone.'

Having originally shot to promi-nence by winning the 1955 Syracuse Grand Prix at the wheel of a Connaught, Brooks subsequently established himself as a leading Formula 1 contender at Vanwall. He'd held on, waiting to see if Tony Vandervell would continue in 1959, but by the time the British industrial-ist decided to quit, the only available competitive seat was at Ferrari. It was a decision which undoubtedly put Jean Behra's nose out of joint, but political tensions, such as they were, were water off a duck's back to the quiet Englishman.

Brooks came close to winning the 1959 Championship. The high points of his year were brilliant victories in the French Grand Prix at Reims and German GP on the super-fast Avus track in Berlin, a heady mix of auto-bahn and a daunting, near-vertical 180-degree banking.

Behra, who had led at Monaco before blowing up his Dino's engine, worked himself up into a fine old lather over his disappointment with the season, culminating in his thump-ing team manager Romolo Tavoni in the pit lane at Reims after trashing another V6 engine. Losing his temper in such a manner also lost him his place in the Maranello line-up and the gallant Frenchman died soon after-wards when his Porsche sports car flew over the top of the Avus banking during a supporting event at the German GP meeting.

'I didn't have any problem with Behra,' says Brooks, 'but we didn't communicate much, because I didn't speak French and his Italian was not very good – mine was quite compe-tent – but there were never any nasty words.

'I don't know what Behra's problem was. Perhaps he thought he should have been appointed number one driver. For my part, I just joined the team on the understanding that I was going to get a car as good as every-body else's. And at Ferrari I did get a car which was always the equal of my team-mate's – which is more than I can say for my time with Vanwall.'

Carlo Chiti believes that Behra was cut adrift emotionally by Ferrari, having joined the team believing he would be designated team leader. At Reims, when he threw that punch at Tavoni, he had got it into his mind that his Dino 246 was somehow

Great partnership. Ferrari's 1959 Formula 1 line-up included (from left), Phil Hill, Dan Gurney and Tony Brooks. (LAT)

mechanically deficient – and even reportedly made a protest to the sport's governing body to the effect that Ferrari had stitched him up, providing him with a chassis which had recently been shunted by Dan Gurney in testing at Monza.

'Jean was certainly not a very likeable character,' recalled Chiti with a brutal frankness. 'They called him "the gypsy" because of his passionate temperament. He also had a particularly vulgar way of expressing himself.

'But the way he died led me, even so, to think deeply about it. We had completely abandoned that man to himself, with his brooding determination to win. We had obliged him to take refuge in his own desperation.'

Brooks was unusual in that he seldom had any aggravation from the ultra-critical Italian media which was always quick to home in on a Ferrari driver's shortcomings. But at Monaco he felt he was hard done by. Feeling as sick as a dog from exhaust fumes building up in the Dino's cockpit, he struggled home second to Brabham's Cooper only to be given a pasting by the media.

'If I hadn't been ill, I'd have been able to give him [Brabham] a better run for his money,' reflects Tony, 'even though a front-engined Ferrari versus a well-sorted rear-engined Cooper round Monaco would have been a tall order anyway.

'This was followed by suggestions in the Italian press that I was rather sick and weakly. I suppose if I'd retired they'd have said "well, he did his best" but to carry on in your own vomit to finish the damned race, feeling like nothing on earth with a splitting headache, round that circuit, I thought I did damn' well finishing second.'

Unfortunately the Belgian GP was cancelled in 1959, robbing Brooks of

another good prospect, and one of the traditional Italian metal workers' strikes meant that the Dino 246s were not present at the British GP at Aintree where Behra and Brooks had finished first and second in the non-title Aintree 200 mile race earlier in the year.

More disappointment was waiting for Brooks at the Italian GP at Monza where he qualified in the middle of the front row between the Coopers of Moss and Brabham. This race followed on immediately after a disappointing performance in the Portuguese GP at Lisbon's Monsanto Park circuit where the Dino 246 was off-form and Tony could only finish ninth.

'At Monza I had done some very fast laps in practice and finished up about one-tenth of a second slower than Stirling,' he explains. 'But I came into the pits afterwards and told them that there was a smell of Ferodo linings, but I wasn't sure whether it was the brakes or the clutch.

'So apparently they decided to change the clutch overnight, but didn't bed it down properly as they could only drive it round the paddock – there were no race morning warm-up sessions in those days!

'You just don't get the same grip with a brand new clutch and, of course, with a racing start, when I let the clutch out, it slipped momentarily and burnt out. I did about 100 metres! I think it was just unfortunate; I hadn't burnt a clutch out before or since in my racing career.

'So there were some more possible points thrown away. Stirling won, going through non-stop with the Walker-Cooper, but I think I might have been able to go non-stop since I was always fairly easy on tyres.'

Brooks and Championship rival Jack Brabham then had a nerve-rack-

ing three-month wait before the Championship clincher took place in Florida, the United States GP on the Sebring airfield circuit.

Brooks qualified as the fastest Ferrari runner on the inside of the second row, but was rammed on the opening lap by team-mate Wolfgang von Trips's sister car. Brooks reflected his own very firm personal philosophy by making a precautionary pit stop to check for damage. It cost him his chance of the title.

He explains the rationale thus: 'Life is a gift from God, I believe, so you don't have the right to take your own life. In a war, or some set of threatening circumstances, I'm prepared to put my life on the line with the next man. But what we were engaged in was a sport.

'So I reasoned that I didn't have the right to take a totally unreasonable risk with my life. What I interpreted as loading the dice against me unreasonably was driving a mechanically deficient motor car. I had earlier had two lessons on that subject; one was a sticking throttle in the BRM at the 1956 British GP, which resulted in it turning over and throwing me out, and the other trying to get the Aston Martin out of fourth gear and rolling at Tertre Rouge, ending up trapped underneath the car.

'Both of those were stupidity errors rather than driver errors. They reminded me that motor racing was dangerous enough and I decided that if I was ever faced with that dilemma again, I would definitely come in and get the car checked.

'At Sebring, this was a terribly difficult decision to make. It wasn't the biggest shunt of all time, but the point is that when you stress a component in a direction it isn't design to be stressed, relatively low impact speeds can cause a problem.

Cliff Allison tries a Dino 246 at Modena in 1959. Carlo Chiti (left), Romolo Tavoni and Enzo Ferrari look particularly pensive in the background. (Peter Coltrin)

'Clearly, if I came in, I was going to have blown my Championship chance, but I felt that I would have not been true to myself if I hadn't honoured the promise I had made to myself after those previous two accidents. So I had to force myself to come in to be true to myself. The easiest thing would have been to continue, but I would have betrayed myself. One likes to live comfortably with oneself and not have regrets.

'Ferrari never castigated me in any way, but I don't think he was very pleased. I think it was completely contrary to what Ferrari expected and he was less than pleased. But I don't think he understood this sort of philosophy, perhaps many people don't. I finished third, but needed to win to take the Championship.' It was his last race for the Prancing Horse.

'I really enjoyed my year at Ferrari,' says Brooks. 'Vanwall was great, but there was a more convivial atmosphere in the Ferrari team. There was more life and emotion there, particularly when you did well.

'I think I only saw Enzo Ferrari perhaps two or three times during the whole time I was driving for him. I did my deal with him in about half an hour – in those days we didn't have lawyers, managers and advisors involving us in three months of negotiations. You got peanuts and just signed the contract; it was all very straightforward.'

Not that Brooks had to get involved in much testing with the Italian team. 'Fortunately, dear Phil [Hill] lived at the Albergo Real in Modena' – the hotel used by most of the Italian racing set – 'and as he was on the spot, and a pretty darn good driver anyway, they tended to use him.

'I always preferred to drive down to the factory, as I still do in Europe. There were no motorways, of course, but I could still do England to Maranello in a day. Did I have a company Ferrari road car? You must be kidding! I still had my Aston Martin DB 2/4 from 1957, but I think I used to tactfully park it away from the Ferrari pits. But, no, I never owned a Ferrari road car. There was never one on offer.'

By the end of the year, Brooks left Ferrari as he wanted to put more hands-on effort into the development of his fledgeling garage business at Weybridge, close to his Surrey home. Tempted by the possibility of a Vanwall return, he agreed to pick up the threads of the relationship with Tony Vandervell. But then the bearing magnate changed his mind and Brooks found himself with no choice but to drive an uncompetitive Cooper for the private Yeoman Credit team in 1960.

To this day, Tony believes that Vandervell – still deeply upset by Stuart Lewis-Evans' death at Casablanca 18 months earlier – was trying to coax him in the direction of retirement. 'I think he always had rather a soft spot for me,' admits Brooks.

The Dino 246s continued as the mainstay of Ferrari's effort into 1960, although by this time the writing was on the wall for any front-engined Grand Prix car. Carlo Chiti's engineering team reworked the cars with Squalo-style pannier tanks on either side of the chassis and the V6 engine moved back in the frame by almost 10 inches. They also now had Dunlop disc brakes and had switched from Engelbert to Dunlop rubber.

Despite the strength of the central-engined opposition, the Dino 246s could be expected to give a decent account of themselves at the faster circuits, but disappointment was in store at both Spa-Francorchamps and Reims. Then the British constructors boycotted the Italian GP at Monza, claiming that the banking was too mechanically punishing. The race went ahead without them, leaving Phil Hill, Richie Ginther and Willy Mairesse to drive the Dino 246 into the history books with a dominant 1–2–3 finale.

Another taste of the realities involved in being a member of Ferrari's Formula 1 and sports car racing team in the 1950s is provided by Cliff Allison, the garage owner from Brough, Cumbria, who handled the Dino 246s in 1959 and 1960. Allison believes that Mike Hawthorn may have mentioned both himself and his Lotus Formula 1 team-mate Graham Hill as possible candidates to replace him on his retirement at the end of the 1958 season.

'I got on very well with Mike and we spent a lot of time together,' recalled Allison to the author in 1984. 'I rather think that Graham was a little bit too pro-British to be interested, but I went down to Modena and did a deal for the following year [1959].

Opening lap of the 1959 German GP on Berlin's Avus circuit with Jo Bonnier's BRM leading from Phil Hill's Dino 246, Bruce McLaren's Cooper and the Dino 246s of winner Brooks (No. 4) and Gurney (No. 6). (LAT)

'Of course, this involved me racing on the sports car scene and standing in as a reserve driver on the Grand Prix team to start with.'

These days, Ferrari's top drivers criss-cross Europe in their private jets, fitting in test sessions around appointments with their Swiss bankers, but in the distant days of the mid-1950s, Ferrari drivers were just human beings like the rest of us. Listening to Allison's travel arrangements to get from rural Cumbria to Modena is enough to make the most seasoned traveller turn grey with apprehension.

'Oh, it wasn't really a problem,' he shrugged. 'I used to drive to Darlington, get the express train to Kings Cross, taxi to the Cromwell Road air terminal, bus to Heathrow, plane to Milan, taxi to the station, train to Modena . . .'

Cliff's desire and need to keep in touch with the family business meant that he made this trip every couple of weeks. It was just routine. He knew of no other way, so it never bothered him in the slightest.

The easy-going, undemanding Allison slipped into Maranello's way of life without any fuss. He developed comfortable relationships with the other drivers on the team, in particular having happy memories of Wolfgang von Trips.

'He was a really charming, delightful man,' he remembers. 'I think it was Peter Collins who had first nick-named him "Taffy" because, at first acquaintance, his English accent sounded rather Welsh. I remember, he used to confuse words like donkey and monkey.

'I got on with most of the other drivers pretty well. Phil Hill was fun, but, heavens, was he jumpy! And Tony Brooks, of course; slightly aloof, rather in a world of his own, but in the most pleasant possible way.'

Ferrari finally allowed Allison his Formula 1 debut at the wheel of a Dino 246 in the 1959 Dutch GP at Zandvoort where he finished ninth, but a fifth at Monza strengthened his prospects of a full-time drive in 1960. Despite this, he recalled his biggest disappointment being his retirement from the 1959 US GP at Sebring.

'I was lying third behind the Coopers of Brabham and McLaren, and I really think I could have got on terms with them in the closing stages. Then the clutch flew apart – God, was I sick!'

Clutch failure also accounted for his retirement from the first part of the two-heat German GP at Avus, although he was satisfied to have posted fastest time during practice 'but I was only a reserve entry and had to line up at the back, rather than taking pole position.'

The beautiful Fantuzzi-bodied 1959 Dino 246 in the old Monza paddock prior to the Italian GP. This is the car which would be raced by Phil Hill.

Allison was taken on to the full-time Formula 1 team in 1960, opening the year by sharing the winning Testa Rossa with Phil Hill in the Buenos Aires 1000km endurance event, a week before the Argentina Grand Prix. Despite tyre problems, he still managed to finish second with the Dino 246 in that race, behind Bruce McLaren's winning Cooper.

'Dunlop's engineer Vic Barlow told us that there were tyres with two different tread depths available for this race,' he explains, 'the 5mm version of which would mean starting with a light fuel load and then making a pit stop for fuel and fresh rubber. There were also the 7mm ones on which we could go through non-stop.

'I said I wanted to go non-stop, but there was some confusion and I wound up with the 5mm treads and a full fuel load. The tyre fitters had done it wrong, so I had a marginal time towards the end, waiting to see when the breaker strips appeared.'

This was the best result of Allison's season, but his Formula 1 career with Ferrari came to an abrupt and unfortunate end when he crashed heavily during the second qualifying session for the 1960 Monaco Grand Prix.

Cliff was waiting to go out with full tanks on unscrubbed tyres when he realised that his good time from the previous day had been wiped from the slate, all the times having apparently been disallowed because of a glitch with the official timing equipment.

Coming through the chicane on to the harbour front, Allison clipped the wall with his right front wheel and the car spun wildly, hurling him out on to the road. He was bundled off to hospital where he 'woke up 16 days later, speaking French – which was quite strange, because I didn't know any French.'

Allison took the best part of a year recovering from the facial injuries sustained in that accident. Yet cut off from the narcotic life of an international racing driver was almost too much for him to bear.

He returned to the Formula 1 fray at the start of 1961 to drive a UDT/Laystall team Lotus, but crashed badly on his first practice lap at Spa and broke both his legs. Cliff Allison's racing career was now over for good and he admits that he returned to the life of a rural garage owner, at the age of just 29, nursing a burning sense of resentment and annoyance which took many years to evaporate.

Chapter 5

Mille Miglia disaster and the winning habit at Le Mans

By the mid-1950s, international sports car racing had grown to the point where it was every bit the equal of Formula 1 from the point of view of sheer excitement, prestige and manufacturer involvement. Of course, motor racing's infrastructure was different in those days. In the last decade of the century, Formula 1 has turned into a high-profile televised sport and the financial lifeblood of the competing teams is derived from whatever possible global television exposure it feels it can sell to a potential sponsor.

Companies like Ferrari, Maserati and, to a lesser extent, Jaguar and Aston Martin, lived on their wits. Their financial bottom line was dependent on car sales, and their racing income by how many customer cars they could pass on to private entrants. The races took place on the top circuits of the time, which inevitably meant that the contests could become pretty dangerous as professional and amateur both shared some of the most dangerous stretches of tarmac in the world.

By 1957, however, the Mille Miglia – Italy's glorious 1000 mile road race – had run its course. As long ago as 1938, a Lancia Aprilia had plunged into the crowd at Bologna, killing

three adults and seven children. Mussolini's regime immediately banned the race, but it had been revived in 1947. In 1956 the death of John Heath, Wolfgang Piwke and several spectators increased the clamour for its abandonment. Then came the carnage of the following year.

It had originally been intended that 'Fon' de Portago would drive the 1957 race in a Ferrari 250GT, sharing with his old friend and fellow bobsleigh competitor, Ed Nelson. However, the Spaniard damaged it beyond repair on a reconnaissance run and was promoted to the cockpit of one of the four-cam 4.2-litre 315S roadsters used by fellow front-liners Piero Taruffi, Peter Collins and Wolfgang von Trips.

De Portago drove well. By the time they reached Rome he was fourth, then moved up to third after Collins retired. Enzo Ferrari was at the Bologna depot on the return run to watch his lads come through on the final sprint back towards Brescia.

'The difficult parts were over, the game was played,' he wrote later. Streaking northwards towards the finish, with 975 miles behind them and only 25 left to run, the left front tyre on de Portago's Ferrari burst as he drifted through a long curve between the villages of Goito and Guidizzolo.

The car swerved off the road, uprooted a granite marker stone, then flew through the air, snapping off a telegraph pole and cutting to pieces spectators who were pressing forward at the roadside, regardless of the danger. The Ferrari bounced into one ditch, then shot back across the road. De Portago and Nelson were virtually decapitated by the 315S's bonnet. Nine spectators, including five children, were killed.

Taruffi won the race from von Trips, but it was the last Mille Miglia. As de Portago was buried with all due ceremony in Madrid, so Enzo Ferrari faced a whirlwind of criticism. He and Englebert, his company's tyre suppliers, were prosecuted for running de Portago's car at speeds of up to 280kph on tyres only rated for 220kph. It took four years for the defendants to be absolved of all blame, it being established that the tyres had been slit when 'Fon' drifted the powerful Ferrari over the 'catseyes' reflectors on the Volta Mantovano bend.

Interestingly, Olivier Gendebien finished third on that tragic, final Mille Miglia at the wheel of a 250GT fitted with a 3-litre V12 which had been developed by Andrea Fraschetti's design team. Even by this stage in the year it looked pretty certain that international sports car racing would be governed by a 3-litre limit as from the start of 1958, this being a move to try to sustain Jaguar and Maserati interest – and perhaps even tempt Mercedes to return with the 300SLRs, or derivatives thereof.

Unfortunately, Mercedes was not inclined to reverse its decision to quit, which had been taken at the end of 1955, while the only Maseratis represented on the international stage were now private entries. The works team had effectively been wiped out in a series a horrifying accidents in Caracas, Venezuela, in the final round of the 1957 Championship and did not reappear at the start of the following season. Aston Martin was still in the fray, but the onset of the 3-litre limit had caused Jaguar's interest to cool, although Porsche was steadily developing into a force to be reckoned with in the smaller capacity classes.

Eventually, Ferrari would settle on a single-cam, Chiti-developed V12 which was finally launched as the definitive 250TR in November 1957. Customer cars would be available only in left-hand drive, but the works cars were generally right-hand drive machines. Drum brakes and a sturdy chassis were essential elements of the TR design. It was the start of Ferrari's most consistently successful era on the international sports car racing stage.

Ferrari's strong driver line-up helped the 250TRs to open the 1958 season with a hat trick of victories in the Buenos Aires 1000km, Sebring 12-hour and Targa Florio rounds of the sports car World Championship. However, at the Nürburgring, Stirling Moss's Aston DBR1 simply waltzed away from the opposition, this race being marred by one of the most unfortunate accidents in motor racing history – after the chequered flag had been shown.

German amateur Erwin Bauer, sharing a private 250TR with Austrian Gottfried Koechert, mistakenly continued racing on to the slowing-down lap, crashed and sustained fatal injuries. It was an episode which perhaps highlighted the risk involved in allowing private entrants to purchase racing sports cars of such fearsome calibre.

With 30 points scored, compared with Porsche's 15 and Aston Martin's eight, Ferrari could hardly lose the World Championship as it went into the Le Mans 24-hour race, but the French classic was now the most important event on the sports car racing calendar now that the Mille Miglia had been consigned to the history books.

For this race there were three works 250TRs on hand for Peter Collins/Mike Hawthorn, Olivier Gendebien/Phil Hill and Wolfgang von Trips/Wolfgang Seidel. In addition, there were seven privately owned TRs in the field, plus a 2-litre 500TR from Luigi Chinetti's North American Racing Team for two young Mexicans, Pedro and Ricardo Rodriguez. When it was discovered that Ricardo Rodriguez was only 16, he was not permitted to start and his place was taken by José Behra.

Moss's Aston Martin led from the start only to break a con-rod after just over an hour, after which the heavens opened and most of the pack slowed to a crawl, apart from Phil Hill who kept up a consistently impressive pace and surged through into the lead with his works TR. Hawthorn and Collins steadily dropped back with clutch problems caused by Mike's over-exuberant getaway at the start.

Others in trouble included von Trips and Wolfgang Seidel, the latter being a nice guy but not really a top line driver – he spun at Arnage and got stuck in the mud. The Hawthorn/ Collins machine then retired with major transmission problems.

Elsewhere, amongst the privateers, there was plenty of grief as well. Luigi Chinetti had also brought to Le Mans an ex-works 250TR which he had acquired after the Targa Florio and had subsequently been rebuilt at the works. Entrusted to Dan Gurney and Bruce Kessler, it endured until late evening on Saturday when it was almost wrecked in a massive accident with a Jaguar D-type entered under the pseudonym 'Mary', the driver of which was fatally injured. Kessler was lucky to escape.

The Francois Picard/Jaroslav Juhan TR later spun and collided with an abandoned Lotus, but throughout all this drama Hill and Gendebien surged onwards to a superb victory. They were under pressure from the Duncan Hamilton/Ivor Bueb Jaguar D-type until almost lunchtime on Sunday, when it had started to rain again and Hamilton crashed heavily on the greasy surface. From there on, Hill and Gendebien cruised cautiously home to win by 10 laps from the Aston Martin DB3S driven by the Whitehead brothers, Peter and Graham.

Le Mans in 1961 was neither the first nor last time that NART had behaved as something of a loose cannon. Chinetti, although fundamentally one of the most ardent of Ferrari supporters, enjoyed it when the works cars were put under pressure by his own machines. However, he was to be seriously less-than-amused at Sebring in 1962 when his TR61 was excluded from the 12-hour race for what he regarded as bureaucratic meddling.

The Rodriguez brothers: fanning the flames of enthusiasm

MENTION OF TESTA Rossas inevitably introduces the subject of the Mexican Rodriguez brothers, Ricardo and Pedro, leading to another detour in the narrative.

Their father, Don Pedro Rodriguez, had raced motorcycles himself and later built up a considerable fortune working for a succession of Mexican presidents, apparently

Baby face. Ricardo Rodriguez – so much talent, so little time. (Günther Molter)

administering the secret service. Reputedly, he even learned to drive railway locomotives in order that he could run the presidential trains himself as part of his security duties!

Pedro Rodriguez de la Vega – so named because of the Spanish and Portuguese habit of including the maternal surname as a suffix – was born in 1940, Ricardo two years later, and while their father's fortune enabled them both to become under-aged racers, the younger brother soon emerged as the most outstanding performer. They had Jaguars, Corvettes and Osca sports cars, but their careers really took off when Luigi Chinetti took them under his wing and started to advance their interests.

In 1959, Chinetti purchased one of the ex-works 250TRs for the Rodriguez family and this was used largely by Pedro in US and Mexican national events, and the following year both brothers drove a 196 Dino, starting at Sebring and then continuing to finish an amazing seventh in the Targa Florio – despite rolling it twice en route to the finish, reducing its bodywork almost to scrap in the process!

Yet it was in 1961 that the Rodriguez brothers really started to ring the international motor racing bell. They were determined, highly competitive and – particularly Ricardo – utterly fearless. They very nearly won the Nürburgring 1000km before being delayed when the spokes on the right front wheel of their 250TR61 prototype broke, and Ricardo had to limp back to the pits on three wheels and a hub.

Then came Le Mans where the works TR61s for Phil Hill/Olivier Gendebien and Willy Mairesse/Mike Parkes were backed up by a third such car for the Rodriguez brothers entered by NART but controlled by the factory's pit crew. Enzo Ferrari was no fool, rightly reasoning that Ricardo and Pedro were out to make their names in a big way by racing the works cars, but team manager Romolo Tavoni privately doubted whether he could bring the two exuberant Mexican lads to heel.

Richie Ginther led from the start in a works 246SP, but Gendebien took the Testa Rossa through into the lead second time round. The two works Ferraris then settled down to run at a disciplined pace at the head of the pack. But this wasn't enough for Pedro Rodriguez who was taking the first stint in the NART car. He piled on the pressure, hauled in the factory cars and swooped past into the lead on the Mulsanne straight as early as the ninth lap of the race.

Throughout much of the night the ensuing battle raged between the three Testa Rossas, the ferocity of the contest becoming so lurid that at one point the Rodriguez car clipped the nose of Mairesse's machine as he lapped the Belgian. It didn't take long before tempers began to run ragged in the pits, Tavoni beseeching the Rodriguez boys to toe the Ferrari line, whilst attempting subtly to remind Papa Rodriguez that they had been loaned the TR61 to support the factory team – not to try consistently to beat it.

Tavoni shrewdly managed to delay the Rodriguez car when it came spluttering into the pits with an ignition problem in the small hours of Sunday morning. A faulty condenser was eventually diagnosed and the mechanics took a leisurely 20 minutes to rectify the fault – thanks to Tavoni's instructions. The Rodriguez brothers resumed fourth, completely unfazed by this delay, and battled flat-out back to second before their over-used V12 eventually blew apart and limped into the pits trailing a cloud of white smoke with only two hours of the race left to run.

Unquestionably, Ferrari was impressed with the Rodriguez brothers and offered them both rent-a-drives with his Formula 1 team. Unfortunately, business commitments prevented Pedro from accepting the invitation, but Ricardo signed up for the deal and would qualify second fastest for the Italian GP at Monza – his first Formula 1 outing – only three months later.

One man who knew Ricardo Rodriguez better than most was Jo Ramirez, today the

Ricardo Rodriguez accelerates the NART-entered Ferrari 250TR out of Mulsanne during the 1961 Le Mans 24-hour race where he and his brother Pedro gave the works cars a real fright. (LAT)

McLaren-Mercedes Formula 1 team co-ordinator but then an 18-year old pal of the Mexican ace who came to Europe with the younger Rodriguez.

'We used to go kart racing together in Mexico,' recalls Ramirez, 'and I came with him to work for Ferrari at some races, although I couldn't get a full-time job with the factory and ended up working for Maserati.

'Ricardo? Oh yes, he was simply born with it. God, he had the talent to go all the way. He didn't have to try hard at all, but Pedro needed to work at it to keep up with his brother. Ricardo was very easy-going, laid-back and extrovert and I got on with him really well. Pedro was quieter, more introspective.

'Papa Rodriguez was obviously very well

off, but he didn't force motor racing on to his boys. But when they were obviously pretty keen, having won everything on motorcycles, he was happy to buy them their four-wheeled toys.

'Before they came to Europe, he bought Ricardo a Porsche RS and Pedro a Testa Rossa. They went up to Riverside (in California) when Ricardo was just 15 – I mean, he was a kid and he looked like a kid. Everybody just laughed when they saw him, but he blew off John von Neumann and Ken Miles, two of the local men to beat, in a race on both Saturday and Sunday.

'When the boys came to Europe the Old

Man came with them, usually with a lot of people around him. The Rodriguez family was always very popular in what you'd call Mexican high society and there were no shortage of rich friends who could afford to travel with him.

'Ricardo was such a natural person. I went with him to most of his Grand Prix races in 1962 and he just couldn't take it all in when the engineers started asking him his opinion about the car. "I mean, me," he used to say. "They asking *me* – where I brake, where I change down into second gear – and my team-mate [Phil Hill] is the World Champion!"'

The NART Testa Rossa was driven in this event by Stirling Moss and Innes Ireland and was ranged against a similar Scuderia Serenissima independent entry handled by Jo Bonnier and Lucien Bianchi. As the Rodriguez brothers built up a lead in the 246SP, so Moss and Ireland became embroiled in a dispute with the officials after Innes was admonished for charging into the pit lane at what the officials clearly regarded as excessively high speed.

Innes might have got away with a verbal warning had he kept his lips buttoned, but in characteristic style he joined Chinetti in giving the Chief Steward a verbal bashing. Later, Ireland made a pit stop two laps short of the regulation 20-lap minimum refuelling intervals and the NART Testa Rossa was duly topped up, but against the regulations.

Nello Ugolini, the former Maserati team manager who was looking after the Scuderia Serenissima Testa Rossa, then lodged a protest and another great row broke out in front of the NART pit, with much gesticulating and raised voices. Eventually the Ireland/Moss car was excluded from the race – black flagged into retirement almost three hours after the original rule infringement.

In his autobiography, *All Arms and Elbows* (Pelham Books, 1967), Ireland really got stuck into the Sebring organisers: 'So we had been driving this car quite unnecessarily for over three hours and this burned up both Moss and myself. I can't tell you how furious I was. My language, I know, was quite unbelievably bad and I told everyone in sight just what I thought of them and their lousy race.

'The organisers allowed Stirling and I to motor on with that car for all that time, during which we could have broken our necks, or anything could have happened. That, I feel, was not only grossly unfair, but damned dangerous. One is left with the impression that the organisers did not want to disqualify Moss, the main attraction of the race, too early and while the customers were still coming in.'

Hair-raising accidents, of course, were routine, part and parcel of the endurance racing business in those days. Before being taken on as a full-time member of the Grand Prix team at the start of the 1960 season, Cliff Allison spent many miles in the Testa Rossas. In 1959 he finished second at Sebring with Jean Behra, fifth in the Nürburgring 1000km with Willy Mairesse and fifth in the Goodwood Tourist Trophy. He was also extremely fortunate to survive unscathed from a monumental accident whilst practising for the Targa Florio.

'I was going flat-out down one of the long straights,' he remembers, 'and I suddenly became aware of a vibration. I backed off slightly and it weaved about a bit, but when I went back on the throttle again it wasn't too bad.

'I wondered if there might be a problem with the steering, but it turned out that a front tyre had deflated and the centrifugal force at 160mph was just about enabling the car to stay under control. When I tried to slow down seriously, I found myself in real trouble, heading straight for the end of a wall on the side of a bridge.

'I managed to swerve away from that, but the car took off, had its floor pan ripped out by a milestone, before crashing down on the opposite side of the road. I looked down to where the floor should have been and just saw mud and earth. You can't imagine how relieved I was, but if I hadn't kept my feet on the pedals, I might well have been in really bad shape.

'The Ferrari team's reaction was most interesting. Until they'd ascertained that the car hadn't broken, they were very worried and preoccupied. When they discovered it had been tyre trouble, and not a chassis breakage, they heaved a sigh of relief!' The fact that their driver had had a lucky escape was not really part of the equation. Ferrari drivers were expendable.

For his part, Tony Brooks has mixed memories of the Testa Rossa. 'Not a match on handling for the Aston Martin DBR1, which was a really great sports car, but the DBR1 didn't have the power of the Ferrari and, with due respect to David Brown, the gearbox was pretty atrocious,' he recalls.

'But the Testa Rossa was a good car, it went well, but not a match for the DBR1 round a circuit like the Nürburgring. Of course, I signed at Ferrari on the condition I didn't have to drive at Le Mans, which I was astonished that he accepted, but I had no problem driving anywhere else. There was all sorts of rubbish written that I refused to drive at Sebring, but that wasn't the case at all. I enjoyed racing, but I preferred Grand Prix cars, and I think that a GP car responded better to a delicate touch. A sports car didn't repay finesse quite as much.'

During this period, Hill and Gendebien emerged as one of the most outstanding of the Ferrari endurance racing partnerships. In 1958, 1961 and 1962 they won Le Mans together, and also Sebring in 1959 and 1962. In addition, Gendebien won Le Mans in 1960 sharing with Paul Frère and the 1958 Targa Florio with Luigi Musso, while Hill won the 1958 and 1960 Buenos Aires 1000km (with Peter Collins and Cliff Allison respectively).

The two men got along pretty well,

Classic Ferrari sports car. The Phil Hill/Olivier Gendebien 250TR heading for victory at Le Mans in 1958. (Geoffrey Goddard)

although Hill recalls that he used to get rather irked over the manner in which his Belgian colleague rather tended to play down his contribution to the overall winning package.

Throughout that time – a period of six seasons – the Testa Rossa remained in the front line of Ferrari's armoury on the international sports car racing scene. The cars evolved steadily in terms of technical specification and, in total, some 36 examples were built, enabling Maranello to do a lucrative business with private entrants across the world. In fact, Ferrari ceased the production of pure 'customer spec' Testa Rossas at the end of the 1958 season, the privateers' ambitions thereafter being met by ex-works cars as they were gradually replaced by new machinery.

By 1959 disc brakes had found their way on to many Testa Rossas as a by-product of the late Peter Collins's enthusiasm, after he had a set of them fitted to his road-going 250GT by Dunlop shortly before his death the previous year. The same year saw ex-Maserati bodywork wizard Medardo Fantuzzi establishing his own coach-building company which took over the manufacture of Ferrari competition car bodies from the Scaglietti company which was by then hard pressed to deal with Maranello's demand for road cars.

Ferrari lost the 1959 Sports Car Championship to Aston Martin. Then the CSI, motor racing's then governing body, made some suggestions for changing the rules the following year. Many people felt that out-and-out two-seater racing cars like the Testa Rossa were only one step removed from Grand Prix machines and therefore didn't conform to the GT image, which was judged as likely to tempt in new manufacturers.

Gendebien drifts the 1958 Le Mans winning Ferrari 250TR through the White House curves.

Tony Brooks at the 1959 Nürburgring 1000km with a Ferrari 250TR. The Englishman reckoned that the Aston Martin DBR1 was a far more manageable proposition round this challenging circuit. (Francis Penn)

Luigi Musso bares his forearms at the wheel of a 250TR at the 1958 Nürburgring 1000km. (LAT)

Cliff Allison at the wheel of the works Ferrari 250TR en route to victory in the 1960 Buenos Aires 1000km where he shared the car with Phil Hill.

At one point it was suggested that the 1960 Championship should be run for GT cars only, with the sports cars permitted to continue competing but not to be eligible for points. Eventually a compromise was reached, with changes to the rules to make the out-and-out sports cars vaguely identifiable with GT road cars; a full-width windscreen with a vertical depth of at least 34cm, operational windscreen wipers and space for a 'suitcase' measuring a certain size were now demanded.

Ricardo Rodriguez (right) and Juan Manuel Fangio at Modena in 1962. (Ramirez collection)

For the 1960 season there were also changes on the driver front, the most notable switch being Dan Gurney's decision to move to BRM. Having carved his way into prominence on the US racing scene via a succession of sports cars including a 4.9-litre Ferrari fielded by wealthy vineyard owner Franck Arciero, Gurney was earmarked by Luigi Chinetti as a promising lad and was duly taken to Le Mans as a NART driver in 1958.

The following year he was promoted to the Formula 1 line-up on an occasional basis alongside Phil Hill, who advised him in advance of the pitfalls and problems involved in being a Ferrari team driver. The affable Gurney, however, found the draconian team discipline, autocratic management style and modest pay all a bit too much to bear. But switching to BRM turned out to be a major career error.

Olivier Gendebien, meanwhile, moved to Porsche, leaving Phil Hill and Cliff Allison to form the core of the Maranello driver line-up, supported variously by Wolfgang von Trips and another Chinetti discovery, Californian Richie Ginther, who was an old pal of Hill from their club racing days. Ginther quickly established a reputation as one of the most astute test and development drivers in the business, much to the satisfaction of his team-mates who were generally quite content to leave such day-to-day drudgery to their wiry little colleague.

In 1961 the CSI firmly decreed that

this would definitely be the final season for the sports car Championship and that a GT series would replace it for 1962. By this stage Carlo Chiti had the benefit of a small, home-brewed wind tunnel at Maranello and the heavily re-designed TR61 benefited from a more aerodynamic windscreen and a cut-off Kamm tail. It would not be long before the TR61s sported a tail spoiler as well, heralding the arrival of Ferrari's aerodynamic age – albeit at a modest level.

The CSI may have intended that GT cars would move into the limelight for 1962, but this approach didn't seem to have taken much account of the race organisers' viewpoint. They were all deeply concerned about the potential pulling power of GT cars alone, so it was decided that a Sports Car Cup should be contested by the 3-litre prototypes over seven races.

For Ferrari the prospects for the 1962 season were frustrated by a wholesale walk-out of key personnel at the end of the previous season; Carlo Chiti, Giotto Bizzarrini (in charge of control and testing management), Commercial Manager Girolamo Giardini – who was at one point slapped in the face in public by Ferrari's increasingly interfering wife Laura – financial wizard Ermanno della Cassa, production and supply manager Federico Gilberto, personnel manager Enzo Selmi, team manager Romolo Tavoni and foundry manager Fausto Galazzi all decided to tender their resignation.

On the face of it, this was a major body blow, but Enzo Ferrari was never one to be intimidated. If anybody was going to do the intimidating at Maranello, then it was the boss, and he treated his staff defection with a degree of lofty disdain.

There was another defection on the driver front. This time Richie Ginther decided to quit, frustrated at lack of front-line Formula 1 opportunities and poor salary. He went to BRM where his testing skills would pay off handsomely in contributing towards the British team's 1962 World Championship victory. His place was taken by the wayward Belgian 'Wild Willy' Mairesse, who also took over testing duties, much to the frustration of team-mates Phil Hill, Lorenzo Bandini, Ricardo Rodriguez and Giancarlo Baghetti, none of whom could make any sense of his chassis settings.

For Le Mans, 1962, Ferrari came up with what's best described as the ultimate Testa Rossa, an experimental car based round a TR61 chassis with inboard rear brakes and powered by a 4-litre Superamerica V12 developing around 360bhp. Come Le Mans, Hill and Gendebien stroked their way to an easy victory with this hybrid machine, designated 330TRI. As far as the factory was concerned, this represented the end of the road for its serious Testa Rossa development. The central-engined route was now the only way to go, and Ferrari concentrated on the development of the new 250P for the 1963 season.

Twelve months later, NART brought the 330TRI back to Le Mans with Pedro Rodriguez and Roger Penske, the man who would later become one of the USA's most successful business-men and owner of the prolific Indycar team which carries his name to this day.

Yet the young Penske was certainly not a match for Rodriguez in terms of speed, much to the frustration of the Mexican family, and the race ended when the V12 blew up spectacularly

Ricardo Rodriguez (hand on car door) in company with (from left), Juan Manuel Bordeu, Jo Ramirez, Lorenzo Bandini and Phil Hill at Modena in 1962. (Ramirez collection)

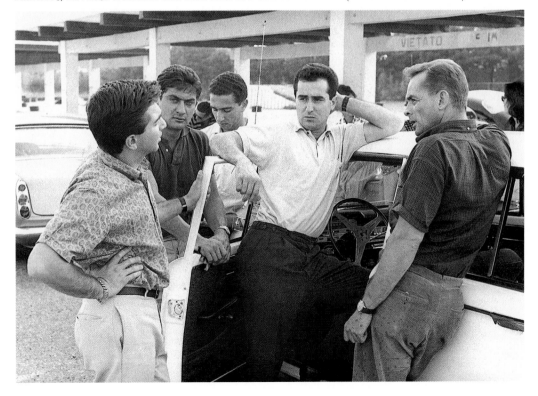

Last time out for the Testa Rossa. Le Mans, 1963, and young Roger Penske, in the NART entry he shared with Pedro Rodriguez, leads a GTO through the Esses early in the race. Penske eventually crashed heavily after the engine exploded. (LAT)

as the American driver was at full throttle between the Mulsanne and Indianapolis corners. The car shot off the road into the trees and Penske was fortunate to escape serious injury.

Thereafter, the Testa Rossas eked out a twilight existence in the hands of privateers, particularly in US domestic racing, but their high-profile racing career had come to an end. The curtain thus fell on one of the most exciting and successful of all of Ferrari's sports racing cars, as well as on the marque's most consistently fruitful period of endurance racing achievement.

Chapter 6

Rear-engined revolution

ALTHOUGH FERRARI RELIED on its Dino 246s to represent the team's Grand Prix fortunes through to the end of the 1960 season, there was no ignoring the rear-engined revolution as pioneered by Cooper and successfully developed by Lotus. By the time Phil Hill sped to the front-engined Dino's final GP win at Monza in 1960, more than two-and-a-half years had passed since Stirling Moss's victory in the Rob Walker Cooper-Climax in Buenos Aires.

The 1960 Monaco GP saw Richie Ginther debut the first rear-engined Ferrari car, an experimental Dino 246 built round a multi-tube spaceframe, using a totally new five-speed gearbox in unit with the final drive and incorporating an overhung clutch at the rear.

However, it was not Ferrari's rear-engined technology which was to prove the key factor in 1961, but his belief that the 1.5-litre formula would in fact be implemented by the CSI. On 29 October 1958, Mike Hawthorn and

Factory test driver Martino Severi tries the rear-engined Ferrari Dino 246 at Modena prior to Richie Ginther giving the car its race debut at Monaco in 1960. (Graham Gauld)

Tony Vandervell had attended the Royal Automobile Club in London's Pall Mall to receive the awards for, respectively, the drivers' and constructors' World Championships. Yet what started out as something of a convivial social gathering for the British motor racing community soon turned into a potentially explosive gathering.

Following the formal presentations, the CSI President Auguste Perouse stunned the assembled company by announcing that a 1.5-litre Formula 1, with a 500kg minimum weight limit, would replace the existing 2.5-litre regulations for the start of the 1961 season. The CSI had voted in favour of the new rules by a margin of 5–2 with only Britain and Italy voting for the continuation of the existing regulations.

The British constructors were furious. A meeting of the RAC Competitions Committee on 12 November gave vent to their feelings when Lord Howe reported that 'despite the efforts of the RAC, backed up by technical information offered by leading drivers and manufacturers, a decision had been taken which is most unpopular with British interests.'

Consideration was duly given to the introduction of a separate formula which would be more closely tailored to British requirements. This subsequently manifested itself as a 3-litre formule libre category – dubbed the Intercontinental Formula – which flourished briefly as little more than a UK-based super club racing category. From a historical standpoint it was a complete irrelevance which contributed nothing apart from taking the British constructors's eyes off the Formula 1 ball. By the time Cooper, Lotus, BRM and engine suppliers Coventry-Climax finally took on board the message that the 1.5-litre Formula 1 was coming whether they liked it or not, Ferrari was well down the road towards preparing for the new category.

Throughout the final three years of the 2.5-litre Formula 1, Ferrari concentrated a lot of time on developing a small-capacity version of the Dino V6, initially for Formula 2 applications. Thus, by the beginning of 1961, Carlo Chiti's engine department had a 65-degree V6 all ready to go at the start of the new formula.

As a curtain-raiser to the new season, Ferrari had fielded the rear-engined Dino equipped with a 1.5-litre engine (the 156) in the 1960 Italian GP. It finished fifth in the hands of Wolfgang von Trips, having initially been 'towed' clear of the non-Maranello opposition in the slipstream of Mairesse's regular front-engined Dino 246. Preparation for the new season was rounded off when von Trips finished third in the Modena GP on 2 October 1960 behind Jo Bonnier's Porsche and Mairesse in a front-engined Dino 156 Formula 2 car.

The distinctive new Ferrari 156s were fitted with front 'shark nose' radiator intakes similar to those seen on the late-model Testa Rossa sports racers. Chiti had also developed a 120-degree version of the V6 engine with a view to a lower centre of gravity and the possibility of mounting various ancillary equipment within the vee, but the 1961 season started with the 65-degree engines regarded as the main thrust in terms of motive power and the 120-degree unit initially earmarked as an experimental project.

The driver line-up for 1961 from the outset included Phil Hill, Richie Ginther and Wolfgang von Trips. In addition, Ferrari support was leant to Giancarlo

Distinctive rear-end treatment of the front-running 1961 Ferrari 156. (Phipps Photographic)

Baghetti, the eldest son of a wealthy Milanese industrialist, who was initially entered in the non-title Syracuse GP under the auspices of the Federation Italiana Scuderie Automobilsche. This was effectively an amalgam of Italian racing teams who had got together with the intention of promoting home-grown driving talent. Baghetti would win the races, admittedly against makeweight opposition, thereby marking himself out as a potential future star.

The 1961 World Championship battle began at Monaco where the extra power on tap to the Ferrari 156 drivers wasn't really a benefit. Hill, von Trips and Ginther – the latter using the new 120-degree V6 alone – were comprehensively taken to the cleaners by Stirling Moss's Rob Walker team Lotus 18.

Powered by a four-cylinder Coventry-Climax engine which was giving away at least 30bhp to the Ferraris, Moss drove with relentless precision to score one of his greatest Formula 1 victories. Ginther, a tiger, drove the race of his life to finish second, but simply couldn't push 'Stirl' into a mistake.

Four years later, Ginther would win the final race of the 1.5-litre Formula 1 at Mexico City with the Japanese Honda. Yet the Californian still rated Monaco in 1961 his greatest race up to the day he died.

'My car and my effort were stronger than the opposition when I won in the Honda, which was just plain faster than the opposition,' he later recalled, 'but at Monaco, both Stirling and I were three seconds below the pole time in the race. Staggering, isn't it?

'I set the lap record very late (16 laps from the finish) but Stirling equalled it next time round. That son of a gun! If you did well against him,

Wolfgang von Trips in the pits at Spa in 1961. The popular German count would be poised to snatch the World Championship when he was killed at Monza three months later. (Phipps Photographic)

then you'd really done something special.'

Meanwhile, Hill, who had finished third ahead of von Trips, added his postcript to the proceedings when he noted that chasing the Moss Lotus round Monaco in a Ferrari was like trying to race a greyhound round your living room with a carthorse.

Ironical *bon mots* were certainly Phil's speciality.

On the same afternoon that Moss was trouncing the works cars, Baghetti was enjoying an easy run to win the non-title Naples GP. Then von Trips won the Dutch GP at Zandvoort where Hill battled back to a close second place after grappling with clutch pedal problems, and Ferrari followed that up with a predictable 1–2–3–4 grand slam in the Belgian GP at Spa-Francorchamps.

Amidst the splendid pine forests of the Hautes Fagnes, Hill squared his Zandvoort defeat and won by less than a second from von Trips, with Ginther third ahead of Olivier Gendebien's yellow-painted Equipe Nationale Belge entry. It was during practice for this event that Dunlop engineer Vic Barlow told Chiti that he was extremely concerned about the amount of negative camber on the rear wheels of the Ferrari 156s. Barlow was worried about heat build-up on the inside of the tread and persuaded Chiti that the camber should be wound off slightly. It was, and the handling seemed to improve.

Next on the agenda was the French GP at Reims-Gueux, traditionally a sweltering affair under a relentless sun. The 1961 fixture proved no exception and Baghetti's FISA-entered 156 supplemented the works entry. Hill, who had learned a thing or two about out-psyching his contemporaries, put in a stupendous lap to take pole – over a second faster than the frustrated von Trips.

The German count immediately started complaining that his car must be sub-standard in specification. Phil then offered to take Trips's car out for a trial run, at the same time that he

Phil Hill, the 1961 World Champion, looking suitably animated in the cockpit of his Ferrari 156 at Reims. Carlo Chiti (in white shirt) and Luigi Bazzi (hand on rear tyre) watch with interest.

This magnificent David Phipps shot catches the magic of the splendid Reims circuit with Phil Hill's Ferrari 156 leading the pack out on to the Muizon straight on the opening lap of the 1961 French GP. Behind him is team-mate Richie Ginther, Stirling Moss's Rob Walker Lotus 21, Wolfgang von Trips's Ferrari 156, John Surtees's Yeoman Credit Cooper, Graham Hill's BRM, the Team Lotus 21s of Jim Clark and Innes Ireland and Tony Brooks's BRM. (Phipps Photographic)

heard there was some oil down on the track surface at the Thillois corner. As it transpired, Hill found no oil at all and went like the wind, setting a tremendously quick time before coming in and apologising to his team-mate that he couldn't go any quicker because of the (fictional) oil. Von Trips was left distracted and bewildered.

Ginther led initially, but had an early spin, leaving von Trips and Hill initially to battle over the lead. Von Trips was out after 20 laps with a stone through the radiator, then Hill spun at Thillois and was clouted by Moss's Lotus. Phil stalled and couldn't restart. All this drama allowed Ginther through into the lead, but his chances were thwarted by fading oil pressure.

'Eventually I just had to come into the pits,' said Ginther, 'because I couldn't bring myself to drive the engine until it broke. But I was instructed to go out again, only for the engine to blow up before I even got as far as the first hairpin.'

Unbelievably, Baghetti now came to

Giancarlo Baghetti's Ferrari 156 just pips Dan Gurney's Porsche for an unexpected victory in the 1961 French GP at Reims. (LAT)

Phil Hill and Maranello politics

By the 1961 season Hill was an old hand when it came to dealing with the intricacies and pitfalls of Maranello's highly political atmosphere, even if he hardly found it an easy challenge.

This was an era when drivers were still regarded by Ferrari as light bulbs. If one burnt out, you just screwed in another. It was all straightforward. Yet this approach understandably grated with the intelligent and thoughtful Californian, a man who many of his friends considered was really a little too cerebral to be a racing driver in the first place.

Getting things changed on the car was always a drama. Hill reckoned it had much to do with the Italian social system and the pride it engendered in an individual's work. A mechanic was a mechanic, an engineer an engineer, but, in Hill's words, they tended to suffer from 'the jealousy of jurisdiction'.

In short, any complaints about the car – however mild-mannered and apparently reasonable – were automatically interpreted as professional slights. Two years earlier he'd asked for a slightly higher windscreen on a Dino 246, only to be told by Ferrari to 'forget your head and keep your foot down.'

In 1961, the problem seemed to be excessive cockpit heat in the 156s. Fortunately, things had become a little more reasonable and Hill was able to get his mechanic to make the necessary modifications. But by 1961, one tends to get the impression that Ferrari was rather wearing Hill down.

the fore. Battling with commendable judgement and self-discipline, the Italian new boy found himself enmeshed in a contest for the lead of his first World Championship Grand Prix. His rivals were now the two powerful four-cylinder Porsches driven by Dan Gurney and Jo Bonnier.

Working together, the two Porsche drivers ganged up on Baghetti, pulling every flanker they could think of. Sometimes they would rocket through the start/finish area on either side of the Ferrari, sometimes in front and behind, or fanned out across the circuit ahead of the inexperienced Italian.

Two laps from the finish, Bonnier dropped from the fray and it was down to Gurney – himself a former Ferrari man – to try to get the better of the Prancing Horse. Coming down the long straight into the final Thillois right-hander for the last time, Gurney slipstreamed past in the lead, the two

cars scrabbled through the turn and made for the line.

In a perfectly judged move, Baghetti swung out of Gurney's slipstream and surged past to win by one-tenth of a second. The Milanese new boy had saved the day for Maranello. Nobody could have imagined it would also be the last time in his career that Baghetti would lead past the chequered flag in a major international motor race.

Ferrari's traditional unwillingness to nominate a specific team leader was getting on Phil Hill's nerves. The pressure was building and the Californian realised that von Trips was now emerging as the man he would have to beat if he wanted to become World Champion. For his part, Trips seemed to have matured into a more controlled and restrained performer, although his technical knowledge remained minimal and he was still inclined to be hard on ailing machinery.

Following Reims, von Trips triumphed decisively in a soaking wet British GP at Aintree. Hill was second, but he later recorded a heart-stopping moment in graphic detail. It says much about his frame of mind:

'I had a horrible fright. I hit a groove of deep water going into Melling Crossing and I could see my right front tyre just stop turning. Hydroplaning (or aquaplaning) was not as common then as it became with the advent of wider tyres. I had no steering and I was headed for this metre-thick gate post with that image of the tyre's stationary tread pattern etched on my retina.

'Finally my wheels cut down through the water enough to get a grip and I missed that post by a hair. A few years earlier it would have been forgotten – like a letter dropped in a mailbox – the instant the wheel caught hold. But by 1961 it stayed with me.'

Moss and the Walker Lotus again dished out a beating to Ferrari at the Nürburgring, von Trips scrambling across the finishing line to finish second ahead of Hill. Now there were two races to go; the Italian GP at Monza and the US race at Watkins Glen. But, mathematically, it came down to whichever of the two top-scoring Ferrari drivers – Hill or von Trips – won at Monza, he would become the 1961 World Champion. Yet the boss still issued no team orders, any more than he had done in 1958 when Musso, Hawthorn and Collins were battling amongst themselves in the Dino 246s.

At Monza there were five Ferrari entries. Works cars for Hill, von Trips, Ginther and the dazzling 19-year old

Start of the 1961 British GP at Aintree with Phil Hill (No. 2) alongside Richie Ginther (No. 6) and eventual winner von Trips (No. 4) just behind. (LAT)

The rear-engined revolution extended to Ferrari sports cars too. Here Olivier Gendebien looks anxiously up the track after spinning his 246SP during the 1961 Nürburgring 1000km. The Belgian had huge difficulty restarting because of carburetter icing.

No fewer than six Ferrari 156s on hand for the team's five-car entry in the fateful 1961 Italian GP at Monza. (Phipps Photographic)

Ricardo Rodriguez – courtesy Luigi Chinneti's influence with Enzo and Papa Rodriguez's financial muscle – plus Baghetti now running under the auspices of the Milan-based Scuderia Sant'Ambroeus.

Von Trips qualified on pole with the remarkable Rodriguez alongside him on the front row. But the Ferrari drivers were all using a high final drive ratio for this event, so they were slow off the mark at the start, allowing Jim Clark's Lotus 21 to get in amongst them on the opening lap. Coming down to Parabolica for the second time, von Trips came blaring past the Lotus, but then seemingly misjudged his position, moving over to take his line into the right-hander before he was clear of Clark's car.

The two machines interlocked wheels and Trips's Ferrari cartwheeled up against the spectator bank before throwing its driver out on to the edge of the track. Fourteen spectators were killed in this grisly disaster, and von Trips was fatally injured.

Hill survived to win, the only Ferrari to make the distance in front of the team's home crowd. But the satisfaction of winning the World Championship was obviously swamped by the magnitude of the tragedy which had befallen his team-mate.

After the race, Hill admits that he stayed in Modena and was distressed by the political backwash which left Enzo Ferrari apparently beleaguered from all sides. In a moment of emotional loyalty he agreed to stay for the 1962 season. Only after he had done the deal did Ferrari tell him that Chiti and the rest of the senior management team had decided to walk out on him.

Giancarlo Baghetti's Ferrari 156 on the Monza banking during the 1961 Italian GP. The Milanese driver failed to finish. (LAT)

Young bloods. Ricardo Rodriguez (centre) and Giancarlo Baghetti in company with Ferrari team manager Eugenio Dragoni (left). (Ramirez collection)

Ferrari offered a generous tribute to von Trips. 'I was particularly fond of him because of his great integrity,' he wrote. 'He was a descendant from a family of barons, one of those German families who still represent feudal land ownership. [Perhaps Enzo identified with him.]

'He died just as he was about to add the World Championship to his victories in Holland and England. What had been a glorious season for us ended violently; the very day that should have been a celebration of courage, victories and success in shared work brought raw bitterness and sadness instead.'

Chiti's departure might have been regarded as a major disaster from Ferrari's technical standpoint had he not had a young engineer waiting in the wings to slide into the top job. This was the bespectacled Mauro Forghieri, a man whose versatility and design genius made a remarkable

contribution to the success achieved by the Prancing Horse for over 20 years.

The key to Forghieri's special relationship came from the fact that his father, Reclus, had been a pattern maker on the original Alfa 158s during the pioneering pre-war years of the Scuderia. Mauro's grandfather, in turn, had carved himself a niche as poet and social commentator, spending much of his life in the 1920s living on the Cote d'Azur and only being allowed back into Italy when Mussolini's regime took over on the strict understanding that he would not involve himself in any political activities.

Thus there was an excitable, imaginative and theatrical streak coursing through the Forghieri bloodline, as well as a grasp of practical engineering. Yet despite the fact that his father had worked for Ferrari himself, Mauro's ambitions originally extended

beyond racing cars when he was studying at the University of Bologna.

'My great passion was aviation engineering,' he explained. 'I really wanted to go to the USA and work with Lockheed or Northrop, but just as I left university with a diploma in mechanical engineering at the end of 1958, I was called up to do my national service.'

His plans to decamp to the USA were shelved, never to be revived. Reclus Forghieri got on well with Mr Ferrari on a personal level and the boss suggested that Mauro should have a place in the company. One thing was for certain; Forghieri junior was in no doubts as to what awaited him. In 1957 he had spent some time at Maranello gathering information for a university project and he eventually joined the company at the end of 1959, working with Chiti on detailed calculations for the new 120-degree V6 Formula 1 engine.

'Engines have always been my principal interest,' he said, 'and when I went to Ferrari I didn't know anything at all about chassis design. I suppose in the following 20 years you could say that I became equally interested in chassis, suspension and gearbox work, but engines were always my first love. I regarded my work on the 1.5-litre Ferrari 156 as my schooling period in the art of chassis development.'

Unfortunately, the 1962 season was a complete and unmitigated disaster for Ferrari. Hill was now paired with Baghetti, Ricardo Rodriguez, Mairesse and, increasingly, Lorenzo Bandini. The last-named was the protégé of Ferrari's new team manager, the Machiavellian Eugenio Dragoni – Phil Hill and he immediately developed a mutual dislike.

It had originally been intended that Rob Walker would run a private

Ferrari 156 for Stirling Moss – a move which would certainly have rattled the works drivers – but the English driver's career came to an end with his dreadful accident at Goodwood on Easter Monday, and the plan was never implemented.

However, as a token of his esteem for Moss, Ferrari loaned a works 156 for Stirling's pal Innes Ireland to drive in the non-title BRDC International Trophy race at Silverstone. Innes finished fourth – and then submitted a number of suggestions to improve the car's handling direct to Maranello.

One of the items on his list was a proposed wide-track suspension set-up. It was adopted by Forghieri, proved less than effective and, since Phil Hill didn't hit if off with the new designer anyway, simply added to the tensions. In fact, the truth of the matter was that Ferrari was eclipsed in 1962 simply because the new V8 engines from BRM and Coventry-Climax were much more powerful than Maranello's V6. And the combination of Jim Clark's Lotus 25 and Graham Hill's BRM were also in a different league.

The personal relationship between Dragoni and Hill deteriorated steadily throughout the season. Phil's frustration with the Ferrari's lack of competitiveness was attributed by the new team manager to the after-effects of von Trips's death. Hill, he reasoned, had been 'psychologically impressioned' by the tragedy. In any event, Dragoni had his own agenda in advancing Bandini – he wanted to be the architect of an Italian Formula 1 driving renaissance – and if that meant undermining the American, then so be it.

Nevertheless, Hill produced Ferrari's best result of the season with a strong second place to Bruce McLaren's Cooper at Monaco. He was also third at Zandvoort, a result matched by Ricardo Rodriguez in the Belgian race at Spa-Francorchamps after Mairesse rolled his car into a ball in a horrifying, fiery high speed accident.

At the end of the season, Hill and Baghetti quit the team and followed Chiti, Tavoni et al to the abortive ATS squad which had been established in a vain attempt to beat Ferrari at his own game. It was effectively the end of these two drivers' serious Formula 1 careers and, in essence, an important victory for Dragoni in his attempts to position Bandini in the most favourable possible light.

Ferrari was sparing in his praise of Hill's talents. 'Phil Hill, who was von Trips's team-mate, was a solid, emotional racer. He wasn't first rate, but he was dependable and profitable mainly on high-speed circuits. He preferred wide curves and long straights to winding roads – the so-called demanding circuits which required constant driving precision. He displayed great precision where speed was the determining factor.

'He excelled even more in the

Ricardo Rodriguez made his Formula 1 debut at Monza in 1961, qualifying his Ferrari 156 second behind von Trips on the front row of the grid. (Phipps Photographic)

sports cars because in long distance races he was able to combine his innate gifts for speed and respect for the machinery – a winning combination.' Given Phil's achievements at Le Mans and elsewhere, he could hardly say otherwise!

'In his annuals, the only way you came off any good was either to be on especially good terms with him, or to die,' said Phil perceptively. 'If you died, you got your picture in colour – with big ruby lips. I can't imagine where he found a guy to paint those things.'

Sadly, Ricardo Rodriguez was killed practising Rob Walker's Lotus 24 in front of his home crowd at Mexico City in October 1962. Nine years later, brother Pedro would also perish in action when he crashed in a minor-league sports car race at Germany's Norisring circuit.

Poignantly, he would again be driving a Ferrari – a privately entered 512M – at the time.

Chapter 7

Surtees and the British influence

TALK OF FERRARI in the 1960s and one automatically thinks of John Surtees, in many ways the most remarkable driver ever to have thrown in his lot with Maranello. Nuvolari may have had superhuman tenacity and Michael Schumacher a God-given talent which enables him to dwarf his contemporaries, but Surtees, sure enough, had a blend of both those qualities in varying degree. The trouble was, he never quite succeeded in channelling them to best effect.

Surtees was quite a complex character. He came from a humble background and was suffused with a tremendous sense of family loyalty. The author collaborated with him in producing his autobiography *John Surtees, World Champion* (Hazleton Publishing, 1991) and never failed to be impressed at just how much respect and affection he displayed when referring to both his father Jack and mother Dorothy.

Jack Surtees was an accomplished pre-war amateur motorcycle racer, and his fierce passion for two-wheeled competition was passed down to his son who became one of the very greatest of international motorcycle champions. John competed officially for the first time in 1948 when he rode in the sidecar of his father's Vincent in the Trent Park speed trials, and his own personal career began the following year when he raced an Excelsior-JAP at the Eaton Bray grass track meeting.

By 1951 young Surtees was a regular competitor on both Vincent and Norton, quickly rising to prominence as the most likely challenger for Geoff Duke's unofficial crown as the top British rider. By 1955 he was poised for great things on the international stage riding a Norton, and the following year he signed for the works MV Agusta team based at Gallarate, near Milan.

By the end of 1956 Surtees had clinched the 500cc World Championship. Two years later he took both the 350 and 500 titles, repeating that achievement in 1959 and 1960, by which time he was ready to switch to car racing, a transition which he was to achieve with distinction.

Count Domenico Agusta was an autocrat out of a similar mould to Enzo Ferrari. For the 1960 season he told Surtees that MV would not be contesting any races outside the World Championship series and that John was contractually bound not to race for any other manufacturer in other events. Such a restricted programme was not to Surtees's taste, and the only way round Count Agusta's restrictions was to make the switch to four wheels.

In motorcycle circles, Casina Costa, the MV headquarters at Gallarate, was regarded respectfully in much the same way as Maranello was to the car racing world. Moreover, the Agusta and Ferrari families had their own eccentricities, but whereas Enzo Ferrari's personal life was dominated by memories of his late son Dino, the Agusta brothers lived totally in the shadow of their mother, the Countess.

Surtees recalled the meeting at which he signed for MV. 'The door opened and a lady completely clothed in black and wearing a black veil came into the room,' he said.

'I stood up and she came across, looked me over, and went back to the table where she addressed Domenico.' This was the Countess and she was just giving him the once-over to see whether he was suitable to be admitted to the Agusta family. It seemed he passed muster. It was hard to imagine Laura Ferrari doing the same at Maranello.

Surtees was imbued with a great love of Italy whilst riding for MV. He was attracted to the people, the style of life and the overwhelming enthusiasm for motor sports, which seemed to be part of their psyche. More than ever, his two-wheeled championship years laid the perfect foundations for him to hold his own as a member of the Ferrari squad.

In 1960 he drove for Lotus, then switched to the Yeoman Credit Cooper team run by the highly respected Reg Parnell. At the end of that season he received an approach from the Prancing Horse, went down to Maranello for an interview with Enzo Ferrari and then – very shrewdly, as things turned out – decided against joining the team in 1962.

'The actual meeting with the man himself came almost as an anti-climax,' John recalled. 'We were led into a room, about 30 feet by 20, with a sort of old-world atmosphere which immediately reminded me of Count Agusta's office at Gallarate. To describe it as musty would be unkind; that suggests it was dirty, which it most certainly was not. Perhaps "mellow" would be a better word.

'As I was soon to discover, Enzo Ferrari could be a man of many or few words, depending on his mood. Foregoing the usual pleasantries, he came straight to the point: "I would like you to drive for us next year; Formula 1, sports cars and anything else we might decide to race."

'It was as simple as that. Or was it? Was I really ready to drive for Ferrari?' After a trip round the racing department, and a chat with Carlo Chiti, Surtees decided on balance that he was not ready for this sort of commitment. Instead, he drove the Bowmaker team's Lola-Climax Formula 1 cars in 1962. The following summer came another offer from Ferrari and, this time, John correctly judged that the timing was more

appropriate. He accepted the deal.

'It had to be the finest time to go to them,' he recalled. 'They were on the floor, but they also wanted to pick themselves up and have a bit of a go. Forghieri had come in and I got on with him fine. He was a new boy and I think I was able to inject a little of my experience into things, so there was something of a fresh approach.

'It was all a hotch-potch, really, because we had to choose from a great pile of bits and pieces to put something together. We started with this hacked-about tubular chassis car which I thrashed round Modena. That little V6 was a good engine . . .'

From the outset, John would find life in the Maranello fold made extremely difficult by the machinations of team manager Eugenio Dragoni. The Milanese businessman clearly had some very deep links with Enzo Ferrari and was out to make it very clear that he ran the team his way. It was a recipe for confrontation.

Yet Surtees was no run-of-the-mill Italian hopeful driven on by nationalistic fervour. Here was a man coming into the team with impeccable credentials, not only from the motorcycle world but in car racing as well. He may not have yet won a Grand Prix, but his exploits with Lotus, Cooper and Lola had clearly established John's top-drawer potential. He wasn't about to be messed around by Dragoni – and had the strength of character, call it stubbornness if you like, to sit it out with Ferrari's team manager when it came to a row.

Central to Ferrari's 1963 racing efforts was the brand new 3-litre, rear-engined 250P sports prototype which was scheduled to run in all the season's endurance classics. Surtees spent a lot of time setting up the cockpit of his race car to his personal taste in preparation for the first outing at

Sebring, so he wasn't amused to find that the chassis had been switched when he arrived at the Florida airfield circuit.

He drew Dragoni's attention to this apparent discrepancy, but he just shrugged his shoulders and turned away. Mairesse and Nino Vaccarella now seemed destined to race the 250P which Surtees, who was to drive with Lodovico Scarfiotti, had so painstakingly set up during those pre-season tests at Modena and Monza.

John just wasn't having this. An explosive row followed with Dragoni, and the Englishman stormed back to his hotel and began packing his suitcase. Then came a knock on his bedroom door. It was Scarfiotti. He successfully coaxed John into agreeing to drive, and the two men vowed they would take the 'uncomfortable car' and beat their team-mates at Dragoni's own game. Despite exhaust fumes seeping into the cockpit, which made both men feel extremely unwell, Surtees and Scarfiotti did just that and won the race.

There was another crucial dimension to the Surtees/Dragoni relationship as well. While the other Ferrari drivers had to rely on the team manager for all their information as regards lap times, and so-on, John's wife Pat was an accomplished timer and lap scorer and kept her husband independently appraised of his own progress. Thus Dragoni took against John Surtees almost from the very start of his Ferrari career.

On the Formula 1 front, Ferrari had clearly been badly bruised by his team's humbling experience during the 1962 season. The revised Ferrari 156 saw Forghieri borrowing from Lola and Lotus suspension configurations, and Swiss fuel-injection specialist Michael May had been engaged to help with the development of a new

Bosch high-pressure fuel-injection system which was now fitted to the V6 engine.

Gradually, the Prancing Horse began to regain its position as a credible Formula 1 force. Surtees raced the new 156, clad in sleek new Fantuzzi bodywork, at the non-championship Silverstone International Trophy meeting where he was up to second place, chasing hard behind Jim Clark's Lotus 25, when an oil leak forced him to pull out.

That was followed by fourth place, and fastest race lap at Monaco, but then a string of retirements blighted the team's progress. Prospects brightened again when Surtees finished second in the British GP at Silverstone, reaping the benefit of an all-nighter prior to the race helping to fit a three-gallon auxiliary fuel tank to the car. He finished second behind Clark after Graham Hill's BRM spluttered out of fuel on the final lap. John also set fastest lap.

It was now quite clear that only a sliver of good fortune would be required for Surtees to score his first Grand Prix victory. That moment finally came in the 1963 German race at the Nürburgring where Clark's Lotus lapsed on to seven of its eight cylinders and Surtees sailed away to a convincing win. It was just the pick-me-up that Maranello needed, and Surtees cemented this feeling of upbeat optimism by following it up with victory in the non-championship Mediterranean GP at Enna-Pergusa in central Sicily.

Forghieri, meanwhile, was clearly keen to learn from British chassis construction techniques and came up with a new semi-monocoque chassis in time for the Italian GP at Monza. This car had originally been intended to accommodate the all-new four-cam V8 engine which had been developed by Angelo Bellei's design team.

This new engine was intended to be installed as a stressed member in the chassis, but quite late in the day it was decided that the V8 was insufficiently reliable at this early stage in its development. Consequently the 156 'aero' was re-worked to accept the 120-degree V6 in time for the Monza race where Surtees proved its potential by slamming round the combined road and banked circuit to take pole position.

Disappointingly, neither Ferrari entry would finish the race and Jim Clark was allowed to celebrate his first World Championship title with a masterly win.

From the start of the 1963 season, Surtees had been partnered in the Formula 1 squad by Willy Mairesse, the somewhat wild, unpredictable, yet great-hearted Belgian driver. But Mairesse had a bad season. First he suffered burns when their Ferrari 250P ignited at Le Mans after fuel had been spilled into its undertray at a pit stop. He recovered from those injuries just in time to pile off the road in the Formula 1 car at Nürburgring, an accident which effectively wound up his front line international career.

Mairesse has frequently been characterised as a headstrong driver who could not judge his own personal limits. Yet Surtees speaks about him with obvious affection. 'He was quite talented, but there was an awful lot of emotion inside him,' he recalls. 'Very sadly, he eventually committed suicide in 1969.

'His world was so shattered when motor racing finally gave him up a few years later that I imagine he felt there was nothing left to live for. It was a great tragedy, for I had real respect for his ability to handle a racing car.'

John Surtees in 1994. In the background is a painting of his Ferrari 158 in NART livery in the 1964 Mexican GP where he clinched his four-wheeled World Championship.

Surtees and Bandini: mutual respect, outside tensions

LORENZO BANDINI WAS recruited into the Ferrari Formula 1 squad as Willy Mairesse's replacement in mid-1963. He was a man whom Surtees would also come to like enormously but who, unwittingly, would be used to undermine the Englishman's position in the team three years later.

All those who knew Bandini testify to the fact that he was a lovely man. Born in North Africa on 21 December 1936, Lorenzo would become without doubt Italy's best Formula 1 driver of the decade. Although much of his career was spent dutifully playing second-fiddle to the brilliant Surtees, it was a role which he fulfilled happily and without any tension.

Bandini's father had died when he was very young, apparently abducted in the early months of the war and shot by some sort of mercenary execution squad, according to Enzo Ferrari's recollections.

The details of this tragedy are vague in the extreme. Lorenzo was nine when the war ended and he was barely into his teens when he moved to Milan and gained employment in the Milan garage owned by a Signor Freddi, whose daughter Margherita he would later marry.

Yet it was a hard apprenticeship. Bandini lived on sandwiches and often spent the nights sleeping on the back seats of cars in the garage. This was long before Sig. Freddi loaned him a Lancia Appia in which he won his class in the 1958 Mille Miglia, although this event was now a much milder rally-type affair compared with the no-holds-barred road race which had come to an end with the de Portago tragedy the previous year.

By 1959, Bandini was working his way through the cut-and-thrust of Formula Junior before moving into Formula 1 for the first time in 1960 driving an old Cooper-Maserati for Gugelielmo Dei's Scuderia Centro-Sud. He was then fleetingly included in Ferrari's Formula 1 line-up in 1962, but was dropped in favour of Mairesse the following year.

Bandini then stepped down slightly to drive the ex-works BRM fielded by Centro-Sud, but was reappointed to the Ferrari Formula 1 team after Mairesse's Nürburgring accident, only weeks after the Italian had shared the winning Ferrari 250P at Le Mans together with Scarfiotti.

In 1964 he won the first Austrian Grand Prix on the bumpy Zeltweg military airfield circuit a stone's throw from the site where the superb Osterreichring track would eventually be constructed five years later. He would continue as Surtees's loyal lieutenant through to the end of the 1.5-litre Formula 1 in 1965, but the following season he found himself propelled into the limelight as *de facto* team leader after John's patience with Dragoni finally snapped and he left Ferrari.

Bandini was bitterly disappointed not to have won the 1966 Italian GP at Monza, a race at which the new 3-litre Ferrari 312s demonstrated a considerable performance advantage. That victory fell to Scarfiotti, a man with whom Lorenzo was apparently feeling increasingly ill-at-ease.

The curious strains between the two men were pinpointed by Ferrari in his privately published volume *Pilote che gente*. In particular, it seemed that Bandini was under stress just prior to the 1967 Monaco race. Lorenzo wanted to take things steadily and didn't want Scarfiotti to be at the race. If Ferrari's analysis of the situation is to be believed, Bandini slightly envied Scarfiotti's patrician status – he was a second cousin of Fiat patriarch Gianni Agnelli – which so dramatically contrasted with his own modest background.

Ferrari says he remembers the Bandini 'who begged for tranquillity before that fateful 1967 Monaco race.'

He claims that he accommodated Bandini's worries by including Chris Amon in the team for that race, although on the face of it this seems demonstrable nonsense on the part of Ferrari, who had signed the young New Zealander simply because he was regarded as a much better driver than Scarfiotti.

That year, Bandini led the opening stages of the Monaco race only to be displaced by Denny Hulme's more agile Brabham-Repco. As he struggled to counter-attack Bandini's Ferrari 312 clipped the chicane and rolled over, bursting into flames. He died three days later from burns and serious internal injuries, shortly before his wife Margherita suffered a miscarriage in the same hospital.

Surtees is perceptive in his assessment of Bandini's driving abilities. He likens him to John Watson, the mild-mannered Ulsterman who drove for Brabham and McLaren in the late 1970s and early 1980s. Like Watson paired with Niki Lauda, Surtees felt that Bandini performed at his best when stimulated by rivalry within his own team. When highly motivated, the Italian proved able to raise the standard of his personal game.

'He thrived in a situation where I gave him a standard to aim for,' said Surtees. 'He quite liked the car set up in the way I did, so we felt comfortable together. He was a nice man, straightforward and uncomplicated, a good person to work with.'

This is a generous tribute from Surtees who is not a man to toss around superficial compliments. Bandini was 30 years old when he died, possibly just approaching the absolute peak of his career.

When one looks back at photographs of this well-groomed and handsome Italian, one senses an easy-going and tolerant nature. And many others firmly endorse John Surtees's opinion of him. In fact, nobody has anything bad to say about Lorenzo Bandini.

For the 1964 season Ferrari would be armed with the 120-degree V6, the new V8 and an ambitious new 1.5-litre flat-12, a jewel of technical packaging which was very much Forghieri's baby but which would not break cover in public until the Italian GP at Monza.

By now, anybody who drove for Ferrari had to come to terms with the hard commercial reality of the team's commitment to winning the Le Mans 24-hour sports car classic. By 1964 this race took on even more symbolic importance as Ferrari's position was now being challenged by the might of Ford, the Detroit company having invested lavishly in its GT40 programme after a bid to buy Ferrari had failed.

With that in mind, the Grand Prix cars always tended to take something of a back seat until after Le Mans, and the 1964 season was no exception. Moreover, a succession of fuel injection problems with the new V8 engine caused additional difficulties early in the season and it was not until the inaugural British GP at Brands Hatch that Surtees finished third, on the same lap as Jim Clark's winning Lotus and Graham Hill's second placed BRM. It was a step forward.

Surtees would then score his second straight win at the Nürburgring, this time having to tackle a formidable challenge from Dan Gurney's

Brabham, and Bandini then won the Austrian GP in the old V6 car after John spun off when the rear suspension broke on his V8.

Then came Monza and another dust-up between Surtees, Gurney and Clark, this time resolved gloriously with the opposition wilting and 'Il Grande John' – as he was increasingly known amongst the fans – slamming home to score his second win of the season with the V8-engined car.

However, the Italian GP had been held under something of a cloud. The Automobile Club Italia – Ferrari's national club – told the Old Man that they were not prepared to forward

John Surtees rounds Clearways at Brands Hatch during his run to third place in the 1964 British GP in the Ferrari 158. (Phipps Photographic)

homologation papers to include the new 250LM coupé in the GT category as it was certain that the car did not comply with the CSI's production requirements.

The 250LM – essentially a roofed and refined version of the cars which had won Le Mans in 1963 and 1964 – was required in Ferrari's armoury to do battle in the GT category where the front-engined GTO was now getting a bit long in the tooth. In order to conform with the GT rules, a manufacturer had to show that he had built, or at least laid down, a run of 100 cars.

Nobody in their right mind believed that Ferrari had got anywhere near building so many 250LMs, but that was hardly the point. Several rival manufacturers had 'fiddled' the figures and the CSI usually took a relaxed view of these homolgation requirements. But the ACI would not play ball.

Enzo Ferrari was fit to be tied. He handed in his competition licence, vowed that he would never again compete in Italy and, henceforth, his works cars would not compete carrying the country's red livery. He was true to his word – in the short term, at

least. For the two remaining Grands Prix of the season, Ferrari's Formula 1 cars were prepared in the blue and white racing livery of the USA and entered officially by Luigi Chinetti's North American Racing Team.

Surtees finished second in the US GP behind Graham Hill's BRM. Going into the final race at Mexico City, Hill had 41 points – of which he could count 39 – Surtees was second on 34 and Clark had 30. If Surtees won the race, he would be champion no matter what happened to the opposition. He could also take the title with second place if Hill was not in the first three. For Jim Clark to win the title, he had to win the race with Surtees

Surtees celebrates his Championship title with the chequered flag at Mexico City in 1964. (LAT)

lower than second and Graham Hill lower than fourth.

Despite grappling with fuel injection problems, John opted to race the V8 rather than the new flat-12 which was prone to high oil consumption and surge on the long fast corners at the Mexican circuit. Instead, the new car was earmarked for Bandini to drive.

In the event, Lorenzo rather blotted his copybook when he dived inside Hill's BRM under braking for a tight hairpin and spun his rival off into the barrier. The BRM's exhaust pipes were damaged, so Hill had to come into the pits for makeshift repairs. Nothing, it seemed, could now stop Clark from taking his second Championship crown.

Yet fate dealt another unexpected blow on the last lap. Clark's Lotus expired with a broken engine, allowing Dan Gurney's Brabham through into first place. Bandini, worried by wildly fluctuating oil pressure on the flat-12 Ferrari, backed off, allowing Surtees through to finish second. In doing so, he became the only man in history to win the World Championship on both two wheels and four.

It was a somewhat fortuitous victory. Clark's Climax-engined Lotus had been the class of the field for most of the season and it was clear that, for all its resources, Ferrari's engine department was not really making sufficient progress. This became abundantly clear to Surtees when he drove the 158 in the first race of the 1965 season, the South African GP at Kyalami. Sure enough, he was

John Surtees at his Edenbridge business headquarters, summer 1983, with one of the Angelo Bellei-designed 1.5-litre Ferrari V8 engines which helped power him to the 1964 World Championship. (Author)

John Surtees celebrating the 1964 World Championship with Mexican GP race winner Dan Gurney (left). (LAT)

Surtees in the pit lane at Syracuse, Sicily, in the Ferrari 158 in the spring of 1965. (Denis Jenkinson)

competitive with Hill's BRM, but there was no way he could get on terms with the winning Lotus.

The story of the final 1.5-litre season in 1965 was one of Jim Clark's domination at the wheel of the Lotus-Climax 33. By the time the German GP was over he had clinched his second World Championship. At Ferrari, the challenge was to develop the compact flat-12 into a fully competitive tool.

However, it was not until the Italian GP at Monza that the new engine was equipped with revised cylinder heads and finally began to show its true potential. Surtees qualified second alongside Clark's Lotus on the front row of the grid, but even before the start the Ferrari's hydraulic clutch control mechanism was beginning to play up, with the result that John got away from the line very slowly indeed.

He completed the opening lap in a lowly 14th place, but thereafter underlined the terrific potential of the new car by catching up with the front runners to battle for the lead before the clutch slipped out of business for good. Unbeknown to John at the time, this would be his last Formula 1 outing of the season – and very nearly the last motor race he ever contested.

Surtees recalls that during the course of the 1964 season he had become increasingly aware that the Ferrari team was isolated from the mainstream development of the UK-based racing teams. On reflection, it seems that he had homed in on one of the key problems facing Maranello, the realisation of which would eventually prompt Ferrari to establish a research and development facility in Britain over two decades later.

Surtees was also concerned that he wasn't really earning much money with Ferrari and he could see oppor-

Flat-12 in anger. Surtees forges ahead into the lead of the 1965 Italian GP at Monza with the 1.5-litre Ferrari 1512 ahead of the BRMs of Jackie Stewart (eventual winner) and Graham Hill, and Jim Clark's Lotus 33. (LAT)

tunities in the lucrative Can-Am sports racing car series which was beginning to become established in North America. In the closing months of 1963 he had taken a loaned – and lightened – 250P prototype to the Canadian GP sports car race at Mosport Park, followed by races at Riverside and Laguna Seca in California and the Nassau speed week.

This excursion yielded little in the way of hard results, but the 250P performed quite promisingly against its ostensibly lighter opposition. It prompted John to discuss with Mr Ferrari the prospect of running his own cars, fielded by Team Surtees, in these races during 1965. Enzo said he had no objection, provided that JS did not compete in any categories which the Ferrari company did not make cars for.

As a result of all this, Surtees began fielding a team of elegant Lola T70 Group 7 sports racing cars, powered by Chevrolet V8 engines, in these North American sports car events during the 1965 season. Unfortunately, on 24 September while practising at Mosport Park, Surtees's machine lost a front wheel going into the fast right-hander beyond the pits at the Canadian track.

The car hurtled into a barrier, somersaulted over it and landed on top of its hapless driver. Surtees would not remember anything for another four days, but he was extremely seriously injured, with ruptured kidneys and a badly fractured pelvis. Frankly, he was not expected to live.

Lorenzo Bandini tackles the Clermont-Ferrand circuit during the 1965 French GP with the Ferrari 1512 flat-12.

Understandably, the accident was headline news across the world. The reigning World Champion appeared to be hanging between life and death, but thankfully the initial physical crisis passed and Surtees was able to apply his enormous powers of gritty determination to the process of recovery.

In many ways, this was much akin to the battle that Niki Lauda would find himself fighting 11 years later. Ahead of John lay painful operations, physiotherapy and gradual rehabilitation. Thanks largely to the medical talents of the staff at London's St Thomas's Hospital, and his own sheer doggedness, he pulled through to race again.

Surtees was impressed that Ferrari's accident insurance paid out to help with his medical costs, even though

he wasn't driving one of the Italian cars at the time of the accident. Yet it would be early in 1966 before John was sufficiently recovered to be able to fly to Italy and discuss his future plans with his employer who, with perhaps uncharacteristic loyalty, never mentioned the prospect of replacing him with another driver – in public, at least.

Of course, the 1966 season was crucial for Ferrari. It was the first year of the new 3-litre Formula 1 regulations and the team held out high hopes for its new V12-engined 312 challenger.

When Surtees made his first post-accident appearance at the Maranello race shop, a wave of emotion came over much of the workforce, many of the mechanics fighting back tears as they crowded round to welcome

'their man' back into the fold. Yet there was a nagging question lurking beneath the surface. Was Surtees fully recovered? Would he ever be able to regain his old form? He soon answered the doubters, pounding round Modena at competitive racing speeds in the little 2.4-litre Dino Ferrari V6 which had originally been built for him to drive in the Tasman series in Australia and New Zealand, but which had remained unused after his accident.

Prior to the start of the season, Surtees began discussing with Ferrari the prospect of spending more time in Italy and getting more deeply involved with the team's activities. To this end, John was offered one of Mr Ferrari's flats close to the home of Lina Lardi, the mother of Ferrari's second son Piero. It seemed like an ideal arrangement.

Yet there were problems on the horizon. The new four-overhead-camshaft 3-litre Formula 1 Ferrari was not an unqualified success from the start, as Surtees immediately realised after driving it for the first time. It was two-and-a-half seconds slower round Modena than the little 2.4-litre Dino. Alarm bells began ringing in John's mind and he spared no time telling Forghieri and engine department chief Franco Rocchi precisely what he thought about this gutless creation.

Surtees had been well on the way to recovery by the time Ferrari's official off-season press conference took place at Maranello on 12 December 1965. The team used this occasion to take the wraps off the new 4-litre, four-cam V12 330P3 sports racer which they would use to contest the following year's classic endurance races.

Because of industrial unrest in Italy and delays in securing the delivery of key components, the works cars did not contest the opening round of the Sports Car Championship at Daytona, although there was one of the new 365P2 single-cam V12s on hand for factory approved privateers Ecurie Francorchamps. This car, driven by Lucien Bianchi and Gerald Langlois van Ophem, disappointingly failed to finish.

The P3 made its race debut at Sebring in March, seven weeks after the Daytona fixture. The single factory entry for Bob Bondurant and Mike Parkes was a highly competitive machine, even challenging the works 7-litre Fords, but it was forced to retire three hours from the finish when the gearbox failed.

Mike Parkes played an increasingly prominent role in Ferrari technical affairs at Scuderia Ferrari during the mid-1960s. The son of a former chairman of the Coventry-based Alvis company, he was born into a world of cars and motor racing, training as an engineer with the Rootes Group and staying with them until 1962, by which time he had established a reputation as a Jaguar saloon car driver in British events.

He joined Ferrari as test and development engineer in 1963 and quietly worked away establishing himself behind the scenes. Yet he was not destined to hit it off with John Surtees. Despite the fact that the two men were English – which might have been expected to draw them together in the Ferrari environment – they developed a studied disregard for each other.

In fact, they were as oil and water. Parkes had an upper-crust image about him; he knew he was an accomplished engineer, but perhaps regarded himself as a far better driver than he actually was. Surtees, the fighter who had come from modest surroundings, was by far the superior driver, but clearly felt that his engineering training at Vincent motorcycles put him on an even footing with Parkes when it came to handling technical matters.

Whatever the truth of the matter, Surtees and Parkes won the 1966 Monza 1000km on 25 April to give the P3 its first race victory. However, Surtees was not impressed with the level of development work which had been carried out on the new car in his absence and, reading between the lines, felt that Parkes and Dragoni might be ganging up on him. Whether this was really the case – or simply a matter of Surtees getting slightly paranoid about the situation – is now largely lost in the mists of time. Moreover, Parkes, is no longer around to give his side of the story as he was killed in a road accident in 1977.

Prior to his first race back with Ferrari, Surtees took the P3 out for a test run at Monza and was not happy with what he found. After a few laps he came into the pits and told Forghieri that it seemed to want to swap ends going into the Curva Grande and the Curva Ascari. John suggested some modifications which improved the car considerably.

'This didn't put me in very good odour with Mike, who had done the initial testing,' he recalled. 'Then, come the race itself, which we won, the P3's windscreen wiper failed and the story was reported back to Mr Ferrari that I had wanted to retire the car and that Parkes had been the one who insisted on continuing.'

In fairness to Surtees, this ludicrous story must have been perpetrated by Dragoni, for he had quickly realised that at high speed the P3's windscreen would be kept clear by the slipstream. In any event, he wanted to win to prove that he had completely recovered from his accident injuries. And he achieved that superbly.

The P3 was a terrific car, but nothing could alter Surtees's sense of disappointment with the new 3-litre Grand Prix machine. 'I'd been round and round Modena in that little Tasman 246,' he said, 'then, of course, the V12 was wheeled out – and it looked absolutely enormous. But people were saying 'Ah, Surtees has no problems, he'll walk the Championship' but when I took this thing out it was as flat as a bloody pancake.

'It was two-and-a-half seconds slower round Modena than the V6. Everybody was saying that poor old Jack Brabham only had around 290/300bhp from his Brabham-Repco, but this bloody V12, which weighed God-know's how much, was really only giving about 270bhp. OK, so I went off to win at Syracuse, but I had to row it along like hell.'

Surtees's worries seemed to be

Side-exhaust three-valves per cylinder Ferrari V12 engine at Monza 1966. Lodovico Scarfiotti went on to win the race in one of these cars. (Phipps Photographic)

vindicated when Brabham beat him convincingly in the Silverstone International Trophy race, although Mauro Forghieri later dismissed John's suggestions that the Ferrari V12 was giving less than 300bhp at the start of the 1966 season.

In any event, it transpired that the Formula 1 V12 was in fact by no means a totally new engine, many of its parts being interchangeable with the contemporary sports car units. 'The engineers knew full well what

the situation was,' claimed Surtees, 'and I used to go to the engine test house, so I knew exactly what the engines were giving – even though they were saying all sorts of other things.'

The first major row of the season with Dragoni came over the question of which car Surtees was to drive in the Monaco Grand Prix. John wanted the Dino 246, but Dragoni told him that he would be driving the V12. Meanwhile Bandini was allotted the

more agile, if lower powered machine. 'You are the lead driver,' Dragoni told Surtees. 'We make 12-cylinder cars and so you will have to race the 12-cylinder.'

This was a stupid remark which indicated just how little Dragoni really understood about motor racing. Fuming, Surtees took the V12, led the race to fend off Jackie Stewart's 2-litre BRM – and then succumbed to gearbox failure, handing the Scot an easy victory. It was all too predictable and John's frustration was compounded by the fact that Bandini finished a strong second. If only . . .

For the second round of the Championship at Spa-Francorchamps, the V12 sported new cylinder heads with revised ports and different valves. That boosted its output to over 300bhp and Surtees drove brilliantly to win the Belgian GP from Jochen Rindt's Cooper-Maserati in treacherous conditions of heavy rain which saw half the field spinning in a sudden storm on the opening lap.

Yet still Dragoni kept up his campaign of niggling antagonism. In those days, long before Grand Prix racing was developed into its current position as a television spectacular, Ferrari relied on his team managers to provide information from the races. And Dragoni made very sure that all this news was given a suitably biased edge – against Surtees's interests.

Then came Le Mans and the final bust-up. Surtees arrived at the French circuit to be told that, as Gianni Agnelli was visiting the race, Lodovico Scarfiotti would do the opening stint – and Dragoni also pointed out that Jean Guichet (the winner in 1964 with Nino Vaccarella) would be the reserve driver. Surtees felt his position was now becoming impossibly undermined. He stormed out, leapt into his Ferrari 330GT road car – and drove off to Maranello for a showdown with Mr Ferrari, taking with him journalist Eoin Young to play the role of impartial witness.

I must say that I had hoped John Surtees might finally shed some light

John Surtees in the unwieldy Ferrari 312 leads Jackie Stewart's Tasman BRM in the opening stages of the 1966 Monaco Grand Prix. Surtees, who wanted to drive the Dino 246 in this event, correctly predicted that the V12 would break its transmission. The episode fuelled the mutual distrust between himself and team manager Eugenio Dragoni. (Phipps Photographic)

Enzo Ferrari in expansive mood. Was there something between him and Dragoni – or did he just get fed up with Surtees? (Author)

on precisely what was behind his divorce from Ferrari which was hammered out in private when he arrived at Maranello. Yet when I collaborated on his autobiography he stopped one hurdle short of providing a full explanation.

He wrote: 'I do not know to this day quite what relationship existed between Mr Ferrari and Dragoni. Frankly, there must have been a deep involvement somewhere, probably attached to funding. There was a lot of political activity with regard to the Fiat involvement, so perhaps the answer lies there.

'Mr Ferrari showed considerable

emotion, not anger – in fact, certain things were discussed during the meeting which to my mind showed that he genuinely felt very hemmed in by the whole situation. He made comments that explained a lot, things that he never talked about again in his lifetime, so I am certainly not going to raise them after his death.'

On reflection, Surtees admitted that Enzo Ferrari was rather like a puppeteer. He liked pulling the strings, having everyone dancing to his tune. So perhaps John ended up being squeezed out of Ferrari because he was too down-to-earth, unwilling to bend the knee to Maranello's many

acolytes. Or, as some people have speculated, perhaps he was just a little too awkward himself.

Either way, the loss of John Surtees effectively wiped out any chance of Ferrari winning the 1966 Formula 1 World Championship. Dragoni's ridiculous assertion that the cars would be so superior that they could win races with a lesser driver was another indication of his inability to grasp the realities of the situation facing the team.

Bandini was certainly by now a very accomplished driver, but the promotion of Scarfiotti and the inexperienced Mike Parkes to the Formula 1 line-up in the middle of the year could not provide the strength in depth that was really necessary to win races on a consistent basis.

For his part Surtees switched to the Cooper-Maserati team and at least had the satisfaction of rounding off the year with victory in the Mexican Grand Prix. Yet he would always find himself pondering on what might have been achieved had he stayed with Ferrari through to the end of his professional racing career. Had he done so, the Formula 1 results sheets in the second half of the 1960s might have made very different reading.

Eugenio Dragoni died in 1974 without ever shedding any further light on the whole mysterious affair. However, the author vividly recalls an episode six years after the Surtees/Ferrari split which suggested that there was still a fair deal of edge between him and his former driver.

The occasion was the 1972 Mediterranean Grand Prix at Enna-Pergusa, by then a round of the prestigious European Formula 2 Championship. Surtees was contesting the race as a team owner, fielding a couple of Hart-engined Surtees TS10s for Mike Hailwood and Carlos

Pace. During one practice session I was standing on the pit wall watching the cars, together with John, his wife Pat and team manager Peter Briggs.

What I hadn't realised was that Eugenio Dragoni was the Clerk of the Course at this meeting. At one point, for some unknown reason, he decided to instruct his officials to clear the pit wall of all team personnel.

Dragoni and his men started at the opposite end of the pits from where we were standing. One by one, the team managers – including future McLaren Formula 1 boss Ron Dennis – were shooed off away from the edge of the circuit. But as Dragoni drew closer, Pat Surtees hissed at me 'don't move!'

Eventually Dragoni and his officials reached our position. Just as it seemed that a confrontation would ensue, the elderly Italian walked back across to the pit counter, along behind us and then resumed clearing the personnel the other side of the Surtees enclave.

The four of us were not bothered, left as a little cluster of humanity on the now otherwise empty pit wall.

'He wouldn't have dared,' said Pat triumphantly. She may well have been right, but throughout the whole episode I couldn't help noticing that Dragoni's face wore an ironic, slightly mischievous smile.

It was as if, after all those years, he was still gaining pleasure from winding up John Surtees.

Chapter 8

Le Mans, the P-series and Enzo's privateers

THE 1961 SEASON was not only high-lighted by Ferrari's Formula 1 domination, but it also saw the debut of one of the most important sports racing machines in the company's history. The Dino 246SP created a sensation when it was unveiled, as it was the first sports car to emerge from Maranello with a centrally mounted engine.

Developed by Carlo Chiti with the benefit of wind tunnel testing, it was powered by a slightly detuned version of the 2.4-litre V6 engine which had powered Mike Hawthorn to the Formula 1 World Championship only three years earlier. The central-engined car would be run alongside the highly developed front-engined TR61s which were now approaching the end of their highly successful lives.

The then-traditional Le Mans test days confirmed the potential of the 246SP when Richie Ginther came within two seconds of the record time established by Phil Hill in the 3-litre TR61. The car went on to score its first win in the Targa Florio, thanks to the efforts of Gendebien and von Trips, and this duo would get as high as second place at Le Mans before running out of fuel early on Sunday morning.

The 1961 sports car regulations required long sloping windscreens, but for 1962 things changed and the FIA agreed on a reduction of windscreen height, which in turn allowed Chiti to lower the rear deck of the shark-nosed SPs. In Ferrari's characteristically confusing style, these were now offered in 2-litre (196SP) and 2.8-litre V6 (286SP) form, now also supplemented by a 90-degree V8 designated 248SP, although this was quickly increased in capacity to 2.6-litres.

The works team's first 1962 victory came courtesy of Ricardo Rodriguez and Mairesse with the 196SP in the Targa Florio, followed by Gendebien and Phil Hill at the Nürburgring. At Le Mans victory again fell to Hill and Gendebien in the 4-litre TR, with second overall going to Pierre Noblet and Jean Guichet in a private 250GT, which was one of the most creditable international performances ever to be produced by these front-engined classics.

The lessons learned from the 246SP and its sisters about the complexities of a central engine installation certainly served Ferrari very well when it came to unveiling his 1963 sports car challenger. This was the classic 250P, a 3-litre V12 central-

engined car which would be backed up in the GT class by the 4-litre 330LM – really a heavily revised GTO fitted with the ultimate Testa Rossa engine used at Le Mans the previous year.

The 'P', as it would become affectionately known, was one of the most balanced and elegant of the prototype sports cars ever to emerge from Maranello. Its Testa Rossa V12 was proven and bullet proof and the whole package was clad in a Pininfarina body which was an anthem to uncluttered simplicity compared with the spats, louvres and spoilers of the TRs and SPs. Moreover, throughout the 1963 season it was the star of the show.

We have already seen how Surtees and Scarfiotti took the 250P to a maiden victory at Sebring, that being followed up by total domination of the Le Mans test day. Then followed the Targa Florio – the only race that the 250P lost all season – and further victorious outings at Nürburgring and Le Mans, where Scarfiotti and Bandini won after the dominant Surtees/Mairesse car caught fire whilst well in command.

In 1964 it was more of the same for Maranello. To start with, Ferrari unveiled the 250LM at the Paris

Motor Show – effectively a roofed, road-going 250P – which would be intended for homologation in the GT category in anticipation of stronger opposition than the old front-engined GTO could cope with. Again, as we've seen, when the ACI refused to submit Ferrari's homologation application to the CSI, the Old Man got a fit of the grumps and relinquished his Italian entrant's licence. But it was to prove a short-term hiccup.

Most of the racers were now fitted with 3.3-litre engines, thereby becoming 275Ps, and with one of these machines Guichet and Nino Vaccarella won at Le Mans. By that time Parkes and Umberto Maglioli had won at Sebring and Scarfiotti and Vaccarella at Nürburgring. Then came the Reims 12-hours and the first win for the 250LM entered by Maranello Concessionaires and driven by Graham Hill and Jo Bonnier. Hill also won the Tourist Trophy at Goodwood for the same team, this time using a 4-litre V12 (330P).

Of course, throughout this time, Ferrari's main priority had been to fend off a burgeoning attack from Ford's increasingly competitive GT40s and 7-litre Mk 2s. Ford had originally attempted to buy Ferrari in the early 1960s, but when the Old Man changed his mind and pulled out of the deal, the Detroit motor giant vowed to beat him at his own game. It would in the end, but it was quite a fight.

In 1965 the P2 arrived, in four-cam 4-litre (330) and 3.3-litre (275) engine sizes. With 30bhp more power available from the 3.3-litre engine – taking its output to 350bhp – and a whopping 410bhp from the larger V12, the works team seemed confident of dealing with the Ford menace. There was also a 365P available to private teams, this being a 4.4-litre P2

fitted with a two-cam engine derived from the 330P unit.

Ferrari also introduced the lovely little Dino 166SP, effectively a scaled-down P2 which was fitted with a 65-degree V6 1.6-litre engine derived from the 1961 Formula 1 engine. In 1966 it was fitted with an enlarged 2-litre engine and the intention seemed to be to homologate it into the sports car category, which required at least 50 to be built.

This never happened and the Dinos spent most of their time racing as prototypes against their larger-engined brethren, proving adept and remarkably agile on circuits where handling was a key priority. Scarfiotti used one with distinction to win the 1965 European hill-climb championship and to finish runner-up to Porsche driver Gerhard Mitter in this specialised contest the following year.

At the 1965 Le Mans test weekend, John Surtees simply flew to set fastest time in the new 330P2, followed by Parkes, Scarfiotti, Vaccarella and Bandini, all taking turns in the same car. The brilliant young Swiss driver Tommy Spychiger also impressed everybody with a superb sixth fastest time overall in Scuderia Filipinetti's recently-delivered 1964 bodied 365P, but he was then tragically killed weeks later practising for the Monza 1000km, a race won by Parkes and Guichet in a works 275P2.

The 275P2 was also good enough to get the job done on the Targa Florio, courtesy Bandini/Vaccarella, a race where no 4-litre cars attended. Surtees and Scarfiotti then followed this up with victory at Nürburgring and all seemed set fair for Maranello to enjoy a successful outing at Le Mans.

Yet the 1965 race unfolded to produce a strange result indeed. The works P2 prototypes were ranged

against the massively powerful 7-litre Ford Mk 2s and the two biggest-engined Fords stormed away in 1–2 formation at the start, their progress the focal point of worldwide television coverage – not to mention the personal presence of Henry Ford II in an executive box above the pits.

However, by midnight both the giant V8s had wilted and it was now the turn of the works Ferraris to get into the action and battle amongst each other for the lead.

Further back, the NART Ferrari 275LM of Masten Gregory and Jochen Rindt was eighth at the end of the first hour, but in the early evening Gregory was back in the pits complaining about a misfire. Rindt immediately concluded that it was a broken valve and resigned himself to retirement, but it turned out to be electrical trouble. The distributor had to be changed, losing the Chinetti entry almost 30 minutes.

By the time the car was ready for Rindt to resume the race, Gregory found him in the paddock, having changed out of his overalls and about to leave the track in his hire car. It took Masten a few minutes to persuade his team-mate that their car was still running, but eventually Jochen was cajoled back into the cockpit. Thereafter the two men adhered to a personal pact – flat out all the way, win or bust.

Resuming 18th, they had made up four places by midnight, and when the fastest works Ferraris were hobbled by persistent cracking of their ventilated disc brakes, the NART 275LM moved into second place in the early hours of Sunday morning.

By this stage of the race it was a private Ferrari 1–2 at the head of the field, for ahead of Rindt and Gregory lay the Equipe Nationale Belge 275LM driven by industrialist Gustave

The Equipe Nationale Belge Ferrari 275LM of Pierre Dumay and Gustave Gosselin which had to settle for second place in the 1965 Le Mans race behind its NART-entered rival. (Phipps Photographic)

Gosselin and nightclub-owner Pierre Dumay. Then, in a re-run of Tavoni's attitude in 1961, down came word from Ferrari works team manager Dragoni that the Belgians should be allowed to win. And, as in 1961, Chinetti just laughed.

All through the early morning mist and into the sunlight, the NART Ferrari was thrashed to within a few revs of its life. It consumed six sets of tyres and brake pads as its drivers charged relentlessly onwards as if they were contesting a two-hour Grand Prix.

By Sunday morning the 275LM engine was down on power, with the brakes and steering juddering furiously. Yet they were closing on the Belgian car at between four and five seconds a lap. Finally, the Ferrari in front threw a tyre tread, tearing apart its yellow bodywork. By the time it was patched up, Gregory and Rindt were through into the lead for good.

In the closing stages the hardpressed machine developed transmission trouble. Gregory, who drove the final stint, winced as he grappled with the most appalling grating noise from the transmission. They won by 50 miles – but the differential packed up for good as the car was driven back to the paddock. It was Ferrari's final victory at Le Mans.

For 1966 the 330P3 further confirmed Ferrari's increasing trend towards monocoque construction with even more stressed aluminium panels overlaying the tubular space-

Mike Parkes and Lodovico Scarfiotti drove flat-out in the closing stages of the 1967 Le Mans 24-hour race in a vain attempt to catch the winning Ford driven by Dan Gurney/A.J. Foyt but had to settle for second. (Phipps Photographic)

frame, developing the manufacturing technique pioneered with the Ferrari 156 'aero' back in 1963. The ex-works P2s were duly processed into 365Ps, using the 4.4-litre single-cam engine, for customers Ecurie Francorchamps, Scuderia Filipinetti and David Piper.

The Ferrari 330P3 won just twice in 1966. The first time was the memorable Monza 1000km – Surtees's comeback race where he shared with Parkes – and the second was at the Spa 1000km where Parkes shared with Scarfiotti. Le Mans, of course, was marked by Surtees's acrimonious departure from the team

and, when it came to the race, Ford took Ferrari to the cleaners with a 1–2–3 grand slam.

In 1967 Maranello bounced back with the beautiful 330P4 which opened the year on a high note by heading a 1–2–3 in a formation finish at the end of the Daytona 24-hour race. Parkes and Scarfiotti won from Bandini and new recruit Chris Amon with NART's 412P – effectively a P3/P4 for privateers – the third car

being in the hands of Pedro Rodriguez and Jean Guichet.

Amon and Bandini then won the Monza 1000km only a fortnight before Lorenzo's fatal accident in the Monaco GP. The season eventually wound up with a Championship head-to-head between Porsche and Ferrari who went into the final round, the Brands Hatch 500-mile race, one point apart.

Jackie Stewart was drafted into the

Never was there a more elegant Ferrari sports car than the 330P4. This is the Amon/Bandini car en route to victory in the 1967 Monza 1000km. (Farabola)

Lorenzo Bandini at Monza a fortnight before his death in the Monaco GP. (Mimmo Dabbrescia)

team to share a P4 with Chris Amon, and he recalls the Ferrari as the best car he had ever driven round the bumpy Kent circuit. The pair of them finished in a storming second place behind the Phil Hill/Mike Spence Chaparral 2J and ensured that the Championship crown went home to Maranello.

The CSI's decision to impose a 3-litre limit in 1968 prompted Ferrari to make it clear that he would field no works cars on the World Sports Car Championship scene that year. In 1969, however, Maranello would be back in the fray with the 3-litre V12-engined 312P, although generally only a single car entry would appear in most of the races.

Ranged against the new 4.5-litre Porsche 917 sports cars, the 3-litre prototypes were simply no longer competitive. The German company won its first Sports Car Championship and Ferrari prepared to take on the new Porsche on its own ground with the 5-litre Ferrari 512 V12 which

Amon and Bandini share the winner's laurels after their victory in the 1967 Monza 1000km sports car race.

Ferrari sports car racing classic. Bandini during practice for the 1966 Monza 1000km race on the banking with the Dino 206S.

would be ready from the start of 1970. The Group 5 regulations now required a total of 25 cars to be produced and Ferrari duly committed itself to that aim.

The 512S – and its 1971 successor the 512M – was another elegant Maranello machine, yet it was never really a match for the Porsche opposition. John Surtees was invited back into the works team for a handful of runs in the 512S during the spring of 1970 and really didn't think much of it.

This view was shared by Jackie Oliver, Surtees's former team-mate at BRM in 1969, who would go on to have experience of both the Ferrari and Porsche 917. 'It had a good engine,' said Oliver in 1996, 'but that was about all. The Porsche chassis was far superior.'

Paradoxically, the Ferrari 512S would notch up an epic victory in the 1970 Sebring 12-hour race, where Mario Andretti drove back through the field after a series of delays to beat the private Porsche 908 shared by

Amon shared this Ferrari P4 in the BOAC 500-mile race at Brands Hatch with Jackie Stewart in the summer of 1967, their second place clinching the sports car crown for Maranello. (Phipps Photographic)

The 3-litre Ferrari 312P shared by Pedro Rodriguez (driving here) and Chris Amon in the 1969 Brands Hatch 1000km sports car race. (Phipps Photographic)

Peter Revson and movie star Steve McQueen. Both the works JW Gulf Porsche 917s encountered a succession of problems with wheel bearings, leaving the Ferrari to take centre stage.

With one hour of the race remaining, Andretti and co-driver Arturo Merzario were waltzing away at the head of the field after the works Porsches stumbled. Then Mario's 512S suddenly broke its gearbox and he was drafted into the third placed sister car being driven by Ignazio Giunti and Nino Vaccarella.

'I didn't really want to get into this strange car,' said Mario, 'but I decided to give it a go, even though I really didn't fit the cockpit. But it was a roofed 512 coupé which handled rather better than our open roadster.

'I started to go really hard, running about four seconds a lap quicker than Giunti. What really drove me on was all this talk about "The McQueen Porsche" when he hardly touched the thing throughout the 12 hours. He was about 12 seconds off Revson's pace, and Peter did most of the driving anyway.'

After 12 hours of wavering fortunes, Andretti saved the day for Maranello by a wafer-thin 22 seconds. You don't often get much closer than that in endurance racing terms.

At the end of the 1971 season the 5-litre Group 5 category was brought to an end by the CSI's latest edict. From then on, only 3-litre sports prototypes would be allowed. It was the start of a non-stop process of tampering with sports car rules by the governing body, which would reduce endurance racing to a husk within two decades.

Ironically, en route, this state of affairs served to provide Ferrari with its most spectacularly successful season of all time.

Becoming a works-blessed Ferrari privateer depended to some extent on whether the Old Man liked the cut of your jib. You had to be financially qualified, of course, and serve your time behind the wheel. But if you were good enough, then there was a degree of assistance and support to be gained as a favoured client of the Prancing Horse.

Ferrari's 1963 decision to leave the GT category pretty much to these private owners produced a huge amount of exposure for that most classic of Ferrari sports cars, the glorious 3-litre V12-engined GTO. Its immediate predecessor was the elegant 250GT short wheelbase berlinetta which dominated the 2 to 3-litre GT racing category from 1960 to 1962.

By the turn of the 1960s, Ferrari sales in Britain were handled by the romantically titled Maranello Concessionaires at Egham, Surrey, a firm which has more recently been transmuted into the blandly named Ferrari UK. Founded by Colonel Ronnie Hoare, a lifelong racing enthusiast who had raced supercharged MGs at Brooklands before the war, the company came into being largely as a result of his meeting the late Hans Tanner in Italy during the 1950s.

Tanner was a Swiss soldier of fortune who started out as an automotive writer and gradually developed into a motor racing 'Mr Fixit', arranging the sale of Maseratis and Ferraris, massaging deals, managing drivers and entering their cars. He lived on his wits, was well-connected throughout the sport and took Hoare on a trip round the Maranello factory. The Colonel was overwhelmingly impressed and vowed one day that he would buy a Ferrari of his own.

In 1958, Mike Hawthorn's TT Garage in Farnham was poised to take

over as Ferrari's official UK importer, but after Mike died in a road accident in January 1959 it was agreed that Hoare would take over the franchise. By this stage he also had a Ford distributorship – F. English Ltd in Bournemouth – but was duly appointed Ferrari importer after a visit to Maranello where he told Enzo Ferrari that he thought he could manage to sell four road-going Ferraris in England during the following year.

Ferrari, in turn, was impressed and did the deal as he had only sold four cars in the UK over the previous 10 years!

The Colonel immediately ordered a 250GT berlinetta. It was raced in partnership with Equipe Endeavour, which was run by Hoare's pal Tommy Sopwith and so named after his father's pre-war America Cup 12-metre yachts. Sopwith, to this day an active director of the British Racing Drivers' Club, helped put Mike Parkes on the road to international recognition with outings in his Jaguar 3.8s and later in this Ferrari.

Stirling Moss also raced a similar car for Rob Walker in which he won the 1961 Tourist Trophy at Goodwood, but the big moment for these privateers really arrived at the start of 1962 when the 250GTO broke cover from Maranello.

The first hint of such a car had come at Le Mans in 1961 when the Ferrari factory fielded what seemed to be a 400 Superamerica fitted with a 250GT engine brought up to Testa Rossa specification and, at 300bhp, developing 20bhp more than the regular 250GT. The following February the definitive GTO was unveiled at Ferrari's pre-season press conference.

The GTO was a handsome beast. Clad in a Scaglietti body, it amounted

Stirling Moss (right) helps with a refuelling churn during a pit stop with the Rob Walker Ferrari 250GT on his way to winning the 1961 Tourist Trophy at Goodwood. (Phipps Photographic)

to a more refined version of its immediate predecessor; lighter, lower, more powerful and equipped with a five-speed gearbox. It was available to approved racing customers at a price tag of $18,000 US which, as British privateer David Piper would discover, translated into £5,000 sterling – which in itself says a lot for how the pound/dollar exchange rate has fared over the past three decades.

The second and third GTOs built came to Britain where they were allocated to UDT Laystall for Stirling Moss, and to Equipe Endeavour/ Maranello Concessionaires for Parkes. There would later be a third car for Bowmaker Racing to be driven by John Surtees, another earmarked for John Coombs to be driven by Roy Salvadori and one for David Piper – delivered in BP green livery in shrewd

consideration of the new owner's fuel sponsor.

Piper – 'the man in the bright green Ferrari' – would become one of Maranello's most loyal and enduring privateers, racing the Italian cars right up to 1970 when he would crash badly during the production of the film epic *Le Mans* with the result that he lost part of one leg.

Yet to this day, at the age of 66, he continues to prepare, enter and race various Ferrari sports cars in historic events. Piper's recollections of racing in the 1960s amount to a wide-lens snapshot of the trials and tribulations of a Ferrari privateer who used his car as a tool of his trade to make a living in his chosen sport.

Having enjoyed trying to make a single-seater career in his own Lotus 16, and then having had an abortive season in Formula Junior in 1961 – by which time he was already 31 – Piper resolved to make the switch into GT racing. He started negotiations for a 250GT SWB berlinetta, but then he saw the first GTO at Goodwood on Easter Monday 1962. That, he decided, was exactly what he needed and, after selling just about everything he owned, stumped up the necessary £5,000 to Maranello Concessionaires.

'At that time, to make a living I was pounding the pavements in Milan and Turin, buying old Lancias and bringing them back to England for sale,' he recalls. 'I used to buy them from these wealthy industrialists around the Milan area and sell them through Danny Margulies, whose Jaguar C-type I'd shared in the Targa Florio back in the mid-fifties.

'Thanks to this, I made enough money to buy my first GTO. Danny said to me that it would be a good idea, once I got it, to do the Tour de France, because I would get to drive on all the circuits and get to know all the organisers, plus all the other people in GTOs.

'So I ordered the GTO in BP green and we duly did the Tour de France together. It was 5000km on the road, five circuit races and five hill-climbs.

We paid 300,000 lire to Ferrari for servicing – assistenza – and started off from Lille in the 1962 event. The private cars were serviced by a van and a couple of Lancias organised by Ferrari's Gaetano Florini, who would check over the cars before the start and maintain them during the event.

'The first thing Florini did when he saw the car – which was new, apart from a couple of races I did at Brands Hatch, or somewhere – was to get some 18-gauge fencing wire and wrap it all round the exhausts and on to the chassis. I thought "Christ, what's going to happen on this event?" and it turned out to be quite a rough old do.

'Every race was two hours – includ-

Innes Ireland, wearing short-sleeved polo shirt, bares his forearms as he steers the UDT Laystall Ferrari GTO to victory in the 1962 Tourist Trophy at Goodwood. (Phipps Photographic)

ing the Nürburgring backwards! – and then we went to Spa. Old Florini didn't know me from a bar of soap, but he was quite impressed with my performance there, and thereafter kept an eye on me after we finished fourth on our first Tour de France outing. He later became one of my best friends in Ferrari and was very helpful.'

At the end of 1962 David took the GTO further afield when he was invited to enter the *Rand Daily Mail* 9-hour race at Johannesburg's Kyalami circuit. He shipped the car to Cape Town and then drove up to Jo'burg in 14 hours, where he would win the race sharing with Tony Maggs – even though they finished with tyres borrowed from a Ferrari in the circuit

car park. He would win this event another five times.

Of course, Piper had to vie with the other privateers for his share of works attention. He was ranged against people like NART, Ecurie Francorchamps and Scuderia Filipinetti which, in David's words, 'certainly had a bit of pull' with Maranello.

'It was a bit of a problem to start with, but there was respect between competitors and it was all much more friendly than it is now in top level racing,' he recalled. 'Everybody would help everybody else.

'Initially I served my time, if you like, with the GTOs and by the time I'd finished with those – I had two new ones from the factory and a

couple or three second-hand ones – I was pretty well established. And I also did so much to them, remember.

'One day at Brands Hatch, Lorenzo Bandini brought Forghieri over to see my GTO and told him "this is the quickest GTO in the world." This was the one which I had taken six inches off the roofline; it had a ridiculously high windscreen, creating a lot of unnecessary frontal area. The regulations stipulated what the height from the seat pan to the roof had to be, and the GTO was simply bigger than it needed to be.

'I wasn't worried about hacking it about. The first GTO I treated with kid gloves, but then I found that to be competitive you had to do your own development. We started off fairly mildly by putting rear wheels on the front and getting some wider wheels at the back, and making some mods to the anti-roll bars at the back, but in the end we had to get quite drastic with it to make it lighter and reduce its frontal area.

'We never touched the engine, but we were free agents when it came to the handling. The problem with those early cars was that they were totally non-adjustable; you couldn't adjust the camber angles or toe-in, and it was quite difficult to adjust the ride height. So really it was quite a lot of work.'

By 1965 Piper had swapped his GTO for one of the newly-homologated 250LMs. 'People were frightened of them to start with,' he grinned. 'They felt that you were sitting too far forward with that enormous V12 engine swinging around behind you. I must say, I wasn't terribly impressed with it myself.

'But I was in a position where I had to make this thing work, otherwise I was going to go out of business. You just had to get on with it. Fortunately,

David Piper used his Ferrari GTOs as a tool with which to earn his living, but he also drove for other teams, finishing in sixth place at Le Mans in 1963 where he shared this NART 330LM with Masten Gregory. Gregory bumped the nose into the sand at Mulsanne, losing a lot of time. 'He apologised about it whenever he saw me for years afterwards,' recalls David. (Phipps Photographic)

David Piper at the wheel of his evergreen Ferrari 250LM. He bought the car in 1964, developed it into the best of that particular breed and retains it to this day. (Phipps Photographic)

I had a very good mechanic – Fax Dunne – a bit of an eccentric. His father was commissioner of police for Sussex; he went to Gordonstoun – a well-educated chap and quite a character.

'We had tremendous rows, but he was a godsend to me. He saved my life on so many occasions and won so many races for us. He was fantastic. But he was eccentric and quite difficult. I remember on one occasion in the Grand Prix of Angola, after the race I said "where's Fax?" and they said "well, they've thrown him in jail for his own safety!"

'We were refuelling from NASCAR churns during the race and, when I came in, Fax prepared to do the job as he didn't want the car to catch fire. But one of the guys from Sacor, the supplying fuel company, felt he should do it instead and Fax settled it by kicking him in the crutch. They didn't let him out until after the prize-giving.'

'This particular year there was a star entry in Luanda. Ecurie Francorchamps were there, with four cars for Willy Mairesse, Lucien Bianchi and a couple of other Belgian chaps, Jean Blaton and so-on. The boat came from England and Keith Schellenberg was there with a Cobra, Filipinetti had a 7-litre Cobra for Jo Schlesser, Denny Hulme in Sid Taylor's Brabham BT8. It was a fantastic circuit round the town, like Monaco.'

Piper recalls it all as tremendous fun. 'The Automobile Club of Angola was an enormously wealthy club and its headquarters was rather like the RAC in Pall Mall,' he said. 'Great big marble pillars, sauna – a lovely place. Angola was the milking cow of Portuguese colonies, if you like.'

Just as in the case of the GTOs,

David Piper's Ferrari 365P2 storms out of Paddock Bend at Brands Hatch ahead of a Can-Am McLaren in the 1965 Guards Trophy race. (Phipps Photographic)

Piper subjected his 250LM to a rigorous programme of development. 'We really had to tune the LM, to get the weight off it,' he remembers. 'By the time we'd finished with it, I loved it. I still own that car to this day, although I had several others as well, and it never went out of my ownership.

'I also developed the long nose for the LM with Mike Parkes which was subsequently put on the short-nose 275GTB. I was at school with Mike and we got on well together.' Parkes, of course, by this time was living in Modena with his girlfriend, English teacher Brenda Vernor who had originally gone to Italy as Piero Lardi's language tutor.

Brenda would later become the enormously popular and helpful Ferrari racing department secretary – although woe betide anybody who ever got on the wrong side of her. Mike Parkes died in a road accident 20 years ago, but Brenda continues to live in Italy, now working as Piero Lardi's personal secretary. She remains a close friend of David and Liz Piper and – by happy coincidence – was staying with them when I visited to tape anecdotes for this chapter.

Piper recalls Parkes telling him: 'If you want to get on with Mr Ferrari, what you want to do is to turn up at the gates of the factory with a fancy car, blow your horn and have a nice looking blonde with you.

'I got on very well with him, in fact. Many years later, when I asked him for permission for Didier Pironi to drive the 330P4 in a historic event at Montlhéry, he gave it, and Pironi blew up the engine after driving it into the ground.

'He was leading by miles. Anyhow, he did quite a comprehensive job on the engine. So I went down to the factory and said to the Old Man "thank you very much for letting Pironi drive the car – I now know what you have to put up with!"

'We went to lunch and I said I could do with a few bits and pieces. He told me that there were three or four old engines down at the test house and perhaps there were some bits on those I could use. So I went down there with Piero and we had a look. There were two Formula 1 engines, one very nice two-valve P3 engine and another bottom end with no heads.

'I thought these were quite useful bits and bobs, and we also found a couple of gearboxes – one for a P3 and one for a 206S Dino. So I asked Mr Ferrari how much he wanted for them. "A couple of million lire, I suppose," he replied. That was about £800 . . .'

Enzo Ferrari was effectively giving Piper historic Ferrari spares worth many thousands of pounds. Granted, David Piper was an old friend and one of the company's most loyal privateers. But that wasn't the point. Ferrari regarded old cars as junk. Just as he pushed the old Formula 1 801s out under a lean-to at the back of the factory when they were replaced by the Dino 246s at the end of 1957, so an old sports car engine was just that. Best to let it go for a song to an old pal.

The 250LM was eventually succeeded in the Piper front line stable by a Ferrari 330P2 in Can-Am trim for the 1965 season. 'The car was delivered in Can-Am form because I was going to do that series,' Piper explained. 'We flew the car over to Canada on a swing-tail Canadair aeroplane. But round about that time the CSI changed the regulations so that you could have a slightly narrower, slightly lower screen and you had to incorporate a luggage box of sorts.

'We also put a P3 screen on it in order to run in the World Championship races. Each year we did the same events, of course: Daytona, Sebring, Monza, Spa, Nürburgring, Le Mans and the Targa Florio, also the Paris 1000km, Reims, Norisring and so-on.

'Then the P2 got a bit long in the tooth and we moved on to having a really good run with the P3, but that got tangled up with the CSI reducing all the engine capacities to 3-litre. Ferrari wouldn't help me with a 3-litre engine, so we did a few non-championship races with the 4-litre which was very good.

'I tried to make it into a 3-litre machine and actually toyed with the idea of a BRM V12 – we paid a deposit of £750 but they couldn't deliver and I lost my deposit, which was a disaster. As a result of this we ended up buying a Lola T70 and the old 250LM was still going strong in which I still managed to beat the GT40s.'

Piper recalls having a wonderful run with the 250LM over the years. 'Of course, the final thing which I wanted to do, which I never was able to do, was to supercharge it,' he grins. 'We actually had a Rootes supercharger, plenum chamber and low-compression pistons made, because 3.3-litres supercharged would have brought us into the 5-litre category which was where the GT40s were running.

'We had it all worked out, all ready to go, then they changed the formula again and that was the end of it. But a supercharged LM would have just paralysed the GT40s. It would have been great with all that torque. It was certainly a car which responded to torque. When the LM first came out it was just 3-litres, a bit disappointing, but when they made it 3.3-litres it made all the difference in the world to its torque coming out of the corners.'

By the end of the 1968 season Piper had enjoyed a pretty good year. At the start of the 1969 season he then received a phone call from Porsche team manager Huschke von Hanstein, inviting him to drive one of the new Porsche 917s in the Nürburgring 1000km.

'We went out and did that race, after which they asked me whether I would like a 917,' he recalls. 'They were offering a special deal; full factory support, providing I drove with Jo Siffert in some non-championship events. So I said, "yes, great." It was expensive at £14,000 but I thought it would be worth doing with works support.

'Anyway, as I said, I'd had a good year in 1968. I mean, you'd get about £3,000 bonus from Firestone for winning, £500 from BP, £350 from Champion and £250 from Ferodo. Sponsorship, of course, was the icing on the cake, but if you won a race like Hockenheim or Norisring you probably earned £6,000–£7,000, which was a lot of money in those days.'

Of course, by running two cars, a private entrant like Piper could double his money. In those circumstances, David would often ask Pedro Rodriguez to handle the second car. 'I used to get on very well with him, because I was first asked to drive with him by Chinetti at Sebring in 1963 with a GTO.'

Piper occasionally drove the works 3-litre V12-engined Ferrari 312P during 1968, finishing second in the Spa 1000km with Pedro, and also competing at Le Mans. He would then switch to one of the gorgeous 5-litre 512S machines for 1970, but his international career ended when he crashed a similar machine during the filming of Steve McQueen's screen epic *Le Mans* and had part of one leg amputated.

Throughout his Ferrari racing career, Piper acknowledges the considerable assistance and support he received from Maranello Concessionaires. 'They always played fair,' he said. 'Ronnie Hoare was very good, even though there was never really any opposition – when Dickie Attwood was racing the Maranello Concessionaires LM, I could always take care of him with my car.

'But Ronnie was fabulous. He made it very easy for me to buy my first GTO. He couldn't have been nicer, and often asked me to drive for him. He was a great chap to drive for, and when I had my accident he offered me a job. It was a nice gesture, but I couldn't have worked for him.'

In many ways Piper was the archetypal Ferrari sports car privateer, paying for his cars and having to race with an eye always to the financial bottom line. By contrast, Chinetti's NART outfit, which won Le Mans with Masten Gregory and Jochen Rindt using an outdated 275LM – the last-ever Ferrari victory at the Sarthe – was buttressed by his Ferrari business in the USA.

It was the same for Maranello Concessionaires in Britain and Equipe Nationale Belge, which was owned by Belgian Ferrari importer Jacques Swaters. Of course, in Switzerland there was Scuderia Filipinetti, but to a large extent their racing activity was the part-time indulgence of its patron Georges Filipinetti.

The glorious 512M was the last outright sports prototype which was financially within reach of international motor racing's private teams. By 1972–73, the imposition of a 3-litre limit meant that the World Championship would be dominated first by the works Ferrari 312PBs and latterly the rival Matra MS660s and 670s.

Yet Luigi Chinetti still reckoned it might be possible to soldier on as a front-line Ferrari privateer. Ronnie Hoare recalled to author Doug Nye:

'During 1972/73 when the works were running their 312P flat-12 prototype cars and winning everything in sight, Chinetti approached me and said "why don't we four concessionaires take over last year's cars and run them in support of the works team, so they have eight cars on the grid instead of four?" We went to the Old Man and suggested the idea; perhaps we could resurrect the old maintenance deal.'

Mr Ferrari took him into the engine department, picked up a 312P con-rod off a bench and asked his old collaborator how much it cost? The answer was £1,000, making £12,000 alone for each engine. Ferrari's front-line privateers had clearly reached the end of the road.

Chapter 9

Unfulfilled promise: Formula 1 in the late 1960s

THE DEPARTURE OF John Surtees from the Ferrari team in 1966 had immediate and serious implications for the competitiveness of the organisation. This impinged more seriously on the Formula 1 team where Bandini was now to be joined by Mike Parkes, the Englishman being immediately promoted to fill the vacancy, even though at 34, it was quite late in the day for a graduation to the sport's most senior category.

Bandini looked set to win the French GP at Reims, the first race after Surtees's departure, but succumbed to a broken throttle cable. Parkes finished second, but it was a performance from the team as a whole which served to flatter. The Ferrari 312s were only competitive on circuits where they could stretch their legs.

At Zandvoort, home of the Dutch Grand Prix, the cars were simply out of contention. Thankfully, the team had taken the decision to miss the British GP at Brands Hatch because of the metal workers' strikes in Italy, a device used frequently by the Old Man over the years to justify his team's absence from a race. The 312s would have been a joke on the tortuous Kent circuit.

At Nürburgring, where Jack Brabham's Brabham-Repco and Surtees's Cooper-Maserati jousted energetically for the lead in the wet, Bandini was the sole Maranello survivor, slinking home an outclassed sixth. Parkes spun off and Scarfiotti, who'd been allocated the little Dino 246 and managed to qualify on the outside of the front row, gave best to electrical problems.

Coming up to Monza, Ferrari simply had to pull something out of the bag for the Italian GP. Approaching the end of a season in

Bandini at speed in the 1966 French GP at Reims. He was leading the race comfortably when his Ferrari 312 broke its throttle cable. (LAT)

which they had experimented with a variety of revised cylinder head configurations for the V12, Forghieri and the engine department settled on three-valve heads (two inlet, one exhaust) for the team's outing on home ground.

The team claimed that this development boosted the power output to around 370/380bhp – which makes one wonder about Forghieri's insistence that the average for the season was 360bhp, particularly if Surtees was right that the first time the 312 ran it was only kicking out around 270bhp. Of such political complexities are Ferrari nightmares manufactured.

Parkes qualified brilliantly on pole position at Monza ahead of Scarfiotti and Jim Clark's H16 BRM-engined Lotus 43, while Surtees's Cooper-Maserati headed Bandini in the third Ferrari on the second row of the grid. Although Scarfiotti's 312 was first on the move, Bandini came bursting through to lead by the end of the opening lap.

Victory at Monza would have confirmed his position as the top Italian driver of the moment, but his hopes were cruelly dashed when a fuel pipe split and he came trailing into the pits at the end of the second lap. That left Scarfiotti to work his way ahead of Parkes, after which Gianni Agnelli's nephew stayed ahead to the chequered flag.

Parkes came home second in a split-second finish with Denny Hulme's Brabham-Repco, so a Ferrari 1–2 at Monza had duly been achieved. Ferrari's final Formula 1 outing of the season came at Watkins Glen where Bandini drove the single three-valve 312 entered for the US GP. He took the lead on the second lap, battling energetically with Jack Brabham before the V12 suffered an internal failure which caused his retirement. It was a dismal note on which to finish a season that had started with such obvious promise.

This was certainly not how Enzo Ferrari had anticipated things, so for 1967 Maranello made an even bigger effort on the technical side with a further revised V12 engine developing a reputed 390bhp. This unit was distinguished by its extraordinarily complex tangle of exhaust pipes emerging from the centre of the vee. It was one of the most attractive Formula 1 cars of its era.

Responsibility for racing the latest 312s was firmly entrusted to Bandini, again supported by Parkes and Scarfiotti, but with 23-year-old New Zealander Chris Amon now included in the team for the first time. Amon, a

Lost talent. Lorenzo Bandini (left) talks to Ricardo Rodriguez in 1962. Both men would die in action – Rodriguez in a Lotus at Mexico City that same year and Bandini in a Ferrari at Monaco in 1967. (Ramirez collection)

genial and laid-back young man with a sunny temperament but charmingly shambolic attitude towards organising his personal life, had been on the fringes of front-line Formula 1 since first arriving in the UK at Reg Parnell's behest in 1963. Now it seemed as though he would at last be rewarded with a car worthy of his undoubted talent.

Amon was first due to drive for the team in the non-title Brands Hatch Race of Champions, but while driving to the circuit he was involved in an unpleasant road accident. He was badly bruised and, after a handful of practice laps, opted to withdraw from the race rather than make an idiot of himself.

'Practice at Brands Hatch wasn't until Friday morning, but I thought I would pop down to Brands Hatch on the Thursday to see the cars being unloaded, just have a look and be fitted into the car,' he recalled.

'I was driving my Sunbeam Tiger, and some woman just turned sharply across my bows and I hit her straight in the side. I was terribly lucky, getting away with a badly bruised hand and ribs, because my passenger went right through the windscreen.'

Bandini raised Ferrari hopes with a splendid fighting second place behind Dan Gurney's Eagle-Weslake in the 40-lap final, and the trend continued in apparently the right direction when Parkes strolled away with the 52-lap Silverstone International Trophy race a few weeks later. To some extent these races were inconsequential curtain raisers to the season proper, but at least the Italian cars looked pretty reliable.

Bandini went into the opening round of the 1967 World Championship with high hopes of success. The mood in the Ferrari camp was buoyant, and even when the

Italian driver had a slight brush with the wall at the Mirabeau turn during practice for the Monaco GP, breaking a steering arm, the sense of optimism seemed hardly dented.

With characteristic pragmatism, Bandini effected makeshift repairs to the damaged car in order to get it back to the pits, reasoning that his mechanics needed to start repairing the consequences of his personal error as promptly as possible. At the end of the day he did a good job to qualify second on the front row of the grid only 0.7sec behind Jack Brabham's more agile pole-position Brabham-Repco.

Having finished this race second in 1966, Bandini now wanted to prove that he had finally emerged from the shadow of John Surtees and could be seriously regarded as a front-line driver in his own right. Just before the start he jokingly warned Clerk of the Course Louis Chiron that he would run him over if he didn't move out of

the way quickly after waving the starting flag. 'If you do that, then who will be there to wave the chequered flag for you when you win?' shot back Chiron in a similarly lighthearted vein. It was a poignant observation.

Bandini led the opening lap, but then dropped to third behind Jackie Stewart's BRM and Denny Hulme's Brabham-Repco. After the Scot retired with broken transmission, Hulme was left to dominate the race with Bandini struggling to keep in touch. Yet Lorenzo tried to launch a counter-attack with about 20 of the race's 100 laps left to run.

Whether he was trying too hard, or simply tiring with the effort of battling with the heavy Ferrari on that tortuous circuit, we will never know. But as he came through the chicane on to the harbour front on lap 82, Bandini clipped the inside wall with the car's right-hand wheels. It was enough to throw him off-line to the left and, as the car exited the corner, it climbed

The final day. Lorenzo Bandini hustles his central exhaust Ferrari 312 through Casino Square during his fateful pursuit of Denny Hulme's Brabham-Repco in the 1967 Monaco Grand Prix.

the straw bales, turned over and erupted in flames on the track.

Watching on television back in Maranello, Enzo Ferrari says he was struck by a sense of apprehension. Instantly, it seemed, he felt that this was one of his cars in trouble even before Bandini had been identified by the commentator. Of course, whether this was really so, or simply another case of the Old Man putting a melodramatic spin on his personal recollections is another matter altogether.

In those days Grand Prix cars did not have self-sealing fuel cells, nor on-board fire extinguishers, nor life support oxygen supplies piped into the drivers' helmets. Rollover bars were still skimpy, helmets not yet full-face and overalls capable of offering nothing but the most superficial protection. In truth, the most amazing aspect of the whole grisly business was that Bandini survived the initial accident.

Italy's great hero was desperately injured and, despite fighting grimly for three excruciating days, eventually lost the battle for his life. As this catastrophe was unfolding, so Chris Amon – on his first outing for Ferrari – had to drive past the accident scene again and again. After a pit stop to change a tyre punctured on the accident debris, Amon eventually finished third behind Hulme and Graham Hill's Lotus.

Bandini's death was one of Formula 1's most gruesome episodes, but it kick-started the sport into thinking, at least in general terms, about improved safety standards. Coming only a year after Jackie Stewart was badly hurt when he crashed his BRM in that opening lap rainstorm at Spa, it brought the whole rationale of motor racing into tighter focus. Were drivers being paid to demonstrate their skill or take absurd risks? Bandini's death endorsed Stewart's view that his

Chris Amon on Lorenzo Bandini

CHRIS AMON WOULD always remember his lost team-mate, Lorenzo Bandini, with respect and affection. 'I have to confess that I was a little wary about him when I first joined the team,' he reflected. 'I suppose his reputation had rather gone before him from the occasion when he knocked Graham Hill off in Mexico back in 1964, so I suppose I thought he might turn out to be a little aggressive towards me.

'Yet he was utterly charming. He was *so* pleasant and really helpful when it came to sorting out problems with the car. He really was one of the nicest guys I ever came across, and the greatest tragedy of the whole affair is that he was just maturing into a first-class number one in his own right.'

Chris Amon swings his Ferrari 312 through La Source hairpin on the way to third place in the 1967 Belgian GP at Spa-Francorchamps. (LAT)

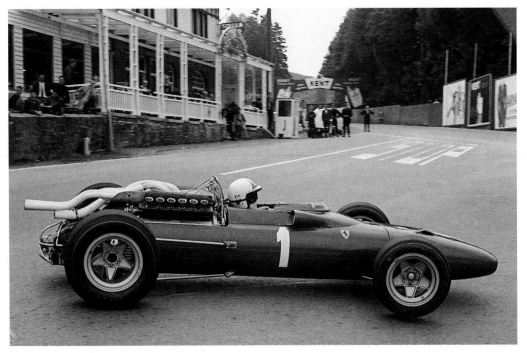

safety crusade was correctly judged.

In the immediate aftermath of the Monaco tragedy, Scarfiotti and Parkes staged a dead-heat for victory in the non-title Syracuse GP, after which the Dutch Grand Prix at Zandvoort saw the debut of the sensational Cosworth DFV-engined Lotus 49. This machine rewrote the contemporary parameters of Formula 1 performance – and meant that there was another car out on the circuit which Ferrari was hard-pressed to get on terms with.

Amon at least managed to avoid being lapped at Zandvoort, but then the Belgian GP at Spa-Francorchamps produced another Ferrari disaster. Although Amon qualified two seconds faster than Parkes to line up fifth on the grid, the Englishman nipped past

Chris Amon at Silverstone on his way to a hard-fought third place in the 1967 British GP with a Ferrari 312 in a season when he was often Maranello's lone Formula 1 representative. (Phipps Photographic)

him on the opening lap to run fourth behind Clark's amazing Lotus 49, Jochen Rindt's Cooper-Maserati and Stewart in the BRM H-16 which was spewing oil even at this early stage.

On the long haul back from Stavelot through the fast Blanchimont left-hander, Parkes lost control in the biggest possible way, almost certainly on that lubricant from Stewart's car ahead of him. His Ferrari somersaulted spectacularly high in the air, leaving a horrified Amon to pass underneath his team-mate's car as Mike was hurled out on to the trackside.

Chris was understandably shaken and took some time to get back into the swing of things, although eventu-ally a reassuring 'MIKE OK' sign was put out from the Ferrari pit. Not quite OK, in fact, for Parkes had sustained terrible leg fractures. He would recover, but his Formula 1 career was now over.

Amon finished third at Spa, but now found himself increasingly obliged to shoulder the entire responsibility for Ferrari's Formula 1 efforts. Scarfiotti, who was also racing in Belgium, seemed deeply affected by Parkes's accident and all-but lost his nerve. But Chris enjoyed some good races; third at Silverstone and Nürburgring, sixth at Mosport Park after a spin. It wasn't bad, but the engines were still relatively gutless.

'No question about it,' said Amon. 'That chassis was a dream, but they'd got an oil scavenging problem which prevented them from realising the engine's full potential. The Old Man really got quite annoyed when I insisted that it wasn't as quick as a Repco V8, telling me that we'd got more power, but I'd sat behind them at Silverstone and the 'Ring, and I told him I knew otherwise.

'Forghieri touched on the problem

Ferrari had two 312s at Chris Amon's disposal for the 1967 Italian GP at Monza. These evocative photographs show the cars being prepared in the old Monza lock-up garages. One wonders why Forghieri bothered with inboard front suspension given the aerodynamically appalling tangle of uprights and outboard springs at the rear of the car!

briefly and we went testing at Modena that summer with me under instructions to drop the clutch and cut the engine at high revs before coasting into the pits. Then they took off the sump cover to see how much oil was round the bottom of the engine – a bit crude, in a way, because I was never sure they knew how much oil they should be expecting anyway!'

Whatever the real problem, Forghieri produced a 48-valve engine for the Italian GP at Monza where Chris qualified only 0.8sec slower than Clark's pole position Lotus 49. Chaos at the start, when Amon was forced to dip the clutch to avoid running into the back of Jimmy's car, resulted in the V12 losing its edge before the start of the race. Chris trailed home seventh, four laps down, while John Surtees squared his account with Maranello by winning the Italian GP at the wheel of a Honda.

Come the US GP at Watkins Glen, Amon really got stuck into the Lotus 49s and was challenging for the lead of the race when his V12 blew up only 12 laps from the end of the 108 lap event. 'It was one of the few occasions when we'd got a Ferrari engine which was really on a par with the DFV,' he recalled. 'That was one of the famous races I feel sure I could have won if the engine had lasted.'

Amon rounded off the season with a fifth place in the Mexican GP, and then squared up to the business of preparing for 1968. Interestingly, he admits that he would have liked Jackie Stewart to have signed on as his team-mate 'to give me something to aim for.' But the canny Scot went to Tyrrell now that his contract with BRM had come to an end, leaving Chris paired with Belgian rising star Jacky Ickx.

Amon admits that he never quite hit it off with Ickx and was annoyed when Mr Ferrari paid him a healthy retainer for the 1968 season – whilst obviously intending to leave Chris on the same pay scale as during the previous year. The situation was eventually rectified, and suitable adjustments made, when Amon complained about the situation to the Old Man.

In 1968 the 48-valve Forghieri-designed Ferrari V12s were at the absolute peak of their development. Their acclaimed handling qualities were complemented by an engine which was almost – almost – good enough to get on terms with a Cosworth DFV in a straight fight. But everything seemed to go wrong for Amon.

His goggle strap broke when he was mixing it for the lead with the McLaren M7As of Bruce McLaren and Denny Hulme during the Silverstone International Trophy. His engine failed when he was 25sec ahead in the Spanish GP, and then the team missed Monaco, possibly because of memories of Bandini's accident the previous year. Amon asked if he could drive the spare Tyrrell Matra alongside Stewart, but Mr Ferrari wouldn't allow it.

For the Belgian GP, both Ferraris appeared with aerofoils positioned above the gearboxes, and Chris slammed round to put his 312 on pole position. The car felt fantastic, but more disappointment was waiting once the race began.

'Ever since the advent of the British specialist chassis manufacturers in Formula 1 at the start of the 1960s, I think most people accepted that Ferrari always tended to lag behind in chassis development,' said Chris. 'But I honestly think that, in 1968, things were the other way round. I think we surprised quite a few people when we turned up with that aerofoil

at Spa. The 312 really worked well there. On the lap I set my quickest time, I came down the Masta Straight and pulled up to Brian Redman's Cooper-BRM as we approached Stavelot. I remember going by him into the corner, with my foot buried on the throttle, as he was braking and changing down. The thing felt tremendous.

'There's absolutely no way I shouldn't have won that race. I got a bloody good start and must have been 150 yards ahead at the end of the opening lap. I thought I was going to pull away quite easily, but on the second lap I found Jo Bonnier limping back to the pits right on the fast line, as I came out of the Masta kink.

'I had to back off and Surtees slip-streamed past me in that Honda. I knew full well that, once he was in front, the Honda was quick enough in a straight line to give me hell's own job to get by again. I was really furious.

'Then I suddenly almost lost it at the Masta kink – a horrifying experience. The Honda kicked up a stone which went straight through my oil radiator and I lost it because the oil was now spraying on a rear tyre. I felt sick about that one, but I was absolutely convinced that Ferrari would win a race.'

Chris was correct in his judgement, but he would not be the man in the cockpit. It was Jacky Ickx who emerged victorious from a streaming wet French GP at Rouen-les-Essarts, while Chris never featured. As a result, the Ferrari management began to have doubts about the New Zealander's wet weather capability, but Chris totally vindicated himself with a brilliant performance at Nürburgring, running third in the pouring rain behind Graham Hill's Lotus before he spun off at North Curve.

'Before the start Franco Gozzi – the Ferrari team manager – and Forghieri told me to get the best start I could and hold the others up while Ickx got away,' he recalls, 'but at the start we all got on with it and Ickx never got within half a mile of me in the race.'

Separating those two wet-weather races was the British GP at Brands Hatch where Chris managed to celebrate his 25th birthday with a superb second place 4.4sec behind Jo Siffert's Rob Walker team Lotus 49.

'We were being blown off by the Cosworths out of the slow corners,' he remembers, 'but I still think if we'd had a bigger wing on the back of the car, we would have won. I drove absolutely balls-out for the entire race, but I was running short of rubber towards the end. I think the Ferrari people were slightly annoyed that I didn't win that one, but when they saw the rear tyres after the race they were slightly more understanding.'

In time for the Italian GP at Monza, Forghieri's engineering team had come up with a very sophisticated adjustable aerofoil driven by hydraulic power. The wing remained 'up' when the driver was in first, second or third gears – or when he went on the brakes in fourth or fifth – but feathered when he was on the throttle in the two highest gears. There was also a manual override which Amon admitted he preferred.

In the early stages of the race, Chris stayed with the leading bunch, only to spin off and fly into the densely packed trees after oil sprayed on his left-hand rear tyre going through the fast Lesmo right-handers. Amon found himself hanging from his seat harness – his legs having come up out of the cockpit without injury – before

Apart from an arm beckoning for a way through, Chris Amon's Ferrari 312 is almost concealed from view behind Jo Siffert's Lotus 49B as the pair battle for the lead of the 1968 British GP at Brands Hatch. Amon celebrated his 25th birthday with another close second place. (Phipps Photographic)

Star shot. Photographer Nick Loudon captured this superb shot of Chris Amon in a full-blooded power slide through Old Hall corner during the 1968 Oulton Park Gold Cup. The 1968 Ferrari 312 was a joy to handle – just lacked steam. (Nick Loudon)

being rescued from this parlous state by an obliging marshal.

Amon's rotten luck continued. Despite the fact that the clutch had packed up early on in the race, he dominated the Canadian GP at Ste Jovite. But with 17 laps left, the final drive pinion could no longer endure these clutchless changes. Chris was out – as indeed he would be from the final two races of the season, at Watkins Glen and Mexico City.

The 1968 season represented the absolute zenith of Chris Amon's three-season Ferrari career. At the end of that year Ickx left the team to join Brabham, leaving Amon effectively the team's only front-line Formula 1 driver. This was the year in which Enzo Ferrari successfully sought financial salvation from Fiat for his company which now had its back to the economic wall. Gianni Agnelli personally met with Mr Ferrari and a deal, whereby Fiat took 50 per cent of Ferrari SpA's stock, was hammered out which ensured the future of the Prancing Horse. But it was not agreed until 18 June, by which time any renewed commercial stability had simply

Mauro Forghieri was Ferrari's chief engineer for more than 20 years. He had an enormous respect for Chris Amon in particular, rating the New Zealander on a par with Jim Clark. (Phipps Photographic)

arrived too late to help Amon's cause.

It was hopeless. For some complex political reasons, Forghieri had been banished to a special projects department and the technical leadership entrusted to Stefano Jacoponi, the man who had previously worked on the 212E flat-12-engined European Hill-climb Championship contender.

'God, I gave Jacoponi a hard time,' remembers Amon. When his 312 dropped out of the Spanish GP at Barcelona's Montjuich Park circuit with a broken gearbox, Chris really lost his cool. He was also diagnosed as suffering from measles, which couldn't have helped matters.

'I hadn't been feeling at all well through the Spanish GP weekend,' he remembers. 'I mean, I didn't fancy a drink after the race, which was pretty unusual for me. But I forced myself to have one, and I felt dreadful!'

After that fleeting moment of promise, Chris never again led a Grand Prix at the wheel of a Ferrari. He continued: 'we were in bad shape at Monaco, no steam at all. The engine was useless. I'd made up my mind to try to have a big go at Stewart's Matra, but there was no way because we had to fill the thing up to the brim with fuel for it to go the distance.

'That was followed by a great dice to third at Zandvoort. Amazing! My last finish in a Ferrari. Then off to the French GP at Clermont where I was running third when a piston blew. I was screaming the guts out of it, though. Then Silverstone . . . another

Chris Amon: where did it go wrong?

'HE'S BECOME A bit of an Amon.' Any Formula 1 driver of the 1990s earning such a label probably won't quite understand its significance. But the Kiwi's contemporaries won't need reminding. It refers to an uncanny knack of being in the right places at the wrong time – consistently. It is amazing that Amon remains sane.

Only 53, he has been retired from F1 for more than two decades and lives in rural New Zealand with his wife and three children. Although Chris was never to win a Grand Prix, he was regarded by Mauro Forghieri as possibly the only driver of his era who was genuinely a match for Jimmy Clark.

Yet when it came to making strategic career decisions, this mild-mannered son of a prosperous farmer could be relied upon to pick the joker from the bottom of the pack. Ngaio Amon, Chris's father, bought him an old 1.5-litre Cooper-Climax back in 1960 which he drove to second place on his maiden outing. He then switched to an old Maserati 250F and in 1963 drove a Cooper-Climax in the Tasman Championship. He was spotted by British team boss Reg Parnell who plucked him from this rural backwater and placed him in the cockpit of a Lola Formula 1 car at the age of 19.

After a patchy European apprenticeship, he did the deal with Ferrari for the 1967 season. This upset his compatriot and friend Bruce McLaren who had plans for Chris to drive one of his BRM-engined Formula 1 cars that season and for whom Amon had been driving sports cars in North America. Chris was paid no retainer in 1967, just a percentage of the prize money. 'Which was fine by me,' he recalls.

With Ferrari, he started from the front row on 19 occasions, yet could not improve on a hat trick of second places. His switch to March yielded no better fortune, nor his subsequent move to the French Matra squad at the start of 1971. He held the 1972 French GP in the palm of his hand; then he got a puncture . . .

After Matra came a fruitless liaison with the hopeless Tecno team. Things got worse when he embarked on a project to build his own Formula 1 car in 1974. Thankfully, it was eventually scrapped. After a brief stint with BRM, Amon enjoyed something of an Indian summer with Morris Nunn's little Ensign Formula 1 team in 1975/76.

Chris was helping to bankroll the tiny Walsall, UK-based operation, and drove some sterling races before quitting the team after being caught up in the traffic jam backed up behind Niki Lauda's burning Ferrari in the 1976 German GP.

'I was simply sick and tired of watching that sort of spectacle in Formula 1,' he told me only a week or so later. 'I've sat about and seen too many blokes fried like that over the years. It simply proves to me that we're raving mad to be driving round the Nürburgring as it is at the moment.'

There was one more Formula 1 outing remaining; that year's Canadian GP at the wheel of one of Walter Wolf's ex-Hesketh 308Cs. It was a disaster. Chris spun and was T-boned by another competitor during practice. It was the end of his Formula 1 career.

Chris Amon returned to farm in his native New Zealand later that same year. He has never attended a Grand Prix since. However, on his 50th birthday, a group of us telephoned our congratulations from the press room at Hockenheim during free practice for the 1994 German GP.

With wailing Renault V10s and Ferrari V12s going about their business in the background, Chris seemed quite touched. Yet at the same time, he sounded quite content with his life after motor racing.

diabolical engine. Jumping out of gear. I packed it in.'

Late in August, Chris would be invited to have his first run in one of the new 1970 Ferrari Formula 1 prototypes. It went well, felt strong – but kept suffering major engine failures. He thought, 'Oh God, I can't stand any more of this' and did a deal to drive a March-Ford for the following season.

It was yet another crucial career wrong-turn. The new Ferrari was powered by the 3-litre flat-12, the engine which would become Maranello's most successful Formula 1 power unit of all time.

Chapter 10

The fabulous flat-12s

So Chris Amon made the wrong decision. Forghieri had spent most of late 1968 and early 1969 tucked away working on the sensational new Formula 1 car/engine package which would herald in Maranello's most consistently successful era.

Think about it. From August 1970 through to October 1979 – that's 10 seasons – Ferrari's flat-12-engined machines would win a total of 37 races out of 169 Grand Prix starts. That represents a 22 per cent success rate. Yet Ferrari was starting from quite low down on the overall achievement scale when the new car first broke cover in August 1969.

'Graceful' is the best word to describe the 312B1. The chassis construction followed the traditional Ferrari manufacturing methods of the time – a latticework of small diameter tubes overlaid with aluminium panelling. Its suspension was conventional, its water radiators front-mounted.

Yet its very heart, the 180-degree 12-cylinder engine, was the key. Forghieri and his colleagues had produced a remarkably compact power unit of 78.55 x 51.55mm, producing a total capacity of 2991.01cc. Its four chain-operated overhead camshafts ran on needle

rollers, operating 48 valves, and the crankshaft ran on four main bearings.

Its reputed 460bhp-plus at an 11,700rpm maximum was judged to be more than enough to deal with its Cosworth DFV-propelled rivals, even though the Ferrari was clearly thirstier and needed more fuel. Some of that fuel was contained within a rearward extending pontoon under which the flat-12 engine was neatly slung. It was a cleverly executed package.

'I decided on the 180-degree engine configuration for two reasons,' recalls Forghieri. 'There was a slight weight saving as compared with the earlier V12s and the centre of gravity would be significantly lower in the chassis. There was the added benefit of a smooth upper surface to the rear bodywork and we decided to hang the "boxer" from beneath a rearward extension of the monocoque which could also be used to carry extra fuel.

'The 312 engine had four main bearings, the crankshaft was machined from a special alloy billet imported from the USA and it had four chain-driven overhead camshafts running on needle rollers. To cure those early crankshaft failures, we had a specially developed coupling between the crankshaft and flywheel,

the purpose being to transfer flexing stresses along the length of the crankshaft.

'I began to think of the "boxer" configuration at the end of 1968 after a year of pole positions, leading races and disappointing retirements with Chris Amon.'

Back into the Ferrari fold as team leader for 1970 came Jacky Ickx, the 23-year-old Belgian driver. Ickx was a well-brought-up lad who came from straightforward surroundings – his father was one Belgium's leading motor sport journalists – yet somehow the young man contrived to project rather an aloof, almost patrician air. If it was contrived, it certainly worked well for him.

Ickx tended to get his own way. He was shrewd, motivated and, in the author's opinion, one of two drivers over the past three Formula 1 decades who obviously deserved to, but never pinned down, a World Championship title. The other was Carlos Reutemann.

Ickx hadn't really wanted to leave Ferrari at the end of 1968, but he was driven by the force of commercial circumstance. 'It was an easy decision to return there,' he recalled. 'I only left because of my Gulf Oil contract clash.

Chris Amon accelerates the prototype Ferrari 312B1 out of the pits at Modena during preliminary testing in summer 1969. Chris knew the car was better, but felt he couldn't gamble with another season with Ferrari. So he left, and he lost out. (Roebuck collection)

'I was driving for the JW Gulf team in long-distance events at the time and Gulf didn't want me driving a Formula 1 Ferrari running on Shell. I rejoined Ferrari at a time when it was clear that Fiat generally, and Gianni Agnelli in particular, were having more influence. I stayed at Ferrari for almost four seasons and I believe I was subsequently one of the few people who could go to Maranello and visit Mr Ferrari without an appointment.'

Ickx drove alone in the early part of the 1970 Formula 1 season. It was a fascinating year, for although he was ranged against the new Ford DFV-engined March 701s – driven most notably by Stewart and Amon – from the start of the year it was the long-promised arrival of a brand-new Lotus which everybody was really bracing themselves for.

In due course it arrived. It was, of course, the sensational torsion-bar-sprung, side-radiator Lotus 72 with which Jochen Rindt would mount his World Championship challenge. It would take a few races for the new car to be massaged into competitive form, but Ferrari would certainly have some serious opposition.

For Ickx, however, the 1970 season almost ended in spectacularly premature fashion. On the opening lap of the Spanish GP at Jarama, Jackie Oliver's BRM broke a front stub axle under heavy braking and T-boned the Belgian driver's Ferrari.

The impact ruptured the Italian car's fully laden fuel tank and the 312B1 simply erupted into a fireball of orange flame. Amazingly, both men escaped with their lives, although Ickx sustained minor burns which would cause him some degree of irritation for several months ahead.

For the Belgian GP at Spa, Ferrari decided to enter a second car. Not since Scarfiotti in 1967 had an Italian been seen strapped into the cockpit of one of the Formula 1 cars from Maranello, but now that all changed with the arrival of 28-year-old Ignazio Giunti. He was a charming, self-effacing young man who had served his motor racing apprenticeship in Alfa Romeo GTA saloons and T33 sports cars, later joining the Ferrari sports car team and, as we have seen, shared the Sebring-winning 512 earlier that same year.

On his debut outing at Spa-Francorchamps, Giunti drove in purposeful style to finish fourth. Yet Ferrari, typically, was not prepared to allow the young man to rest on his

The 312PBs: flat-12 domination

THE FERRARI 312PB was little more than a two-seater Grand Prix car built for the 3-litre Group sports car category at the start of 1971. A single car was fielded throughout that season as a trailer for the first full year of the 3-litre limit in 1972 and the cars raced through to the end of the 1973 season before Maranello abandoned endurance racing to concentrate on the rebirth of its Formula 1 operation.

The first 312PB – *prototipo boxer* – was completed at the end of the 1970 season. It was powered by a detuned version of the Formula 1 flat-12 engine, now delivering a more modest 440bhp at 10,800rpm – 1,800rpm lower than the GP engine's operating limit. The new machine was gloriously compact, scarcely bigger than its rivals in the 2-litre category.

Tragically, the 312PB's race debut in the 1971 Buenos Aires 1000km race was marred by the death of Ignazio Giunti. The Italian was leading the race, almost due to hand the car over to Merzario, when he was killed in a violent collision with the stricken Matra MS660 which its driver, Jean-Pierre Beltoise, was attempting to push back to the pits after encountering trouble out on the circuit.

Giunti's death was a huge blow to Ferrari's morale, but the team soldiered on throughout the 312PB's development season, achieving a succession of distinctly promising results. Then at the start of 1972, Maranello launched itself on the Sports Car Championship season with a three-car squad of these formidable racers.

The driver line-up was equally impressive, composed as it was of Jacky Ickx, Clay Regazzoni, Mario Andretti, Ronnie Peterson, Carlos Pace, Tim Schenken and Brian Redman. Andretti had experienced his first taste of PB motoring in the late 1970 season Kyalami 9-hour race. His comments sum up his affection for the little red racer.

'Those were race cars you could really grow an affection for,' he told the author. 'It's amazing how much you grow into part of a car when you are in it hour after hour. You hand it over to your co-driver and then, when you get back in it again, it still feels the same. It's still got brakes, it's still got oil pressure, it's still got a gearbox.

'I've driven Fords and I've driven Alfas, but Man, to drive a Ferrari sports car, well, that's on a level entirely of its own. Six hours, 12 hours, 24 hours, they just keep on running.

'That Kyalami race was the best of all. We lost 45 minutes with fuel pump trouble and when I stopped at Clubhouse corner with battery problems, a mechanic came out to the car and gave me some "assistance" and then we were away again.

'Jacky and I agreed that he would just go flat-out, and if it broke, then it broke. Jeez, we'd lost 14 laps, so we settled down to an eight-hour Grand Prix! We made five laps on everything else on that race track and, in the end, we took second place, only 45 minutes from the finish.

'The next day, both cars were on show down at a local garage and we went down to have a look. Clay and Brian's, it was immaculate, really nice. Jacky and mine looked as though it had just done the Battle of Normandy. It was just used up.

'But it is a fantastic feeling when you

Sports car stars. From left: Ronnie Peterson, Clay Regazzoni and Tim Schenken debate the merits of the 1972 Ferrari 312PB sports racer in the pits at Monza. (Associated Press)

Clay Regazzoni, Tim Schenken and Mario Andretti head a Ferrari 312PB 1–2–3 on the opening lap of the 1972 Daytona 24-hour sports car classic. (Phipps Photographic)

know you can go flat-out, hand it over to your team-mate, and it only needs a click on the dampers next time you get into it. One thing, though, the mechanics used to cover everything with graphite grease – you got out of a Ferrari looking as though you had been under it, rather than in it.'

Through 1972, the Ferrari PBs won every race they entered; Buenos Aires, Daytona, Sebring, Brands Hatch, Monza, Spa-Francorchamps, Targa Florio, Nürburging, Osterreichring and Watkins Glen. All these races fell to the Italian cars. However, the team decided to miss Le Mans, thereby

shying away from a direct confrontation with the works Matras, the rival French team having opted to contest only the 24-hour marathon during 1972.

In 1973, the scene was very different. Matra's latest MS670 was, quite simply, a vastly superior chassis to the 312PB. From the very start of the season Ferrari was on the run and, when it came to the crucial head-to-head at Le Mans that summer, Maranello was roundly trounced.

Only the Pace/Merzario car endured the race distance to finish a distant second behind the winning Matra of Henri Pescarolo and Gerard Larrousse. It was a devastating blow for the Prancing Horse which had hoped to add one more Le Mans victory to its already impressive tally.

Tim Schenken well remembered that defeat. 'When we dropped out at Le Mans, the whole team was in tears. I just couldn't believe it,' he reflected thoughtfully.

Ignazio Giunti speeds to fourth place in the 1970 Belgian GP at Spa-Francorchamps in the Ferrari 312B1. It was his first Formula 1 outing. (Phipps Photographic)

laurels. For the next race – the Dutch GP at Zandvoort – the second Ferrari was handled by Swiss Gianclaudio Regazzoni. Like Giunti, he would finish fourth on his GP debut, which was marred by the death of British driver Piers Courage who crashed his Frank Williams-entered de Tomaso.

'Clay' Regazzoni was relatively old at 30 to be getting his Grand Prix chance. Yet he was just the sort of driver Enzo Ferrari liked. Make no mistake, Clay was a tough old boy and had been in plenty of controversial scrapes. In Formula 3, driving for the Italian Tecno marque, he had seemed to crash almost every time he took to the track.

Moreover, Zandvoort was a somehow poignant track for Regazzoni to make his GP debut on. Two years earlier he had been at the source of a terrible controversy when his Formula 2 Tecno became embroiled in an accident with British rising star Chris Lambert who was killed as a result. Accusations flew in all directions. It was an ugly business, but although it touched Regazzoni emotionally, he kept it very much to himself.

Yet Clay was an undeniably charismatic man who took life as it came. At the 1972 Italian GP, Mario Andretti recalls noting with amazement that Regazzoni was drinking wine with his lunch on race day, only a couple of hours before the start. 'I only have a couple of glasses,' said Clay earnestly, as if that explained everything. Yet perhaps it didn't quite sharpen his sensibilities as much as he had hoped as he tripped over Carlos Pace's March and spun out of the lead of the ensuing race whilst lapping the slower competitor.

Despite the advent of the Lotus 72, the Ferrari 312B1 acquitted itself magnificently throughout its first full season. Regazzoni got to lead a Grand Prix for the first time at Hockenheim where Ickx battled with Rindt the entire distance, just finding himself out-fumbled on the final lap. In fairness, Rindt commented: 'A monkey could have won in my car today.'

Yet Jochen would be deprived of victory in his home race, the inaugural Austrian GP at Osterreichring, where Ickx and Regazzoni put on a convincing demonstration run to finish in 1–2 formation. Tragically Rindt was then killed in a crash during practice for the Italian GP at

Jacky Ickx and Clay Regazzoni round the Boschkurve at Osterreichring in line astern formation on the way to a commanding 1–2 victory for the Ferrari 312B1 in the 1970 Austrian GP. (Phipps Photographic)

Monza where Regazzoni won the race – his first – and Ickx retired with a broken clutch.

It was a dark weekend for the international motor racing fraternity, but there remained the tantalising prospect that Ickx, after all, just might beat his dead rival for the Championship crown. Ickx finished the Italian GP weekend with a total of 19 points, way behind the total of 45 which Rindt had accumulated prior to his death.

The mathematics were simple. If Ickx could win the three remaining races – Canada, US and Mexico – he would pick up another 27 points and take the title by a single point. On the face of it, this seemed like a long shot, but he almost did it. He kept the battle open by winning the Canadian race at St Jovite, near Montreal, but a fuel line sprung a leak at Watkins Glen

two weeks later and he could only scramble home fourth.

This now confirmed Rindt as the sport's only posthumous World Champion, but it was a close run thing as Ickx went on to round off the season with a victory at Mexico City. He had thus won a total of four Grand Prix during the course of the season, only one short of Rindt's total, but the Belgian acknowledged that it was only right that his Austrian rival should have emerged as Champion.

The 1971 season opened on a suitably upbeat note. Mario Andretti won the first round of the World Championship, the South African GP at Kyalami, at the wheel of a 1970 spec. Ferrari 312B1. It was a wonder-

ful achievement for the 32-year-old Italian born American who, less than 20 years earlier, had been fired by the sight of Alberto Ascari's Ferrari 500 winning the Italian GP at Monza.

Andretti was one of motor racing's greats. He oozed charisma and will probably go down in history as one of the sport's most versatile exponents. He wanted to drive for Ferrari and, thanks to his Firestone Indycar links, it was not too difficult to arrange a deal with the Old Man which would see him join up as an occasional third-stringer alongside Ickx and Regazzoni.

Pre-race testing at Kyalami had also seen the debut of the brand-new Ferrari 312B2, Forghieri's logical development of the previous year's

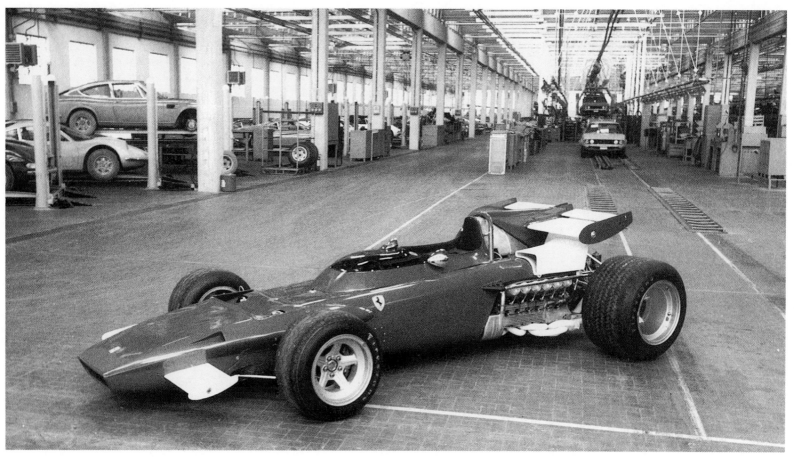

The angular Ferrari 312B2 at its Maranello unveiling in late 1971. The car was bedevilled by acute Firestone tyre vibration problems and many of its drivers reckoned it was never as good as the original B1. (Coltrin)

car. It was visually more angular and less attractive; it certainly looked less than attractive after Regazzoni slammed it into the wall and damaged it quite badly.

Clay made amends with a well-judged victory in the Brands Hatch Race of Champions with the B2, while Andretti triumphed in the unique one-off Questor GP at California's now-defunct Ontario Motor Speedway. It had been a promising start to the season, but the signs were that everybody had underestimated the newly-forged partnership between Jackie Stewart, Ken Tyrrell and Goodyear.

Ferrari remained on Firestones and

had the added benefit of Peter Schetty as a team manager. This even-tempered Swiss came from a family which ran a Basle-based textile business. A keen and accomplished semi-professional racer himself, he retired from Ferrari's sports car team at the end of 1970.

Telephoned out of the blue by the author 11 years later, he recalled graphically the challenge of managing Ferrari – and the drama which unfolded in terms of the B2 track performance.

'When I retired from driving, I had planned to return immediately to my family business, but Mr Ferrari asked me if I would care to stay on as team

manager and do some test driving,' said Schetty. 'I agreed, and indeed, I was delighted to do so.'

Firestone were developing tyres with an increasingly low aspect ratio during the 1971 season and, before long, Ferrari, BRM and most of their other contracted teams were sending back lurid tales of persistent tyre vibration problems. Moreover, these vibrations got worse as the sidewalls became shallower during the course of the year.

In effect, what was happening was that the tread was lifting slightly from the track and trying to run over itself, causing the sidewalls of the tyre to bend. Those with keen hearing could detect the problem as the cars accelerated out of the corners. It was just like a bass drum.

Schetty did much of the test driving

and testified to the seriousness of the problem. 'Those vibrations just knocked you out, particularly when you were hard on the throttle coming out of a corner,' he said.

'They were high-frequency vibrations which wore out every muscle in your body. I can remember testing a B2 on one occasion and the vibrations got so bad that the instruments just became a blur in front of my eyes. What really worried me was the potential mechanical stress that the vibrations were putting through the chassis.'

Today Nigel Bennett is the highly respected Chief Designer on the Penske Indycar team. Back in 1971 he was Firestone's principal Formula 1 engineer in the field. He also had vivid memories of the problem.

'We tried all sorts of constructions to get rid of the problem,' he said. 'It was an absolute nightmare. The answer seemed to go back to taller tyres with stiffer sidewalls. The vibration problem was a cyclic phenomenon which occurred under torsional – traction – and lateral – cornering – loading. No amount of experimentation with different constructions could dampen it out.

'Of course, it was more extreme on some cars than others. I remember we used to get a lot of stick from Forghieri on the subject, although I did think that the B2 had a rather strange suspension system. In fact, we had more complaints from Mauro than we did from everybody else put together.

'From a communication point of view, Ferrari benefited from Peter Schetty's presence as team manager. He was also pretty good as a test driver. Perhaps not quite quick enough, but very analytical. A logical Swiss, phlegmatic and calm. You couldn't exactly say that about Forghieri.

'Eventually we did some tests with a BRM P160, mounting a camera, which had been developed for rocket use, on the front of the car. The camera ran at 400 frames per second. We were absolutely horrified when we developed the film. The wheel was flexing, the upright was distorting – up to an inch-and-a-half – and the tyre was vibrating.

'We didn't dare show the film to BRM. It was reasonable to assume that the Ferrari suspension was doing the same . . .'

After that flickeringly optimistic start, Ferrari's 1971 season plunged downhill all the way. By the time it came to the Italian GP at Monza, Ickx was saying openly that he thought the B1 was still a better car. This didn't please Forghieri, of course, and then Mr Ferrari stuck his oar in by requesting that Goodyear supply a set of their G27 rubber to use in practice. None of this made any real difference and Ferrari failed to win another World Championship GP all season.

By this stage, of course, Ferrari had its own test track at Fiorano, opened at the start of the 1972 season, which would replace the old Modena autodrome where the Italian cars had been tested since time immemorial. The B2 was fitted with a more conventional suspension system for the new season, but only a single GP win would reward the team when Ickx won commandingly at Nürburgring.

Even more remarkably, the Belgian was defeated in streaming rain at Monaco by BRM-driver Jean-Pierre Beltoise. Ickx was regarded as perhaps the greatest wet weather driver of his era, but there was nothing he could do to respond. 'He just drove away from me into the distance,' said the Ferrari team leader.

Ferrari's Formula 1 fortunes dipped

to possibly their lowest ebb in late 1972/early 1973. The B2s were bog slow, unreliable and difficult to drive. For the new season a switch to Goodyear rubber came as no surprise, but there was still nothing seriously worthwhile coming from Maranello's design department.

The volatile Forghieri now seemed to be going through one of his periodic spells 'in disgrace', so former Innocenti engineer Sandro Colombo was entrusted with the design of the 312B3. Because of industrial unrest in Italy, Colombo turned to British specialist sub-contractors, TC Prototypes, based near Northampton, to build the monocoques.

John Thompson, the TC Prototypes boss, was impressed by the standard of technical drawings he received from the Italian team. But working with Ferrari made him aware that the team lacked some of the specialist skills widely available on the UK scene. Just over a decade later, Ferrari would finally come to the same conclusion and establish its own UK-based design studio.

The first part of the 1973 Ferrari Formula 1 season was effectively a waste of everybody's time. Ickx was now contesting many of the races on his own as the team's single entry. Regazzoni had decided to accept a big money offer from the Marlboro BRM team, while Andretti's Firestone commitments meant that it would be difficult for him to drive a Goodyear-shod Ferrari.

Ickx was also fed up to the back teeth with the whole experience. After finishing eighth, a lap down on Peter Revson's McLaren in the British GP at Silverstone, he quit the team. Maranello had now reached a crucial turning point in its Formula 1 history. Where now?

The team missed the following

British Ferrari. The early 1973 312B3 was based round a chassis manufactured by TC Prototypes in the UK. This is Ickx's car being pushed out prior to practice for the Spanish GP at Barcelona's Montjuich Park circuit. (LAT)

Dutch and German GPs. Forghieri was ordered back into the mainstream Formula 1 business and was instructed to oversee an intensive programme of development on the 312B3 in time for the Austrian GP on 19 August. There were 20 days in which to do something about it – and it needed to be good.

By the time the whippet-thin Arturo Merzario drove out of the pits at the Osterreichring, the B3 looked like a completely different machine. It had been transformed absolutely beyond belief. Radiator positions,

front and rear wings, suspension geometry and engine airbox were all totally different.

The B3's weight distribution had been significantly altered by these changes. It was now a very different car, almost halfway decent. Even the jaded Ickx decided to accept an invitation to drive the car at Monza. He acknowledged that it was much improved, but by then his passion for Ferrari had cooled. He wanted out and was in no mood to seek a rapprochement.

Niki Lauda joined the Ferrari team

at the start of 1974 and won two Grands Prix with a further-evolved version of the 312B3 which had been the subject of Forghieri's interim revamp the previous summer. This car had conventional longitudinal gearbox and Lauda found that it was always prone to a touch of understeer. But when Forghieri unveiled its successor, the new 312T, immediately after the 1974 United States GP, the Austrian recalled that he was deeply concerned and sceptical.

The plan Forghieri had in mind was to pursue the lowest possible polar moment of inertia by packaging as much of the car as possible between the front and rear wheels. This was a philosophy which Lauda had already tasted when March designer Robin Herd penned the hideously unsuccessful March 721X in 1972. Lauda raced it to no effect whatsoever and his career suffered. Little wonder that he was apprehensive about the new Ferrari design concept.

The 312T's transmission cluster was positioned across the car ahead of the rear axle line, the shafts lying at right-angles to the centre-line of the car, the drive being taken via bevel gears on the input side of the gearbox.

'When I was first shown the drawings of the 312T I felt indifferent about the whole project,' he later recalled. 'I didn't really appreciate the advantages that it would offer, because it seems such a very big change from a chassis about which we knew everything.

'Then, when I got to drive it at Fiorano, I quickly appreciated that it was a much more competitive proposition. The problem with the B3 had been its inclination towards understeer. No matter how you tried to tune the chassis, it always understeered very slightly. We had also used up all its potential, so we had to switch to the new car. There was no choice.'

However, Lauda firmly believed that the 312T's flat-12 engine offered only a marginal power advantage over the rival Cosworth Ford DFV machines from McLaren, Lotus, Shadow and Tyrrell. What the superbly flexible engine *did* provide was totally neutral handling and a wide torque curve. Driveability was the key.

'Those suggestions that we had a 30bhp advantage over the Cosworths really used to infuriate me,' he admits, 'although I did try to push them to the back of my mind at the time. If I had really enjoyed an effective 30 horsepower advantage over the others, I would have been walking

Niki Lauda en route to his first GP victory at Madrid's Jarama circuit in the 1974 Ferrari 312B3. (Phipps Photographic)

Niki Lauda's Ferrari 312B3 shows a clean pair of heels to Mike Hailwood's McLaren M23, Clay Regazzoni's Ferrari and the rest of the pack on the second lap of the 1974 Dutch GP at Zandvoort. Lauda won the race easily, his second win of that season. (Phipps Photographic)

Niki Lauda: too heroic for Ferrari?

ANDREAS-NIKOLAS LAUDA was probably the most remarkable man ever to drive for Ferrari. A scion of a wealthy Viennese banking family, he invested £8,500 to rent a drive from the newly-established March team in the 1971 European Formula 2 Championship, a move which launched his serious international racing career.

Even then, he was an amazingly self-assured young man, but blessed with a quietly controlled temperament and calm disposition. Mature and analytical, Lauda had a purely pragmatic approach to his motor racing, and carefully mapped out a strategy which he judged would take him into the sport's senior category, even though, by the time he reached it, he would be around £120,000 in debt. In the early 1970s, he thought it would take a lifetime to pay it off.

Three years later he was being strapped into the cockpit of a Ferrari 312B3 on the starting grid for the Argentine GP at Buenos Aires. The intervening years had seen him struggling to make his name driving for the March and BRM teams, and it was his 1973 BRM team-mate Clay Regazzoni who recommended him for a Ferrari drive when he himself returned to Maranello at the start of the 1974 season.

Lauda successfully completed the necessary legal gymnastics required to get off the hook from his BRM contract and duly completed his Ferrari contract. His position was assisted by the presence of the newly recruited Luca di Montezemolo as Mr Ferrari's new liaison man at the races. The ghosts of Tavoni and Dragoni had long been exorcised; Luca now reported back to the Old Man in an even-handed and relatively

Niki Lauda, 1997, the international airline owner. (Lauda Air)

objective fashion. Of course, it helped that the cars were winning again.

Niki won the Spanish and Dutch GPs that season, following this up with a five-win run to the 1975 World Championship title. Then, on 1 August 1976, he came close to

death when his Ferrari 312T2 crashed at Nürburgring during the German Grand Prix.

There had long been concern about the 14-mile Nürburgring's suitability for contemporary Formula 1 racing. These worries stemmed not from its fundamental challenge, but from the difficulties involved in marshalling it adequately. Yet, even though Lauda had broken a wrist there in 1973 after crashing his BRM at the Bergwerk corner – close to the scene of his subsequent accident – there is no reason to conclude that the Austrian had become prejudiced against the track.

Having started the 1976 Grand Prix on rain tyres, Lauda came into the pits at the end of the opening lap, changed to slicks and rejoined at the back of the field. Even by the time he reached Adenau bridge, he was making progress back through the field, but he never made it as far as the Bergwerk right-hander.

After what is generally accepted to have been a rear suspension breakage, the Ferrari 312T2 snapped violently out of control on a fast left-hand bend – spinning tail out to the *left*, which defied the obvious centrifugal forces working on the car, and slammed through a catch fence into a near-vertical rock face.

The car erupted in flame and bounced back on to the circuit where it was rammed by Brett Lunger's Surtees TS16. Lauda's helmet also came off in the second impact, but he was rescued from certain death by the selfless efforts of fellow drivers Lunger, Guy Edwards, Arturo Merzario and a nearby marshal. He was airlifted to hospital where it was found that his lungs had been damaged through inhalation of toxic fumes from the burning Ferrari's glassfibre bodywork.

For several days, Lauda's life hung by the slenderest of threads. He was even given the last rites of the Roman Catholic church, an experience which almost prompted him to leap from his bed in terror and stark indignation.

Lauda's recovery from these life-threatening injuries was the stuff of which sporting legends are made. Just over two months after the accident, he returned to the cockpit of a Formula 1 Ferrari for a test at Fiorano. Frankly, he was scared stiff, as he later freely admitted, but he controlled and subjugated that apprehension to race again in the Italian GP at Monza.

Nobody will ever know just how much superhuman effort that restoration took. Most of his hair had been burnt away and the scar tissue on his scalp bled freely each time Niki donned his helmet. Yet twice he set fastest lap of the race in the closing stages of the Grand Prix, a time eventually bettered only by winner Ronnie Peterson's March 761. He finished fourth. He was totally drained, yet already hailed as a hero.

Ironically, such heroism would work against him. During his absence, Ferrari's Formula 1 campaign started to become unravelled and the team realised just how much it had missed Niki's analytical technical input. Now they were torn between wanting him back and fearing he would be no good. When he finally missed out on retaining his Championship by a single point, having pulled out of the rain-soaked Japanese GP, they took the simplistic way out. Lauda was nailed to the cross as a scapegoat for the team's failure.

A lesser man would have wilted under the pressure, but Lauda turned the situation to his own advantage. If that meant destabilising the likeable Carlos Reutemann, the enigmatic Argentine driver who was drafted into the team as Clay Regazzoni's successor for 1977, then that was bad luck.

Perhaps Reutemann was simply in the wrong place at the wrong time. Whatever the reason, Lauda conceived a very violent dislike of the man. This was out of character for Niki who usually weighed his personal assessment of others with meticulous care.

The tone of their relationship could be judged by Lauda's response to the question 'Do you regard Reutemann as a team-mate or a rival?' Niki thought for a few seconds and then replied: 'neither.'

Yet Carlos was also a very great driver and, after Lauda's departure, proved his quality by winning four Grands Prix in 1978, including a particularly notable success in the British GP at Brands Hatch where he caught and defeated his former team-mate's Brabham-Alfa.

Lauda also ruthlessly capitalised on his remarkably intimate relationship with Enzo Ferrari. The Old Man was amused by Niki's candour, which was always spiced with a degree of informal over-familiarity which might have proved suicidal for any other driver's career prospects.

Contract negotiations between the two men were simply amazing. Through Piero Lardi, Niki would lay down such outrageous demands that Ferrari's second son was almost terrified to translate them for his father's benefit. In response, Enzo would accuse his number one driver of being 'a jew boy' and threatened to fire him on the spot. Clearly, both men were having a whale of a time.

Lauda's premature departure from the team was fuelled, in part, by Ferrari's outrageous treatment of his mechanic Ermanno Cuoghi who had indicated that he wanted to follow Niki to Bernie Ecclestone's Brabham team. Ferrari team manager Roberto Nossetto was quite happy to cut Cuoghi loose at Watkins Glen with nothing more than his air ticket back to Italy – and no·means of getting back to New York.

That episode offended Lauda's sensibilities. He took care of Cuoghi and wrong-footed Ferrari by walking out after the race. He would spend almost two seasons with Brabham before retiring from the sport in 1979 to concentrate on his fledgeling airline, then returning in 1982 to win a third World Championship two years later at the wheel of a McLaren.

Today Niki runs and flies for Lauda Air, the chief of his own highly successful international airline. He is also a consultant to Ferrari at a time when Luca di Montezemolo is the company president. In 20 years, their joint destinies seem to have come full circle.

Niki Lauda (left), Mauro Forghieri and Luca di Montezemolo produced a great partnership for Ferrari in 1974. (Phipps Photographic)

The Ferrari 312T2s of Lauda and Regazzoni lead the sprint to the first corner at the start of the 1976 Belgian GP at Zolder. It was in one of these cars that Lauda was so gravely injured at the Nürburgring later that year. (Phipps Photographic)

Niki Lauda's Ferrari 312T leaps the brow at Pflanzgarten during practice for the 1975 German GP at Nürburgring. Only a punctured tyre prevented the Austrian from winning this race, but a year later he nearly lost his life in a fiery accident. (LAT)

away with the races using only one hand – because the 312T chassis was so good, that any benefit of that nature in terms of power would have left me with an enormous advantage.

'The chassis was perfect; it was totally neutral and progressive. It was a permanent monument to Mauro Forghieri's skill, a real gem of a car.'

In 1975 Niki won five Grands Prix to take his first World Championship crown. The following year he won the Brazilian and Argentine races with the 312T, then Clay Regazzoni won at Long Beach, and the evolutionary 312T2 emerged victorious in Belgium and Monaco. Then came a spate of engine failures caused by a machining error which produced infinitesimal cracks at the point where a flange taking the drive to the ignition was pressed into the end of the crank-shafts.

This problem was quickly rectified in time for Lauda to take a distant second place to James Hunt's McLaren in the British GP at Brands Hatch. This was subsequently translated into a victory on appeal to the FIA after Hunt was excluded from the results for a rule infringement following a first lap shunt which resulted in the race being red-flagged to a halt.

Then Lauda almost lost his life in a fiery accident on the second lap of the German GP at Nürburgring. This disaster handed James Hunt a priceless opportunity to have a tilt at the championship, the Englishman squeezing home by a single point after Lauda – who'd made a fantastic recovery to return to the cockpit by Monza – pulled out of the final rain-soaked race at Japan's Mount Fuji circuit.

Unfortunately, Ferrari's chassis development programme had been allowed to drift during the period of Niki's hospitalisation. For 1977, the Austrian turned things round and bounced back to take his second title. Yet there was a gradual, almost imperceptible deterioration in the Ferrari T2's performance in 1977, which served as a reminder that Formula 1 cars are complex technical packages. Maranello was also irked that Goodyear's latest tyres seemed more suited to the rival McLaren M26, a development which resulted in Ferrari switching to Michelin radials from the start of 1978.

The Ferrari 312T3s of Carlos Reutemann and Gilles Villeneuve find themselves squeezed between the two Brabham-Alfa BT46s of John Watson (left) and Niki Lauda as they turn into the first hairpin after the start of the 1978 US GP West at Long Beach, California. (Phipps Photographic)

Gilles Villeneuve scored his first Grand Prix win in front of his home crowd at Montreal in 1978 at the wheel of the Ferrari 312T3. (Phipps Photographic)

Jody Scheckter became Ferrari's most recent World Champion driver when he took the 1979 title in the Michelin-shod 312T4. (LAT)

Scheckter in the Ferrari 312T4 on his home soil at Kyalami in 1979. In this race he had to take second place to team-mate Gilles Villeneuve. (Phipps Photographic)

Gilles the fighter! Undaunted, Villeneuve heads for the pits at Zandvoort as his 312T4 sheds the remains of its punctured left rear tyre. (LAT)

That incredible flat-12 reliability continued to underpin Lauda's 1977 efforts. In the South African GP, his T2 ran over debris from the tragic accident which killed Shadow driver Tom Price and the flat-12 lost all its water and most of its oil as a result. But it still finished, cockpit warning lights flickering, to post yet another victory.

At the end of 1977, Lauda quit Ferrari and joined Bernie Ecclestone's Brabham-Alfa squad. But the flat-12s kept winning through 1978 with Carlos Reutemann and Gilles Villeneuve notching up five more victories. Then in 1979, Jody Scheckter won the Championship with the 312T4, winning three races, a tally matched by Villeneuve. But

that was effectively the end of the story.

Villeneuve had joined the Ferrari squad in the immediate aftermath of Lauda's decision to jump ship after clinching the Championship in the 1977 US GP. The French-Canadian was one of the most talked-about Formula 1 talents of his Grand Prix generation, an endearing blend of spectacularly uninhibited talent and little-boy-lost off-track innocence.

Despite being beaten by his team-mate at both Kyalami and Long Beach, Scheckter never allowed his own confidence to waver. In Gilles, he could identify the same qualities of unrestrained exuberance which had characterised his own early days in

Formula 1 some six seasons before.

'The way I remember it, Gilles always cultivated the image of a dare-devil,' recalled Jody in 1997. 'He would always have the wheels spinning in the pit lane, changing gear without the clutch. I suppose it gave me a certain confidence, because I figured that's where I would get the advantage in the end, by being gentler with the machinery.

'I remember just how enthusiastic about his engines Mr Ferrari always seemed to be. But when I came back from the second race of 1979, in Brazil, and we had a team meeting at Maranello, Forghieri simply wouldn't translate my comments when I said that the flat-12 just didn't have the speed of the Cosworth V8s. And I knew, because I had been following them round Interlagos and they just

In 1980 the revamped Ferrari 312T5 was totally outclassed by the rival Cosworth-engined ground-effect challengers from Williams and Ligier. Even Villeneuve's brilliance could not make up the deficit. (LAT)

dropped me when it came to accelerating out of the corners.

'Forghieri was saying words like "yes, yes, – we'll discuss that later on." I think it's fair to say that Mr Ferrari respected me, but he loved Gilles.'

Being beaten in the South African GP was a bitter pill for Scheckter to swallow. He had started on slicks on a damp track and when Villeneuve, who had started on rain tyres, pulled in for a change to slicks, Jody thought he had it made. 'I was miles ahead and I thought it would be one of the easiest races of my career,' he records.

'Then the Michelins began to wear so badly that I just couldn't touch the brake pedal without the car literally jumping over the bumps. I was furious, so I had to come in for fresh tyres

shortly before the end. Then I was catching Gilles at a huge rate, but there wasn't enough time left before the chequered flag.

'Standing team orders at Ferrari always dictated that when the cars were running 1–2, that was the order they kept through to the flag. Would I have passed Gilles? 'Well, I would have certainly been tempted. Perhaps it's just as well that I never quite caught him and we'll never know!'

At Lotus, Colin Chapman's ambitious work on under-car aerodynamics had ushered in the ground-effect era, and Mario Andretti surged to the

1978 World Championship. Then Williams picked up the challenge, refining Chapman's concept to a brilliantly competitive pitch in time for 1980. Ferrari was being left behind.

The 1980 Ferrari 312T5 was a hopeless waste of time. Forghieri desperately tried to engineer in some ground-effect credibility, but the wide flat-12 engine precluded any serious attempt at harnessing the airflow beneath the cars. Add to that a succession of engine failures and Maranello was relegated from champ to chump in a single season.

Chapter 11

Into the turbo era

THE CLOSING STAGES of the 1980 season saw Ferrari climb aboard the Formula 1 turbo bandwagon which had originally started to roll three years earlier when Renault produced its first 1.5-litre V6 challenger.

There were two major factors taken into account by the Maranello engineering staff. First, the 3-litre flat-12 had pretty well come to the end of its development road with an output of around 525bhp. Second, the 1980 312T5 had been a disaster largely because of the impossibility of designing a decent ground-effect chassis round such a wide engine. A 1.5-litre turbo V6 would at least have a narrow bottom end, allowing Forghieri to produce a better aerodynamic package, as well as around 650bhp with which to propel it.

Ferrari decided on a wide 120-degree four-cam V6 which, in its preliminary incarnation, was dubbed the 126C. Unfortunately, Maranello's chassis manufacturing techniques had not advanced for more than a decade and the car, in fact little more than a travelling test bed, used the familiar multi-tube space-frame overlaid with stressed alloy panelling.

Gilles Villeneuve drove the car for the first time during practice for the 1980 Italian GP – held this time at Imola, for a variety of complex political reasons – and lapped half a second faster than the T5 he was to use, and crash, when it came to the race. But the Ferrari turbo was then put on one side and not used again until the start of the following season.

Over the next few months, Ferrari initiated two very separate programmes of development on the V6. On the one-hand, work continued on a conventional exhaust-driven KKK turbocharging system, but they also tried the Swiss Comprex system of 'pressure wave supercharging', a concept originally developed by the Brown-Boveri Corporation for marine and railway power units.

This utilised a direct-drive supercharger, belt driven from the rear of one of the V6 engine's camshafts, in conjunction with pressure waves developed by the exhaust gases to compress the incoming air as it entered the inlet manifold.

The Comprex-equipped 126CK sounded absolutely magnificent, but there were installation problems caused by trying to mount the supercharger within the vee of the engine, and this badly upset the Ferrari's weight distribution. Although the drivers initially reported that the Comprex system provided more encouraging throttle response, it was eventually decided to shelve the project and concentrate on the KKK turbo set-up.

The affable Jody Scheckter decided to retire from racing at the end of the 1980 season, and his place in the team was taken by the Frenchman Didier Pironi, who had won the Belgian GP the previous year for Ligier. Pironi had come into Formula 1 at the start of the 1978 season. He was talented, impassive and, as things would transpire, totally ruthless. For all his ability, many people regarded him as something of a cold fish.

With characteristic openness, Gilles welcomed him into the Ferrari camp. Pironi was quick to ingratiate himself with his new team-mate, but there was no doubt that Villeneuve was much the faster driver in 1981. At Monaco, where the Canadian won his most memorable Formula 1 victory, Pironi was a lapped fourth by the time both Ferraris reached the chequered flag.

Villeneuve's victory at Monaco was proof that, even in this era of increasing high technology, it was possible for the driver to make a crucial difference. When Alan Jones's Williams faltered with fuel pick-up problems in the closing stages, Gilles sliced through to grab victory.

He recalled it as one of his hardest-ever races: 'The car was extremely hard to drive, the suspension as stiff as a go-kart. I bumped my head on the rollover bar all the time and ended up aching all over.

'It was one of the most tiring races of my life. My brakes were finished, and when they started to go I had to be very brutal with my gearbox. But it lasted OK. I was very lucky!'

Three weeks after this success, Villeneuve held off a train of four closely-packed rivals to win the Spanish GP at Madrid's tortuous Jarama circuit. This was another genuine example of mind over matter. The Ferrari 126CK was holding them up through the corners, but its turbo V6 power enabled it to squirt away on the straights.

Jacques Laffite, a close second in the Ligier-Matra, later remarked: 'You know, no driver can do magic, but Gilles made you wonder sometimes!'

The balance of the 1981 season was bitty in the extreme for the Ferrari squad. Like as not, Villeneuve's sheer exuberance could just as easily race out of control. He was a man who simply couldn't give up and, in a car which was so obviously deficient, the tantalising temptation to over-drive was obvious and ever-present. Yet that was what made him such a romantically attractive member of the Formula 1 fraternity.

It was clear that Ferrari urgently needed to do something about its level of chassis development. To that end, British engineer Harvey Postlethwaite joined the team in the middle of 1981 and set about designing a new car for the following season. Postlethwaite had previously worked for Hesketh and Walter Wolf – joining Ferrari after the latter organisation amalgamated with the Fittipaldi team and clearly began running short of funds.

Winning ways. Gilles Villeneuve heads to victory in the 1981 Spanish GP at Jarama with the unwieldy Ferrari 126CK. Three weeks previously he had also won at Monaco with this car. (Phipps Photographic)

Gilles Villeneuve: the racer's racer

FINDING ANYONE CLOSER to Enzo Ferrari's ideal as a racing driver than Gilles Villeneuve would have been difficult indeed. He had Nuvolari's tenacity, the sheer skill of a Surtees and the even-temperament of a Lauda – out of the car, at least.

In his tragically brief Formula 1 career, the lad from rural Quebec won only six Grand Prix victories, yet earned a status within Formula 1 which many more successful competitors never managed to achieve. He joined Ferrari for the last two races of 1977 after Niki Lauda took the decision to leave before the end of the season. Previously, he had driven a third McLaren in that year's British GP at Silverstone, but thereafter he raced nothing but Ferraris through to his death at Zolder in May 1982.

First or last, Villeneuve always drove flat-out. His racing skills had originally been developed on snowmobiles in his native Canada, and he first made his mark on the international car racing scene when he won the prestigious Trois-Rivieres Formula Atlantic race in Quebec late in 1976. That success attracted the eye of James Hunt who returned to Britain and told McLaren that he'd just seen a guy who was future Championship material.

Not very shrewdly, the McLaren management failed to take up its option on Villeneuve's services. Their loss was Ferrari's gain, although it is fair to say that Gilles never enjoyed a chassis whose handling was worth a light throughout his entire time at Maranello.

What made Gilles Villeneuve special? Perhaps it was his uncomplicated temperament. Maybe just his simplistic desire to drive flat-out on every occasion. Or his total belief in his own judgement and ability. Whatever it was, you could always sense everybody craning their necks waiting for him to come into view. He was one of those rare talents who seemed capable of coaxing 101 per cent from the racing car he was driving.

Some of Gilles Villeneuve's greatest races were the ones he failed to win. Fifth place from the back of the grid at Montreal in 1980, driving in pouring rain with the hopeless Ferrari 312T5. Or third the following year with the 126CK turbo, the car having progressively shed its crumbling nose wing, eventually to leave its hapless driver with no aerodynamic downforce at all on the front end. Or spinning off under pressure from Nelson Piquet's illegally underweight Brabham at Rio. Or following Jody Scheckter home dutifully in second place at Monza in 1979, never even considering overtaking him in breach of team orders.

Gilles Villeneuve was the embodiment of all those primeval urges which originally fired man's competitive spirit. He just happened to find the outlet for his talent in a racing car. Like a comet, he flared brilliantly in the Formula 1 firmament. The light was soon extinguished, but the after-glow continues to linger in the mind's eye of enthusiasts the world over more than a decade after his death.

Gilles Villeneuve (left) and Didier Pironi. Gilles was killed at Zolder less than a fortnight after his French team-mate duped him out of a rightful win in the San Marino GP at Imola. (LAT)

Postlethwaite's initial temptation was to follow the example of McLaren and Lotus and pursue a carbon-fibre composite chassis design, but the Maranello factory did not yet have the experience necessary to tackle such a project. Instead, and as an interim measure for 1982, Harvey built the 126C2 monocoque from bonded Nomex honeycomb sheeting.

It was to be a great improvement on the old car and, with ever-improving throttle response from the V6 engine, Ferrari looked forward to 1982 with great optimism. Yet events early in the year would unfold to produce a bitter tragedy which, in retrospect, should certainly have been avoided by all concerned.

After a row at the Brazilian GP the FOCA-aligned Formula 1 teams opted out of the San Marino GP at Imola. That left Ferrari to square up to Renault and a rather sparse field of also-rans, including the Tyrrell team which broke the FOCA boycott in deference to its Italian sponsor, plus Osella, ATS and the fledgeling Toleman outfit. The Italian fans simply loved it, because after the Renaults wilted, Villeneuve and Pironi were left to battle it out together.

Ferrari team etiquette has always demanded that its drivers hold position the moment they assume first and second places. They are reminded to do so by a 'Slow' signal which is shown to them from the pit wall. Although Pironi theoretically broke this rule by overtaking Villeneuve, Gilles thought that he was simply trying to put on a show for the crowd. It was understandable, given the meagre field.

But Villeneuve was about to be stabbed in the back. Mid-way round the last lap, Pironi slipstreamed by into the lead and, suddenly realising he'd been duped, Gilles found himself unable to get back ahead. His simmer-ing indignation was fuelled by Pironi's bland assurance: 'No, there were no team orders.' It was a lie.

The following week, Villeneuve talked at length to my long-time friend and colleague Nigel Roebuck, the Grand Prix editor of the British weekly magazine *Autosport*. The subject of their conversation formed the basis for his personal 'Fifth Column' in the subsequent issue of the magazine and was later included in Roebuck's book *Inside Formula 1* (Patrick Stephens, 1989).

Villeneuve talked about his brief visit to the rostrum: 'He [Pironi] was there looking like the hero who won the race, and I looked like the spoiled bastard who sulked. I knew it would look like that, but still I thought it was better to get away.

'I haven't said a word to him, and I'm not going to again – ever. I have

Gilles Villeneuve practising the Ferrari 126C2 at Zolder on the last day of his life – 8 May 1982. The brilliant Canadian was killed later in this practice session when he collided with the March 821 driven by Jochen Mass. (Phipps Photographic)

declared war. I will do my own thing in future. It's war. Absolute war.'

Villeneuve rightly made the point that he had followed in Jody Scheckter's wheel tracks at Monza in 1979, knowing he only had to overtake his team-mate to become World Champion. Then he returned to the subject of Imola.

'People seemed to think that we had the battle of our lives,' he fumed. 'Jesus Christ! I'd been ahead of him for most of the race and was a second and a half quicker than him. Second is one thing, but second because he steals it, that's something else.'

Enzo Ferrari followed this episode by taking the unprecedented step of issuing a press release which sided with Villeneuve. Two weeks later, Gilles was dead, his Ferrari 126C2 somersaulting to destruction over the back of Jochen Mass's dawdling

March 721 during qualifying for the Belgian GP at Zolder. Pironi had beaten his time and Villeneuve was trying to respond.

Harvey Postlethwaite recalls him to this day with enormous affection: 'He was great. Given the choice of being in the lead and destroying his tyres, or going carefully and finishing third, Gilles would always choose the former.

'Jody Scheckter would always choose the latter, and he was World Champion. Gilles wasn't. It wasn't that Gilles couldn't have done it – he could have done it as well as any man – but there was something in him that wouldn't *allow* him to do it.'

The 1982 season continued as a dark and dismal nightmare for the Ferrari team. In Canada, Pironi stalled on pole position and was rammed from behind by new boy

Ricardo Paletti's Osella. The young Italian was killed. Then at Hockenheim, practising in the pouring rain prior to the German GP, Didier Pironi ran full tilt into the back of Alain Prost's Renault.

I had just arrived in the press car park behind the Sachscurve grandstand when I heard a fearful metallic clang, looked up and saw a Ferrari hurtling through the air at tree-top level. It slammed back on to the circuit, leaving its hapless driver trapped in the wrecked monocoque with terrible leg injuries.

It was the end of Didier Pironi's racing career, although his newly recruited team-mate Patrick Tambay raised Ferrari morale the following afternoon with a timely second victory of the season. For Pironi, ahead lay more than 30 operations to fix his shattered limbs. Yet the accident in no way impaired his taste for adventure. In the summer of 1987 he would die in a powerboat accident off

Patrick Tambay won the 1983 San Marino GP for Ferrari in the Postlethwaite-designed 126C2 which helped win Maranello its most recent Constructors' World Championship. (LAT)

the Isle of Wight. As usual, he was flat-out at the time.

To say that Ferrari took years to recover from the loss of its two star drivers in 1982 would be no understatement. In 1983, Tambay was joined by former Renault man René Arnoux. They were both fine drivers, inspired on their day, yet neither quite in the same class as the two men they replaced. They would win races occasionally and help Ferrari to retain its 1982 Constructors' crown the following year. Yet how many people recall that?

The first carbon-fibre composite Ferrari Formula 1 car appeared midway through the 1983 season. Postlethwaite's technical recipe was effectively to build a development of the C2 round a chassis made from this new material. It worked well, Arnoux winning on its race debut at Hockenheim and later at Zandvoort. Yet it was not quite enough for the Frenchman to qualify for the final Drivers' Championship shoot-out which came down to a two-horse race between Alain Prost and Nelson Piquet, the Brazilian winning the day.

On the technical side, Ferrari became involved in the development of a complex water injection system in conjunction with Agip, its long-time fuel sponsor. This system mimicked the principle which was used to cool jet engines – the Agip technicians having developed a means whereby a globule of water could be encapsulated within a globule of petrol.

Upon combustion, the globule of water turned to steam and exploded the surrounding petrol, theoretically giving increased atomisation and

Tambay refuelling in the 1983 Dutch GP. Such high-pressure refuelling systems would eventually be banned at the end of the year. (Phipps Photographic)

Patrick Tambay at Zandvoort in the 1983 Dutch Grand Prix. The distinctive sit-up driving position of the Ferrari 126C3 reflected just how much fuel needed to be packaged in behind the driver. (Phipps Photographic)

René Arnoux (left) and Michele Alboreto at the official unveiling of the 1984 Ferrari turbo – the 126C4.

improved mixture control within the combustion chamber. In 1983 this development eventually attracted a protest from Ken Tyrrell on the basis that the water was an illegal power-boosting additive. Technically, he may have been right, but Ken got no change from the governing body after a protracted legal battle.

In 1984, Tambay was replaced in the Ferrari line-up by Michele Alboreto, the young Italian driver who had spent the previous three seasons driving for Ken Tyrrell. 'When Alboreto is available, there will be a place for him in one of our cars,' said Mr Ferrari on several occasions. He was as good as his word, and the curly-haired Michele, one of the nicest guys in the Formula 1 business, duly drove his first race at Rio in a Ferrari 126C4.

Like its immediate forebears, the C4 was quite a decent car, but it found itself ranged against formidable opposition. The 1984 season was all about the McLaren team's dominance with their TAG-Porsche-engined cars and Michelin tyres. Apart from a runaway win in the Belgian GP at Zolder, Michele didn't get much of a look in.

The Italian media clearly didn't think much of this state of affairs. In the run-up to the Italian GP, Mauro Forghieri was under pressure and opted to stay away from Monza. In the meantime, Harvey Postlethwaite took a timely holiday in the UK, not wanting to embarrass his more experienced colleague.

Nevertheless, Forghieri was soon moved sideways into the *Reparto Ufficio Richerche Studi Svanzati* – a department dealing with long-term engineering projects for the whole group. Harvey was left in charge and did his best in the closing moments of another season which the entire team would quickly try to forget.

Forghieri in characteristically agitated debate with Patrick Tambay at the Osterreichring in 1983. (Author)

Enzo Ferrari with Alboreto (left) and Gerhard Berger. Barely a month after the death of the company's founder, these two drivers delivered a 1–2 victory at Monza in their Ferraris. (IPA)

Michele Alboreto at Montreal in 1984, with the Ferrari 126C4 running ahead of Elio de Angelis's Lotus-Renault. (Phipps Photographic)

The 1985 season started with another evolutionary Formula 1 machine, now dubbed 156/85. Alboreto opened the year with a strong second place in the Brazilian GP at Rio behind Alain Prost's McLaren-TAG, but there was a big upheaval after this race when Arnoux and Mr Ferrari agreed to go their own ways, and the Frenchman was abruptly sacked.

No official explanation for his dismissal has ever been offered, leaving the way open to wild speculation that Arnoux had overwhelming problems with his personal life. He was replaced by Stefan Johansson, the Swedish driver being generously released from his commitment to the Toleman Formula 1 team.

Johansson almost won the San Marino GP only for his car to run out of fuel in the closing moments of the race. 'We lost the race, but I have found the driver,' said Mr Ferrari after Stefan's energetic chase through to the front of the field. It was a slightly premature judgement; the Swede was undeniably talented, but perhaps just a little too nice to have the necessary ruthless edge that makes a consistent winner.

The 1985 season saw Ferrari come closer to winning a Driver's World Championship than at any time for six seasons. Alboreto drove brilliantly to finish second at Monaco – only a puncture preventing him from winning. He and Stefan finished 1–2 in the Canadian GP at Montreal, a result which propelled Michele into the lead of the title points table where he stayed for two months before succumbing to the steadily advancing Prost.

Alboreto would also win the German GP at the new Nürburgring, defeating Prost's McLaren in a straight fight. 'Alain had a better car than me, so it was good to be able to stay in front of him,' he said.

Even so, the Ferrari 156/85 development just wasn't sustainable. It wasn't just that the V6 turbos failed to balance fuel efficiency and performance in a way that could put them on a par with the McLaren-TAGs, but the team was

René Arnoux was an unpredictable performer, but on his day could be absolutely brilliant. Here he heads for second place in the one-off 1984 Dallas Grand Prix.

also lacking sufficient facilities for aerodynamic development.

Not until the autumn of 1986 would such a facility be available within the extended premises of the competition department, and its first real benefit was not fully felt until mid-way through the following year.

The 1986 season passed in something of a blur. The new cars were now dubbed F186s, another example of the team's appetite for back-tracking. Endless turbo troubles, brake problems and poor handling relegated the Ferraris firmly to the position of also-rans. Alboreto and Johansson were getting restless, but not as restless as Enzo Ferrari and, particularly, Fiat President Vittorio Ghidella who had become extremely anxious indeed about the whole situation.

Even before the end of the 1986 season, steps had been taken to deal with the situation. A new chief designer was required and an approach was made to John Barnard, the man behind the McLaren-TAGs, who had recently split irrevocably from his former partner Ron Dennis.

But Barnard was not interested in relocating to Italy. Thus a deal was hammered out whereby he would organise a UK-based design department – titled Guildford Technical Office, or GTO, a rather corny acronym in view of the significance of those initials to the Maranello legend.

His main brief was to outline the design of a totally new car to conform to the 3.5-litre naturally-aspirated regulations which were due to start in 1989, as well as doing what he could to influence the performance of the 1987 and 1988 turbo cars, work on which had already been started by Austrian engineer Gustav Brunner.

Alboreto remained on the driving strength for 1987, now partnered by Gerhard Berger who had joined from Benetton. Johansson was this particular year's sacrificial lamb, although he soon arranged a drive with McLaren. 'I don't think I ever got to grips with things at Ferrari, because I didn't know the right channels to use in my dealings with the team,' he would later reflect.

The politics of the turbo revolution

THE 1982 WORLD Championship was fought out against the backdrop of a bitter dispute between the predominantly British-based teams aligned with Bernie Ecclestone and the Formula 1 Constructors' Association, and the 'grandees', a term coined to embrace major car makers Renault and Ferrari (and not too-indirectly Fiat, of course).

The British teams, most of whom used off-the-shelf Cosworth DFV engines, now found themselves fighting a losing battle with the turbo brigade in terms of power output, and there seemed no way of reversing this. In an effort to come to terms with the problem, the British teams fitted their cars with water bottles, ostensibly for brake-cooling purposes.

In fact, this was a clever device to permit the cars to run below the minimum weight limit during the race and then – since the rules permitted all liquid receptacles to be topped up before post-GP scrutineering – bring them back to legality by pouring in water after the finish.

Renault protested against this loophole after the Brazilian GP, with the result that Nelson Piquet's winning Brabham and the second-placed Williams of Keke Rosberg were disqualified. This looked as though it would turn out to be a defining moment in contemporary Formula 1 history. The Brabham and Williams team lodged appeals with the FIA. Both were turned down, Prost's third-placed Renault was confirmed as the race winner – and the FOCA teams boycotted the San Marino GP at Imola.

The eventual outcome of all this was the formulation and signing of the Concorde Agreement, a complex protocol which thereafter governed the way in which Formula 1 rules were implemented as well as the commercial side of the sport, most importantly the television revenues which Ecclestone largely controlled.

'I wanted to have the car tested in a wind tunnel, for example, but it never happened. Maybe I just went about it all the wrong way.'

For the last two years of the turbo 1.5-litre engine regulations, fuel capacity and boost pressure were to be progressively restricted. In 1987 the respective limits were 195-litres/4-bar, while in 1988 they would be 150-litres/2.5-bar. In order to make the best of these new requirements, a new 90-degree V6 engine was introduced at the start of 1987 coupled with a longitudinal six-speed gearbox which had been one of Barnard's key technical requirements from the outset.

Despite all this effort, from the start of the year it was clear that Ferrari could match neither TAG-Porsche nor Honda in the power-versus-consumption stakes. Barnard inevitably found himself called to account by nervous team director Marco Piccinini, and he was summoned to Hockenheim for an embarrassing 'trial by press' over the German GP weekend.

All this was prompted by an interview in the French sporting paper *L'Equipe* in which Alboreto had commented: 'Barnard is like a surgeon trying to carry out a complex operation via a long distance telephone call.' It was not an observation that was calculated to make for an easy working relationship between the two. Alboreto also objected to what he regarded as Barnard's autocratic approach to the design process.

Nevertheless, Ferrari was beginning to come good again. Berger would have won the Portuguese GP at Estoril had he not spun off under pressure from Prost's McLaren. But the Austrian made up for this with a superb victory in the inaugural Japanese GP at Suzuka, a race from which Alboreto also emerged with considerable credit after climbing through to fourth place after his clutch had gone solid at the start, causing him to stall the car and then get away last after a push-start.

This was Ferrari's first win in almost two-and-a-half years, bringing to an end the team's longest-ever period in Formula 1 without a race victory. Berger immediately repeated this with a similarly impressive win in the Australian GP at Adelaide, Alboreto taking second after Ayrton Senna's Lotus-Honda, the original runner-up, was disqualified for a rule infringement relating to extra brake cooling ducts which had been fitted especially for this race.

Barnard had originally been convinced that a switch to the 3.5-litre naturally-aspirated car would be the right route for 1988, an interim season in which teams could either take this option, or retain their turbocharged engines. But eventually he opted for continuing with the turbos.

Just when it looked as though Ferrari was poised to win races consistently, the new McLaren-Honda partnership went into action at the start of 1988. With Prost and Senna on their driving strength, the McLarens won a record 15 out of 16 races. If it hadn't been for the intervention of backmarker Jean-Louis Schlesser (the Frenchman subbing for Nigel Mansell) in a Williams, taking Senna off in the closing stages at Monza, they would have achieved a full house.

This slip allowed Berger and

Ferrari's twin-turbo V6 used water injection specially developed in conjunction with Agip. The size of that huge fuel cell tells you everything about 1.5-litre turbocharged racing engines running on unrestricted boost! (LAT)

Alboreto to finish 1–2 in the Italian GP with their Ferrari Formula 1/87/88Cs. But it was too late for Enzo Ferrari's pleasure. Three weeks earlier, on 14 August 1988, the man who had become the most famous name in motor racing died at the age of 90 years. He had been ailing for some time, and Fiat nominee Pier-Giorgio Cappelli immediately took over the running of the operation; Piero Lardi having been displaced from any position of influence shortly before his father's death.

It had been a complicated season. Harvey Postlethwaite went back to Britain to join Tyrrell, taking with him aerodynamicist Jean-Claude Migeot. Engine wizard Jean-Jacques His, meanwhile, switched to the Renault Sport operation, leaving Ildo Renzetti in charge of Maranello's engine department.

Alboreto was dropped from the

Ferrari line-up at the end of 1988, making way for Nigel Mansell's high-profile recruitment the following year. The pleasant Italian was by then at the end of his rope with Maranello, and said so; candidly.

'By the end of 1987, I just knew that I wouldn't be with Ferrari in 1989,' he confessed. 'The tensions built up to the point where I found myself thinking that I really needed a very quiet winter if I was going to be able to stand another season driving for them.

'Life is extremely complicated at Ferrari. OK, so I got on well with Harvey Postlethwaite, a man for whom I've got a great regard. But when other people in the management decide you are no longer capable of winning, they allow those feelings to filter through the team. You feel it, sense it. It is not comfortable, I can tell you.'

However, Michele was quick to say that he in no way blamed Gerhard Berger's arrival in the team at the start of 1987 for his fall from grace. 'I don't believe this situation had anything to do with Gerhard,' he insisted, 'because in the middle of 1988 we were matching each other's performance. But people are always searching for any excuse if Ferrari is not winning, and a lot of this comes from the Italian media which is afraid to go against Ferrari or be too critical.'

Alboreto really warmed to this particular subject: 'The Ferrari team is so important in Italy that if you want to sell papers and magazines, you must always focus on Ferrari, make it headlines. And if you don't talk about Ferrari in the appropriate way, you won't get any information from them.

'The media is capable of convincing the Ferrari management about any aspect of their cars' performance. They will believe the media far more readily than the driver. For example, during 1984 and 1985, we kept saying that we hadn't got enough power.

'But then some newspaper would say "Ah, but Ferrari has maximum speed in a straight line – the engine is

Michele Alboreto and designer John Barnard – not the most sympathetic of partnerships.
(Phipps Photographic)

good." So the Ferrari management thinks the engine is good. So we drivers say "Yes, maybe the speed is good, but that's because we're not running any wing on the straight. But the driveability of the engine is no good because at the bottom of the rev range we have no power."

'Yet in these circumstances they tend to think this is an excuse. They think the driver isn't trying because he hasn't produced the lap time. That's how these things work at Ferrari.'

Alboreto's position was further strained by his somewhat uneasy personal relationship with John Barnard, Ferrari's then incoming new Technical Director. From the outset the Italian driver had doubted the effectiveness of Barnard's UK-based design studio.

'I have nothing against John,' he insisted, 'but I did not believe he was capable of being the Big Chief as far as running the design department was concerned. He is very good designing some parts of the car, but not to be responsible for the whole team.

'Simply stamping your views on everybody else is wrong, taking his attitude "I'm the chief, so I'll decide." You must understand other people's opinions. With over 150 people in the team, they must be encouraged to pull in the same direction.'

Michele left Maranello with hardly a backward glance. He had no regrets that he would not be around to drive the automatic transmission 3.5-litre Ferrari 640 which he dismissed as over-complex and incapable of offering any worthwhile performance advantage.

'To be honest, I feel very sorry for Nigel Mansell,' he remarked. Twelve months later Alboreto was to be proved wide of the mark; in this judgement at least.

Chapter 12

Life after Enzo

Enzo Ferrari's legacy lived on after his death in the form of the V12 engine which would power the first of the new 3.5-litre generation cars in 1989. True enough, John Barnard was the man who opted for the V12 route, but that he was able to do so was a direct reflection on the Old Man's continuing influence in Formula 1 even in the last years of his long life.

Back in early 1986, when the question of a new naturally-aspirated formula was being discussed, there was pressure from some UK-based teams to impose an eight-cylinder limit. Ferrari signalled his preference for a 12-cylinder limit, discreetly underlining this by designing and building an Indycar chassis and engine.

The sub-text of his message was clear. For many years he'd expressed the view that the one race he'd always been disappointed never to win was the Indianapolis 500. Ever since Alberto Ascari had made an abortive trip to the Brickyard in 1953, and Luigi Musso had so spectacularly taken on the Indy roadsters with the 4.1-litre V12 Ferrari on the US cars' second visit to Monza in 1958, the great American race had continued to fascinate Enzo Ferrari.

By the mid-1980s, however, the Indy 500 had come to be regarded as an anti-Formula 1 totem, somehow symbolic of Grand Prix racing's inability to become established in the USA. In a nutshell, anybody committing to Indycar racing was regarded as an outcast by the Formula 1 fraternity, as if they were throwing in their hand with the enemy. But for Enzo Ferrari to show an active interest in Indycars to the point of actually building a machine for the US race was nothing short of a potential disaster. The Formula 1 rules were changed to accommodate 12-cylinder engines – and the Indycar Ferrari was consigned to the role of museum piece.

Barnard's new Formula 1 design for the 1989 season was a major step forward in several key respects and, in retrospect, can probably be regarded as one of the most imaginative concepts of the British engineer's Grand Prix career.

The prototype of the new Ferrari – dubbed the 639 – was first unveiled at Fiorano in July 1988. Distinguished by its tall side-pods, which extended forward almost to the rear of the front wheels, the new machine was powered by a brand new 65-degree engine producing around 600bhp at 12,500rpm.

The most radical aspect of the car's technical specification was an electronically activated change mechanism for its seven-speed gearbox. This was activated by a pair of levers behind the steering wheel, allowing the drivers to change gear by the application of finger-tip pressure.

Yet it was absolutely characteristic of the jumpy, immediate post-Enzo era at Maranello that the management got nervous at the last moment and suggested that Barnard should develop a manual gearbox version of the car. This very nearly became a resignation issue, for John rightly pointed out that it simply wasn't feasible to try installing a manual gearchange mechanism on a design which was already nearing completion. He got his way and the semi-automatic Ferrari duly made its Formula 1 debut.

This, as we have previously seen, was the reason Michele Alboreto shed no tears at being discarded by Maranello. He reckoned the system would be excessively complex and terminally unreliable. In fact, the definitive Barnard-designed Ferrari 640 – effectively a tidied-up version of the 639 test car – won on its first outing, the 1989 Brazilian GP at Rio.

Nigel Mansell was the man who achieved this notable success on his maiden drive for the famous Italian team. Ironically, a spate of problems in practice had convinced him he had no chance in the race. He had booked first class tickets for himself and his wife Rosanne on the 4.30pm British Airways flight back to Europe that Sunday afternoon, believing his car would be an early retirement, and a quick helicopter flight to the airport would enable him to make an early exit. In the event, the 640 never missed a beat all afternoon.

However, the mood of euphoria surrounding the Ferrari 640's debut victory quickly gave way to concern and alarm. Going into the fourth lap of the San Marino GP at Imola, the second round of the title chase, Mansell's team-mate Gerhard Berger veered off the track to the right and slammed into the concrete wall at virtually the same point where Ayrton Senna would be killed five years later.

The Ferrari made contact with a glancing blow, but it was enough to force its right-hand radiator back into the fuel cell running along the side of the cockpit. The chassis was totally destroyed in the impact, the car bursting into flames on the spot.

Berger was saved by the speedy intervention of the fire marshals. Within 15 seconds of the wrecked Ferrari coming to rest, the crew of an Alfa Romeo 164 fire tender were on the spot and they successfully quelled the conflagration within another eight seconds. A technical post-mortem on the accident indicated that the left-front aerofoil came off the car, possibly the result of it being progressively over-strained by trips over the kerbs during practice and qualifying.

Behind the scenes, however, life at Ferrari was being complicated by pressure to re-establish the Formula 1 team's technical base at Maranello. This pressure now came from Fiat

Nigel Mansell discusses the possibility of joining Ferrari with Marco Piccinini in the summer of 1988. (Diana Burnett)

The all-new Ferrari 3.5-litre V12 engine which powered the new breed of John Barnard-designed Formula 1 cars from the start of 1989. (Phipps Photographic)

Nigel Mansell wins the 1989 Brazilian GP at Rio de Janeiro, first time out in the new Barnard-designed Ferrari 640. (Phipps Photographic)

whose stake in the Ferrari company, which had originally started at 50 per cent in 1969, now rose to 90 per cent following the founder's death.

Barnard was not interested in relocating to Italy and, after lengthy debates with new Ferrari president Piero Fusaro – the first Fiat nominee to take this post – it was announced in June 1989 that John's tenure with the team would terminate at the end of October.

Fusaro also found himself at the centre of a furore later in the season when Mansell, having illegally reversed in the pit lane during a routine tyre change whilst leading the Portuguese GP, was fined $50,000 for repeatedly ignoring the black flag on his return to the race. This lapse

ended in near-disaster when the Englishman punted Ayrton Senna's McLaren off the road.

While Berger went through to win the race for Ferrari, Fusaro had the unenviable task of trying to calm the outraged Mansell, who indignantly threatened to retire from Formula 1. Not that this prevented the FIA from acceding to the Portuguese steward's request that Nigel should be banned from the following weekend's Spanish GP at Jerez. Mansell was duly back in the cockpit in time for the Japanese GP, where he broke a driveshaft accelerating back into the race after a pit stop, but his racing career continued to prosper.

For the 1990 season Alain Prost joined Mansell in the Ferrari line-up,

with Gerhard Berger transferring across to fill the place vacated by the Frenchman alongside Ayrton Senna in the McLaren-Honda squad. On the design side, Steve Nichols joined the talented Enrique Scalabroni – who did much of the updating work on Barnard's original 640 concept – on the technical staff as chief designer in the aftermath of Barnard's departure.

Perhaps piqued at losing a key member of his design staff as well as Prost, McLaren boss Ron Dennis opened the 1990 season by accusing Ferrari, at a press briefing in Brazil, of enticing Nichols away from his team by under-the-table payments. Dennis subsequently considered his position and, appreciating that he had been excessively outspoken, went to meet Fusaro and Ferrari deputy chairman Piero Lardi Ferrari.

A bulletin was later issued, stating:

'After a frank exchange of views, Mr Dennis reassured Mr Fusaro that his comments were never intended to suggest that Ferrari had acted improperly, or in a manner which was calculated to damage the spirit of fair play.'

Later the McLaren chief explained: 'I did not go to that press briefing with a prepared statement; my remarks were unfortunately in response to a well-aimed question, which, I admit, touched a sensitive spot.

'My reaction was to say that, if the questioner was being so direct, I wanted to put the record straight. The most significant reason for these transfers was the personal material benefits offered.'

What Dennis was getting at had long been accepted. Most key personnel regarded a stint at Ferrari as a bonus year, a means of putting something aside for their pension fund. Working for Ferrari in Formula 1 traditionally involved more tangential aggravation and political intrigue than just about any other team in the business.

With that in mind, to get key technical staff to come from the UK, the Italian company *had* to pay over the odds. In the post-Enzo Ferrari era, it was all too-easy to conclude that many people were working for the company simply because it offered a spectacularly good pay day; not

Unveiling of the 1990 Ferrari 641 with new boy Alain Prost (left) and a somewhat disgruntled looking Nigel Mansell.

because they were particularly concerned with any passion for the company's traditions.

Prost and Mansell proved a volatile pairing, particularly as everything seemed to go the Frenchman's way during the first half of the season. By the time they arrived at Silverstone for the British GP, Prost led the Championship with 41 points to Senna's 29, while Mansell trailed a joint sixth on only 13.

Prost had already won three races and would bag his fourth when Mansell's Ferrari gearbox went haywire after he'd qualified superbly on pole position and led commandingly in the early stages. In a knee-jerk response to his disappointment, Mansell announced that he would retire from racing at the end of the year.

Thereafter, everything went wrong for Mansell. He retired an only lightly damaged car at Hockenheim, hurt his wrist in a silly collision with Berger's McLaren in Hungary and then trailed round midfield after being forced to take the spare car following a first corner shunt which saw the Belgian GP red-flagged at the end of the opening lap.

What happened next was that Ferrari negotiated for Jean Alesi to replace Mansell in 1991. Once that was tied up, Nigel announced that he had changed his mind about retirement – largely under overwhelming pressure from his adoring fans – and signed for Williams. Prost, meanwhile, found his position in the team undermined when Mansell, in his view at least, ganged up with Senna to thwart his efforts in the Portuguese GP at Estoril.

The whys and wherefores of this episode have never been satisfactorily explained. Many observers recall seeing Mansell and Senna in deep conversation in a hire car the evening before the race. Was Senna trying to persuade Nigel that Prost was the Diabolical Enemy? And, if so, did Mansell need much persuading?

At the start, Mansell's pole position 640 veered across in front of Prost, allowing Senna to take an immediate lead. Ayrton eventually finished second behind Nigel, with Alain third.

'Ferrari doesn't deserve to be World Champion,' said the furious Prost after climbing from the cockpit. 'It is a team without directive and without strategy trying to win against a well-structured team like McLaren. Berger helped Senna to the maximum to win the race.'

A week later, Prost won the Spanish GP at Jerez where Mansell played second fiddle to finish second. Then came the Japanese GP at Suzuka where Alain's hopes of becoming the first Ferrari champion driver in 11 years were wiped out when Senna used his McLaren as a battering ram going into the first corner and wiped both cars out of the race.

'If everybody wants to drive in this way, then the sport is finished,' said Prost. He was right, of course. Senna had overstepped the boundaries of etiquette and principle, yet such was the force of his dynamic personality that even some of the sport's most senior figures adopted a craven attitude of support towards his disgraceful behaviour. In truth, they should have hung their heads in shame for failing to condemn a suicidal piece of driving which could well have ended in a fatal accident.

Ferrari Vice President Cesare Romiti best summed it up when he hinted that Ferrari might consider withdrawing from Formula 1. 'We do not feel part of this world without rules,' he noted. Piero Fusaro also called upon FIA President Jean-Marie Balestre to legislate against such wayward driving tactics.

Either way, Ferrari's hopes of a World Championship had been wrecked. Prost went into the 1991 season with Alesi as his partner, but there were to be no more Grand Prix victories coming their way. Prost also found himself increasingly at odds with the team who at least ditched Fiorio as team manager mid-way through the season. Yet it would not be enough.

Fusaro then announced that Piero Lardi Ferrari would head up the team together with ex-Lancia engineer Claudio Lombardi and Marco Piccinini, the shrewd and politically astute lawyer who had been Enzo Ferrari's *éminence grise* in the late 1970s and remains a member of the Ferrari company's board of directors to this day. Technical responsibility was now already in the hands of Pier-Guido Castelli, another Fiat-nominated engineer, the bulk of whose experience had been gained in road car development.

All this was followed by an amazing comment by Umberto Agnelli, younger brother of the Fiat overlord, who expressed his public preference for Ayrton Senna. This came at a time when much of the Italian media seemed to be baying for Prost's blood, yet the Frenchman refused to be intimidated.

Fusaro should have told the media where to get off, but it was absolutely characteristic that the Ferrari management should be intimidated by the press after Prost had expressed his personal opinion about the Italian newspapers. Astonishingly, they all demanded what amounted to an apology, and Fusaro suggested that Prost should provide just that.

Rightly, Alain would not be intimidated. 'This is the last straw in a ridiculous sequence of events,' he said. 'I suppose it was the same for John Barnard when he was working here, but I never imagined the influence of the press would be so considerable.'

In the end, after a season in which the Steve Nichols update of Barnard's original design – now dubbed the 643 – failed to win a single race, Prost was fired before the final round of the title chase. His offence was to have described the Ferrari 643 as 'a truck'. But his judgement was correct, and Ferrari's absurd intransigence had now cost them the services of one of the greatest Grand Prix drivers of all time.

Ironically, a matter of months separated the departure of Alain Prost and the return of Luca Cordero di Montezemolo to the Ferrari fold as company President. There wasn't much Luca could do about the indifferent 1992 season which unfolded in

dismal fashion for Alesi and his new team-mate Ivan Capelli. But he could put in place changes which, he believed, would result in an upturn in fortunes for 1993.

Part of this new look involved appointing Niki Lauda as a special consultant to the team. Some dismissed this as window dressing, a nostalgic trip down Memory Lane in an attempt to revive memories of the mid-1970s. But Niki was certainly useful behind the scenes, in particular when he approached John Barnard with a proposition that he return to the Ferrari fold in charge of another UK-based technical studio.

Objectively, one is bound to wonder what on earth Ferrari thought it was doing. Having closed down GTO, and sold the premises to McLaren Cars as

a base for specialist carbon-fibre work for their new Formula 1 super-performance road car, the Italian company now started up Ferrari Design & Development in the factory next door. On the face of it, this was the economics of the madhouse!

Harvey Postlethwaite had gone back to Maranello again for a second stint at the end of 1991 and, although his F92A design had been bedevilled by technical problems throughout the 1992 season, it was envisaged that he would continue to remain in charge at the Italian end of the operation into 1993. The cars would be designed in Britain under Barnard's direction and then built in Maranello under Postlethwaite's control.

In 1993 Gerhard Berger also arrived on the scene as *de facto* team leader.

Ferrari had a dismal 1993 season with the F93A, largely because of unreliability of the car's active suspension system. Here Jean Alesi presses on hard in the Portuguese GP at Estoril, a race he led briefly in the opening stages.

This had the effect of unsettling Alesi, yet this was unquestionably the right strategy to adopt. Gerhard was more mature and experienced in the ways of Formula 1. He was also rather more tolerant than Alesi and would eventually relinquish his priority access to the spare car in an effort to keep his team-mate happy and contribute to the overall atmosphere in the team.

In 1993, Barnard produced what was essentially a revised version of the previous year's twin-floor Ferrari F92A. However, most of this season was written off in developing an active suspension system in preparation for 1994. But they had reckoned without the rule makers who decided to ban active suspension from the end of 1993, although it took until the German GP in late July before any official edict was made.

At the end of that season, Harvey Postlethwaite left to rejoin Tyrrell. 'I was beginning to find the whole thing [Ferrari] a little too cumbersome for my taste,' he confessed. 'I'd had some good times with Ferrari, especially first time round when the Old Man was alive, but by the end I had too many memories of sitting in planning meetings with about 40 other people, all talking, all getting nowhere.'

However, June 1993 also saw the arrival of former Peugeot competitions manager Jean Todt, fresh from master-minding the French team's second straight Le Mans victory. Todt would become a major asset to the team. Calm, pragmatic and very intelligent, he would be regarded by some observers as rather aloof. But within the Ferrari team ranks he quickly came to be admired and respected.

Jean Alesi tries to force his Ferrari 412T1 through on the inside of Damon Hill's Williams during the 1994 Canadian GP at Montreal. (ICN)

Todt was sufficiently shrewd to appreciate that he simply couldn't artificially force the pace of Ferrari's Formula 1 recovery. The 1993 season may have been another dismal affair, but the Prancing Horse began to display serious form in 1994 when the new Barnard-designed 412T1 took to the circuits.

It was at the wheel of this car that Gerhard Berger would win the German GP at Hockenheim, yet there were still development glitches which tended to throw a spotlight on the difficulties involved in designing the car in Britain while the team's engine department remained in Italy.

'We started to fall foul of the politics,' reflected Barnard. 'The fundamental thing which cocked it all up was the cooling, because the engine department did not do what I asked them to do, which was to balance the water flows, side to side.'

This caused enormous problems when the changes in the aerodynamic rules following Ayrton Senna's death at Imola required the fitting of aerodynamic side deflectors – 'barge boards' – ahead of the radiators in order to compensate for limitations on the front wing end-plates.

Eventually the problem was solved by fitting a by-pass tube between the radiators on either side of the chassis, but much time was wasted trying to sort out this seemingly insoluble problem.

During 1994 the team started out with a 65-degree V12, but Lombardi's engine department was also working on a new 75-degree unit which was tipped to develop 820bhp at 15,800rpm in 3.5-litre form, but which was reduced to 3-litre trim in line with the new engine capacity limit introduced as part of a package to reduce lap speeds in 1995.

For 1995 Barnard came up with the classically handsome 412T2 with its much lower nose configuration. This was competitive from the outset, with Alesi pressuring Damon Hill's Williams very hard at one point in the Argentine GP where the two rivals finished in 1–2 formation.

Alesi would use the 412T2 to score

Jean Alesi's Ferrari 412T2 after damaging its nose wing in a collision with Schumacher's Benetton in the 1995 Australian GP at Adelaide. (ICN)

Alesi in characteristic pose, hot-rodding his Ferrari 412T2 through the gravel trap during practice for the 1995 Japanese GP at Suzuka. This was the Frenchman's penultimate race for the famous Italian team. (ICN)

what stands at the time of writing (March 1997) as Ferrari's only Grand Prix victory in Montreal. But the Frenchman always displayed a hair-trigger temperament, and that victory in Canada was not enough to guarantee his future. After several undiplomatic outbursts, Luca di Montezemolo made it clear that there was no longer any place for him at Maranello, once Michael Schumacher's signature was secured on a Ferrari contract for 1996.

Berger also left, but on his own terms. It had been anticipated that the popular Austrian, one of the sport's most sensitive and intelligent souls, would remain at Ferrari to partner Schumacher – he was offered another two-year contract at around $12 million a season to do so. Schumacher, the twice World Champion's stipend was a guaranteed minimum $25 million in 1996.

Yet Berger was playing his cards close to his chest. He knew all about being eclipsed by team-mates, having spent three seasons driving alongside Ayrton Senna in the McLaren-Honda squad. But Senna became a close friend. Privately, Gerhard judged there would be much more aggravation involved in racing on even terms with Schumacher. Just before Monza, 1996, he signed to follow his old team-mate Alesi to Benetton.

After it became clear that Berger had other plans, a deal was brokered whereby the Jordan Formula 1 team released Eddie Irvine to partner Schumacher in 1996. The 30-year-old Ulsterman may have displayed a cheerful insouciance to the outside world which some found grossly irritating, but he was shrewd enough to keep his head down and accept his number two role in the Maranello squad with a degree of equanimity.

In 1996, Barnard came up with his first V10-engined car, the Ferrari F310. Almost at the moment of his return to the team in 1993, the British engineer had confronted the Maranello mandarins with the suggestion that they abandon their symbolic V12 and pursue either a V8 or V10 configuration.

To this end, Barnard recruited former Cosworth engineer Stuart Grove to outline plans for a possible Ferrari 3.5-litre V8 engine. Maranello, however, with its dark suspicion of outsiders, conspired to isolate Grove and his small team of engineers. After a year, he reported to Barnard that it was a waste of time. He left and joined Ilmor, makers of the Mercedes Formula 1 and Indycar engines.

Then there was the question of a V10. In an effort to get such an engine quickly, Barnard took Claudio Lombardi on a visit to British engine specialist Brian Hart who had a new V10 running on his test bed. There were suggestions that Brian's V10 might be badged a Ferrari, or that Hart be taken on as a consultant. Neither happened and it was not until 1996 that Ferrari finally took the plunge and built its own V10.

'To a very large extent, we have been building on what went before,' said Barnard in reference to the F310. 'I am very particular about the aerodynamics of my cars, and I suppose you would have to say that the F310 represents the logical conclusion of more than two years' development work on wind tunnel technology for Ferrari.

'To be honest, when I returned to Ferrari in 1992, its aerodynamic development programme had not

Michael Schumacher, Ferrari's new recruit for 1996, betrays his karting heritage. (ICN)

Eddie Irvine heads towards third place with the new V10-engined Ferrari F310 in the 1996 Australian GP at Melbourne. (ICN)

Schumacher blasts the new Ferrari F310 from a brilliant pole position at the start of the 1996 San Marino GP at Imola. He would finish second to Damon Hill's Williams. (ICN)

really progressed as fast as that of many rival teams. During my stint with Benetton we established an extremely sophisticated wind tunnel at the Farnborough-based Royal Aircraft Establishment, but political considerations conspired to keep me from returning to use that wind tunnel once I had joined Ferrari.

'We therefore decided to become involved in a programme with British Aerospace at Filton, near Bristol, the result of which was the development of a half-scale wind tunnel which we've used in the design process of both the 412T2 and the F310. Even so, I would describe the F310 design as evolutionary in concept, maximising aerodynamic possibilities,

although of course it is a totally new car from front to back.'

One of the most outstanding features of the 412T2 design had been its elegant low nose. On the new F310, the nose section has been raised slightly, but it still could hardly be described as 'high nose' in the manner of either the recent Benetton or McLaren designs. It would eventually be fitted with a full high nose in time for the mid-season Canadian GP.

'This question of high and low nose is something which has caused a great deal of examination and investigation in the wind tunnel,' he explains. 'Whatever you do at the front end of the car affects what happens at the back. It's quite simple. You can have a

high nose and that affects how the rear diffuser behaves in a certain way; you can have a low nose, and the diffuser will behave in a subtly different way. But it is a very closely balanced equation and you can make a case for either concept.'

The F310 was eventually developed into a car capable of winning three Grands Prix. Michael Schumacher's 1996 Spanish GP success was a brilliant tour-de-force in conditions of streaming rain, but his subsequent wins in the dry at Spa and Monza were even more impressive.

Even so, the German driver would complain throughout the season that the F310 suffered from a frustrating cornering imbalance which was never quite rectified throughout the year. Yet, second place behind Damon Hill's Williams FW18 in the final race of the year at Suzuka was good enough for Schumacher to vault Ferrari into second place in the final Constructors' Championship order, leap-frogging ahead of Benetton in the closing moments of the season.

By the start of the 1997 season, it was clear that Jean Todt wanted Ferrari's technical base to return to Maranello. Barnard, whose contract with the team did not expire until July 1997, was not interested in going to Italy and the decision was taken for the two parties to go their separate ways.

It was an ironic development. Less than 12 months had passed since Montezemolo delivered a very persuasive lecture to the British specialist press at Nürburgring, emphasising the importance of retaining an involvement in Britain's 'Formula 1 silicon valley'.

Yet the decision to base incoming Chief Designer Rory Byrne and Technical Director Ross Brawn back at Maranello seemed to fly in the face of such assurances.

As far as the new Ferrari F310B was concerned, John admitted that he was rather painted into a corner over its basic specification. It seemed that di Montezemolo and his sporting director Jean Todt wanted a more conventional design for the 1997 season. They didn't quite ask for Barnard to copy a Williams, but the basic concept of the F310B had to be cleared with them before the button was pressed to manufacture the first such machine.

Such design by committee was not in line with Barnard's proven philosophy, but he allowed himself a smile when asked if this annoyed him. 'Let's just say that the F310B was, on purpose, a rather basic design on which to base future development,' he said. 'It was made very clear to me that what was wanted was something quite conventional.'

Even though he had effectively relinquished any further control of the development of his latest progeny, Barnard was confident about the prospects for the F310B – as long as Ferrari's Formula 1 engine department got a grip on its development programme.

'I think it could go quite well,' he predicted. 'Based on some of the information which has filtered back to me from testing, I would say that the new car is as quick as a Benetton. I suppose that leaves us waiting to see how close that will end up to a Williams.

'All in all, I think the F310B is basically quite a sound car, and I know there is still scope on the aerodynamic side for some further tweaking, and there are still a number of options which can be pursued for fine-tuning the suspension set-up.

'But the real question mark must remain how much progress can be made with the engine. The cars will

Defining moment. Michael Schumacher's Ferrari F310 slices inside Jacques Villeneuve's Williams FW18 to take a lead he would never relinquish in the rain-soaked 1996 Spanish GP at Barcelona. (ICN)

Jean Todt: dealing with the drivers

Back in 1960, Phil Hill asked if he could have a slightly modified windscreen on his Ferrari Dino 246 to reduce the head buffeting. Enzo Ferrari strummed his braces and snapped back: 'just keep your foot down and forget about your head!'

Ferrari driver relations have come a long way since those brutally unsentimental days. At the 1994 San Marino GP, Maranello's present sporting director Jean Todt took a distinctly more enlightened view of Gerhard Berger's dilemma in the aftermath of Ayrton Senna's fatal accident.

Gerhard had thrown himself back into the restarted race with a commitment that suggested he was trying to smother his emotions with driving exuberance. He eventually pitted to complain of a rear-end imbalance. Todt simply told him to get out of the car. Putting a sympathetic hand on his shoulder, the Frenchman realised that his driver had done enough for that day.

Think about it. A works Ferrari driver effectively being invited to retire from a home Grand Prix – by Maranello's team manager. A generation earlier, it would have been incomprehensible.

'What is so fantastic about Todt is that he is prepared to sit down and go through all your problems with you,' said Jean Alesi during happier times at Ferrari.

'When something is not right, you can go to him and he will fix the problem. Even if he doesn't understand what your problem is, he wants to understand it, wants to know what is the matter.'

Ironically, even Todt ultimately failed to come to grips with the complexities of Alesi's character. Which was why the Frenchman left Ferrari at the end of 1995 to drive for Benetton.

race for the first time this season with the same engine specification as they finished in Suzuka last October.

'That looked as though it could be a problem, because all the other manufacturers will have made progress with their engine power outputs – Renault has even made a totally new V10! So that could be the area where Ferrari will have to do the most catching-up.'

In the event, Michael Schumacher finished the 1997 Australian GP at Melbourne second behind David Coulthard's McLaren-Mercedes. The new car looked as though it was a pretty convincing machine, although neither of the Williams FW19s – which started on the front row of the grid in the hands of Jacques Villeneuve and Heinz-Harald Frentzen – made it to the finish.

In fact, Villeneuve's race ended at the first corner after Eddie Irvine came bounding down the inside in an over-exuberant overtaking bid which went wrong when he locked up his front wheels. Characteristically, Irvine was unapologetic and shrugged aside any responsibility for the collision which eliminated Villeneuve and Johnny Herbert's Sauber – the Swiss team now using Ferrari engines – on the spot.

Barnard was also rather irked at the initial criticism focused on the F310B during its preliminary tests. In that connection he was hard pressed to suppress his personal reservations about Michael Schumacher. Sure enough, he admired him enormously as a great racing driver, but he was less convinced about aspects of his personal behaviour.

'On a personal level, I find him difficult to warm to, or to get close to,' he admitted. 'It is hard to develop a close working relationship with him. He is also rather aloof, and certainly

Start of the 1997 Australian GP at Melbourne with Michael Schumacher's Ferrari F310B in fourth place behind the Williams FW19s of Heinz-Harald Frentzen and Jacques Villeneuve, and David Coulthard's McLaren MP4/12. Eddie Irvine is right behind Coulthard, about to swing out to the right on the run to the first corner. (ICN)

doesn't have any shortage of self-esteem. In some ways, I suspect that is because he is surrounded by a group of fawning acolytes who keep telling him how wonderful he is.

'On the other hand, the pressure on a young guy of that age must be enormous. All those millions of dollars, private jets and people falling over themselves to make a fuss of you. It's no wonder their heads get turned.'

Few people better understood the complexities and idiosyncracies involved in working with Ferrari than John Barnard. He had worked for Maranello from 1986 to 1989 and from 1993 to the start of this season, on both occasions from specialist design centres he has established in the UK.

He recalls that his first meetings at Maranello involved Mr Ferrari just over 10 years ago. 'It was quite an experience for a 40-year-old to be subjected to the force of his character,' he recalls. 'He really was somebody. And even though he was in his late eighties, you still felt he was a force to be reckoned with.'

Mention Ferrari in the post-Enzo era and Barnard simply smiles. He clearly feels that a succession of Fiat nominees have found it hard to impose a cohesive structure on the operation. It remains a uniquely challenging, perhaps over-emotional, environment.

By the start of 1997 it did not take a clairvoyant to detect that Barnard felt he had been marginalised by Ferrari's Formula 1 operation in Maranello. So, would Ross Brawn and Rory Byrne end up finding themselves clinging together for reassurance within a potentially hostile environment at some stage in the future? 'Could be,' he grinned.

Yet by the start of the 1997 season it was difficult to judge whether Ferrari

---

Luca di Montezemolo: in Ferrari's corporate driving seat

AFTER ENZO FERRARI it could be argued that Luca Cordero di Montezemolo has been the most significant figure in Ferrari history since 1973. Born on 31 August 1947, he graduated in law from Rome University in 1971 and went on to specialise in commercial law at New York's Columbia University.

He came into the Fiat orbit through a close friend who was a nephew of Gianni Agnelli and, in June 1973, was appointed as Enzo Ferrari's 'eyes and ears' at the Grands Prix. Unlike the highly political operators who had previously filled this role, Luca brought a fresh, unbiased and totally objective focus to this crucial task.

Montezemolo developed a particular rapport with Niki Lauda and remained in Formula 1 until the end of 1975, helping to master-mind the Austrian driver's first World Championship season. In 1976 he became Director of External Relations for the Fiat Group, a post he held until 1981 when he took a year off to manage Operation Azzura, the first Italian entry in the America's Cup yacht racing classic.

Late that same year he became MD of ITEDI SpA, the holding company which co-ordinates all the publishing activities of the Fiat Group, including *La Stampa*, the second most popular Italian daily newspaper.

At the end of 1983 he made another career change and took over the role of MD of Cinzani SpA, another offshoot of the Fiat empire. From 1985–1990 he was the high profile Director General of the organising committee for Italia 1990, overseeing his country's hosting of the Soccer World Cup. Thereafter he took over as MD of the media group RCS Video before being appointed Chairman and Managing Director of Ferrari in late 1991.

Vice Chairman of the company is currently Piero Ferrari, with the board of directors composed of Pasquale de Vita, Carlo Gatto, Carlo Mangiarino, Marco Piccinini and Sergio Pininfarina.

On Enzo Ferrari's death in 1988, Luca di Montezemolo was regarded as the most logical choice to fill the top job at Maranello. Formula 1 fans regret that he didn't arrive a few months earlier. Had he done so he might have preserved the Prost/Ferrari partnership which had started out promising so much in 1989 and 1990.

---

seriously believed it might have a chance of winning the World Championship. Or would it take until 1998? Or, be it whispered, would it ever happen again?

As the year unfolded, nobody needed to be reminded that it was now 18 years since Jody Scheckter and Gilles Villeneuve had stormed past the chequered flag at Monza in 1–2 formation, a result which clinched the Drivers' Championship for Scheckter. Nor that 14 years had passed since René Arnoux and Patrick Tambay together amassed sufficient points to earn the Prancing Horse its most recent Constructors' title.

On the other hand, things certainly looked promising. Michael Schumacher's influence had shaped the team's profile to a very considerable degree. He had worked with both Ross Brawn and Rory Byrne during the period at Benetton which yielded the 1994 and 1995 World Championships.

Moreover, there was no sense of confrontation on the driver front, his dutiful number two Eddie Irvine seemingly still satisfied in that role; and, above all, there was the calming influence of Jean Todt bestriding the entire Formula 1 stage. Arguably, given the self-generated politicking of the previous two years, it was better than the senior management deserved.

Yet, whatever the outcome of the 1997 season, Ferrari would continue to remain centre stage as a pivotal force on the Grand Prix scene. Despite its derailments, disappointments and failure to deliver expected results over the years, in the mind's eye the image of the Prancing Horse is still uniquely synonymous, rightly or wrongly, with proper motor racing in the grand manner.

Some Formula 1 insiders would perhaps dismiss this as a soft-focus, sentimental view – yet it remains no less vivid for that.

Ferrari embarrassment. Irvine gets sideways at the first corner, squeezing Villeneuve's Williams and Johnny Herbert's Sauber. All three were out on the spot. (ICN)

Home base. Scuderia Ferrari's headquarters on Maranello's Via Alberto Ascari. (Ferrari UK)

Appendices

Appendix 1: *Biographical details of Ferrari World Championship drivers*

1952 and 1953
Alberto Ascari (Italy). Born Milan, 13 July 1918. Died Monza, 26 May 1955. 31 Grands Prix, 13 wins, 14 pole positions, 13 fastest race laps.

1956
Juan Manuel Fangio (Argentina). Born Balcarce, 24 June 1911. Died Balcarce, 17 July 1995. 51 Grands Prix, 24 wins, 29 pole positions, 23 fastest race laps.

1958
Mike Hawthorn (Great Britain). Born Mexborough, Yorkshire, 10 April 1929. Died Guildford by-pass, Surrey, 22 January 1959. 45 Grands Prix, 3 wins, 4 pole positions, 6 fastest race laps.

1961
Phil Hill (USA). Born 20 April 1927, Miami. 48 Grands Prix, 3 wins, 6 pole positions, 6 fastest race laps.

1964
John Surtees (Great Britain). Born 11 February 1934, Tatsfield, Surrey. 111 Grands Prix, 6 wins, 8 pole positions, 11 fastest race laps.

1975 and 1977
Niki Lauda (Austria). Born 22 February 1949, Vienna. 170 Grands Prix, 25 wins, 24 pole positions, 25 fastest race laps.

1979
Jody Scheckter (South Africa). Born 29 January 1950, East London, South Africa. 111 Grands Prix, 10 wins, 3 pole positions, 5 fastest race laps.

Appendix 2: *Ferrari Constructors' Championship placings since 1958*

Year	Place	Year	Place	Year	Place
1958	2nd	1971	4th	1984	2nd
1959	2nd	1972	4th	1985	2nd
1960	3rd	1973	6th	1986	4th
1961	1st	1974	2nd	1987	4th
1962	5th	1975	1st	1988	2nd
1963	4th	1976	1st	1989	3rd
1964	1st	1977	1st	1990	2nd
1965	4th	1978	2nd	1991	3rd
1966	2nd	1979	1st	1992	4th
1967	4th	1980	10th	1993	4th
1968	4th	1981	5th	1994	3rd
1969	5th	1982	1st	1995	3rd
1970	2nd	1983	1st	1996	2nd

Appendix 3: *Ferrari Formula 1 World Championship Grand Prix victories*

Race/venue	Driver/s	Car type
1951		
British/Silverstone	Froilan Gonzalez	375
German/Nürburgring	Alberto Ascari	375
Italian/Monza	Alberto Ascari	375
1952		
Swiss/Bremgarten	Piero Taruffi	500
Belgian/Spa-Francorchamps	Alberto Ascari	500
French/Rouen-les-Essarts	Alberto Ascari	500
British/Silverstone	Alberto Ascari	500
German/Nürburgring	Alberto Ascari	500
Dutch/Zandvoort	Alberto Ascari	500
Italian/Monza	Alberto Ascari	500
1953		
Argentine/Buenos Aires	Alberto Ascari	500
Dutch/Zandvoort	Alberto Ascari	500
Belgian/Spa-Francorchamps	Alberto Ascari	500
French/Reims	Mike Hawthorn	500
British/Silverstone	Alberto Ascari	500
German/Nürburgring	Giuseppe Farina	500
Swiss/Bremgarten	Alberto Ascari	500
1954		
British/Silverstone	Froilan Gonzalez	625
Spanish/Pedralbes	Mike Hawthorn	553
1955		
Monaco/Monte Carlo	Maurice Trintignant	625
1956		
Argentine/Buenos Aires	Juan Manuel Fangio/ Luigi Musso	D50
Belgian/Spa-Francorchamps	Peter Collins	D50
French/Reims	Peter Collins	D50
British/Silverstone	Juan Manuel Fangio	D50
German/Nurburgring	Juan Manuel Fangio	D50
1958		
French/Reims	Mike Hawthorn	801
British/Silverstone	Peter Collins	801
1959		
French/Reims	Tony Brooks	246
German/Avus	Tony Brooks	246

Race/venue	Driver/s	Car type
1960		
Italian/Monza	Phil Hill	246
1961		
Dutch/Zandvoort	Wolfgang von Trips	156
Belgian/Spa-Francorchamps	Phil Hill	156
French/Reims	Giancarlo Baghetti	156
British/Aintree	Wolfgang von Trips	156
Italian/Monza	Phil Hill	156
1963		
German/Nürburgring	John Surtees	156
1964		
German/Nürburgring	John Surtees	158
Austrian/Zeltweg	Lorenzo Bandini	156
Italian/Monza	John Surtees	158
1966		
Belgian/Spa-Francorchamps	John Surtees	312
Italian/Monza	Lodovico Scarfiotti	312
1968		
French/Rouen-les-Essarts	Jacky Ickx	312
1970		
Austrian/Osterreichring	Jacky Ickx	312B
Italian/Monza	Clay Regazzoni	312B
Canadian/St Jovite	Jacky Ickx	312B
Mexican/Mexico City	Jacky Ickx	312B
1971		
South African/Kyalami	Mario Andretti	312B
Dutch/Zandvoort	Jacky Ickx	312B2
1972		
German/Nürburgring	Jacky Ickx	312B2
1974		
Spanish/Jarama	Niki Lauda	312B3
Dutch/Zandvoort	Niki Lauda	312B3
German/Nürburgring	Clay Regazzoni	312B3

Race/venue	Driver/s	Car type
1975		
Monaco/Monte Carlo	Niki Lauda	312T
Belgian/Zolder	Niki Lauda	312T
Swedish/Anderstorp	Niki Lauda	312T
French/Paul Ricard	Niki Lauda	312T
Italian/Monza	Clay Regazzoni	312T
US/Watkins Glen	Niki Lauda	312T
1976		
Brazilian/Interlagos	Niki Lauda	312T
South African/Kyalami	Niki Lauda	312T
US West/Long Beach	Clay Regazzoni	312T
Belgian/Zolder	Niki Lauda	312T2
Monaco/Monte Carlo	Niki Lauda	312T2
British/Brands Hatch	Niki Lauda	312T2
1977		
Brazilian/Interlagos	Carlos Reutemann	312T2
South African/Kyalami	Niki Lauda	312T2
German/Hockenheim	Niki Lauda	312T2
Dutch/Zandvoort	Niki Lauda	312T2
1978		
Brazilian/Rio de Janeiro	Carlos Reutemann	312T2
US West/Long Beach	Carlos Reutemann	312T3
British/Brands Hatch	Carlos Reutemann	312T3
US/Watkins Glen	Carlos Reutemann	312T3
Canadian/Montreal	Gilles Villeneuve	312T3
1979		
South African/Kyalami	Gilles Villeneuve	312T4
US West/Long Beach	Gilles Villeneuve	312T4
Belgian/Zolder	Jody Scheckter	312T4
Monaco/Monte Carlo	Jody Scheckter	312T4
Italian/Monza	Jody Scheckter	312T4
US/Watkins Glen	Gilles Villeneuve	312T4
1981		
Monaco/Monte Carlo	Gilles Villeneuve	126CK
Spanish/Jarama	Gilles Villeneuve	126CK
1982		
San Marino/Imola	Didier Pironi	126C2
Dutch/Zandvoort	Didier Pironi	126C2
German/Hockenheim	Patrick Tambay	126C2

Race/venue	Driver/s	Car type
1983		
San Marino/Imola	Patrick Tambay	126C2
Canadian/Montreal	Rene Arnoux	126C2
German/Hockenheim	Rene Arnoux	126C3
Dutch/Zandvoort	Rene Arnoux	126C3
1984		
Belgian/Zolder	Michele Alboreto	126C4
1985		
Canadian/Montreal	Michele Alboreto	156/85
German/Nürburgring	Michele Alboreto	156/85
1987		
Japanese/Suzuka	Gerhard Berger	F187
Australian/Adelaide	Gerhard Berger	F187
1988		
Italian/Monza	Gerhard Berger	F187/88C
1989		
Brazilian/Rio de Janeiro	Nigel Mansell	640
Hungarian/Budapest	Nigel Mansell	640
Portuguese/Estoril	Gerhard Berger	640
1990		
Brazilian/Interlagos	Alain Prost	641
Mexican/Mexico City	Alain Prost	641
French/Paul Ricard	Alain Prost	641
British/Silverstone	Alain Prost	641
Portuguese/Estoril	Nigel Mansell	641
Spanish/Jerez	Alain Prost	641
1994		
German/Hockenheim	Gerhard Berger	412T1
1995		
Canadian/Montreal	Jean Alesi	412T2
1996		
Spanish/Catalunya	Michael Schumacher	F310
Belgian/Spa-Francorchamps	Michael Schumacher	F310
Italian/Monza	Michael Schumacher	F310
1997		
Monaco/Monte Carlo	Michael Schumacher	F310B
Canada/Montreal	Michael Schumacher	F310B

Appendix 4 : *World Sports Car Championship race victories from 1953–73*

Race/venue	Driver/s	Car type
1953		
Mille Miglia	Gianni Marzotto	40MM
Spa 24-hours	Mike Hawthorn/ Giuseppe Farina	340MM
Nürburging 1000km	Alberto Ascari/ Giuseppe Farina	340MM
Sports Car Champions.		
1954		
Buenos Aires 1000km	Giuseppe Farina/ Umberto Maglioli	375MM
Le Mans 24-hours	Froilan Gonzalez/ Maurice Trintignant	375Plus
Carrera Panamericana	Umberto Magliolo	375Plus
Sports Car Champions.		
1955		
Buenos Aires 1000km	Enrique Valiente/ Jose-Maria Ibanez	377Plus
1956		
Sebring 12-hours	Juan Manuel Fangio/ Eugenio Castellotti	860
Mille Miglia	Eugenio Castellotto	290MM
Sports Car Champions.		
1957		
Buenos Aires 1000km	Masten Gregory/ Eugenio Castellotti/ Luigi Musso	290
Mille Miglia	Piero Taruffi	315
Venezuela	Peter Collins/Phil Hill	412
Sports Car Champions.		
1958		
Buenos Aires 1000km	Peter Collins/Phil Hill	250TR
Sebring 12-hours	Peter Collins/Phil Hill	250TR
Targa Florio	Luigi Musso/ Olivier Gendebien	250TR
Le Mans 24-hours	Phil Hill/Olivier Gendebien	250TR
Sports Car Champions.		
1959		
Sebring 12-hours	Phil Hill/Olivier Gendebien/ Dan Gurney/Chuck Daigh	250TR

Race/venue	Driver/s	Car type
1960		
Buenos Aires 1000km	Phil Hill/Cliff Allison	250TR
Le Mans 24-hours	Olivier Gendebien/ Paul Frère	250TR
Sports Car Champions.		
1961		
Sebring 12-hours	Phil Hill/Olivier Gendebien	250TR
Targa Florio	Wolfgang von Trips/ Olivier Gendebien	246SP
Le Mans 24-hours	Phil Hill/Olivier Gendebien	250TR
Pescara	Lorenzo Bandini/ Giorgio Scarlatti	250TR
Sports Car Champions.		
1962		
Sebring 12-hours	Jo Bonnier/Lucien Bianchi	250TR
Targa Florio	Olivier Gendebien/ Ricardo Rodriguez/ Willy Mairesse	246SP
Le Mans 24-hours	Phil Hill/Olivier Gendebien	330P
Nürburgring 1000km	Phil Hill/Olivier Gendebien	246SP
Sports Car Champions.		
1963		
Sebring 12-hours	John Surtees/ Lodovico Scarfiotti	250P
Nürburging 1000km	John Surtees/Willy Mairesse	250P
Le Mans	Lorenzo Bandini/ Lodovico Scarfiotto	250P
Sports Car Champions.		
1964		
Sebring 12-hours	Mike Parkes/ Umberto Maglioli	250P
Nürburgring 1000km	Lodovico Scarfiotti/ Nino Vaccarella	250P
Le Mans 24-hours	Jean Guichet/Nino Vaccarella	275P
Sports Car Champions.		

Race/venue	Driver/s	Car type
1965		
Targa Florio	Lorenzo Bandini/ Nino Vaccarella	275P2
Nürburgring 1000km	John Surtees/ Lodovico Scarfiotti	275P2
Le Mans	Masten Gregory/ Jochen Rindt	250LM
Sports Car Champions.		
1966		
Monza 1000km	John Surtees/Mike Parkes	330P3
Spa 1000km	Lodovico Scarfiotti/ Mike Parkes	330P3
1967		
Daytona 24-hours	Lorenzo Bandini/ Chris Amon	330P4
Monza 1000km	Lorenzo Bandini/ Chris Amon	330P4
Sports Car Champions.		
1970		
Sebring 12-hours	Mario Andretti/ Ignazio Giunti/ Nino Vaccarella	512S

Race/venue	Driver/s	Car type
1972		
Buenos Aires 1000km	Ronnie Peterson/ Tim Schenken	312PB
Daytona 6-hours	Jacky Ickx/Mario Andretti	312PB
Sebring 12-hours	Jacky Ickx/Mario Andretti	312PB
Brands Hatch 1000km	Jacky Ickx/Mario Andretti	312PB
Monza 1000kms	Jacky Ickx/Clay Regazzoni	312PB
Targa Florio	Arturo Merzario/ Sandro Munari	312PB
Spa 1000km	Brian Redman/ Arturo Merzario	312PB
Nürburgring 1000km	Ronnie Peterson/ Tim Schenken	312PB
Osterreichring 1000km	Jacky Ickx/Brian Redman	312PB
Watkins Glen 6-hours	Jacky Ickx/Mario Andretti	312PB
Sports Car Champions.		
1973		
Monza 1000km	Jacky Ickx/Brian Redman	312PB
Nürburgring 1000km	Jacky Ickx/Brian Redman	312PB

Bibliography

Carlo Chiti: the roaring sinfonia, Oscar Orefici (Autocritica Edizione, 1991)

Dino: The Little Ferrari, V6 and V8 racing and road cars 1957 to 1979, Doug Nye (Osprey Publishing, 1979)

Enzo Ferrari The Man, Gino Rancati. (Giorgio Nada Editore, 1988)

Enzo Ferrari The Man and the Machine, Brock Yates (Doubleday, 1991)

Ferrari, Hans Tanner and Doug Nye (Haynes Publishing, 1979 and 1984)

Ferrari: Battle for Revival, Alan Henry (Patrick Stephens, 1996)

Ferrari: Ecurie Garage Francorchamps, Gianni Rogliatti (Giorgio Nada Editore, 1992)

Ferrari: the Grand Prix Cars, Alan Henry (Hazleton Publishing, 1984 and 1988)

Ferrari Sports Racing and Prototype Competition Cars, Antoine Prunet (Haynes Publishing, 1983)

Ferrari Testa Rossa V12, Joel E. Finn. (Osprey Publishing, 1980)

Ferrari: The Man, the Machines, Edited by Stan Grayson (Princeton Publishing, 1975; UK edition by Frederick Muller Ltd)

Ferrari 250GTO 1962–64; competition berlinetta, David Clark (Osprey Publishing, 1983)

Flat-12: The racing history of Ferrari's 3-litre Grand Prix and sports cars, Alan Henry (Motor Racing Publications, 1981)

Formula One: Driver by Driver, Alan Henry (The Crowood Press, 1992)

John Surtees: World Champion, John Surtees and Alan Henry (Hazleton Publishing, 1991)

My Two Lives: Race Driver to Restaurateur, René Dreyfus with Beverley Rae Kimes. (Aztec Corporation, 1983)

Origins of the Ferrari Legend, Gioachino Colombo (Haynes Publishing, 1987)

Pilote che gente . . , Enzo Ferrari (Privately published by Ferrari, 1983)

The Colonel's Ferraris: Maranello Concessionaires' racing team, Doug Nye (Ampersand Press, 1980)

The Enzo Ferrari Memoirs: My Terrible Joys, Enzo Ferrari (Hamish Hamilton Ltd, 1963)

Autosport

Classic & Sports Car

Motor Racing

Motor Sport

Index

Page numbers in **bold** refer to illustrations.